Gerald F Brophy

Proceedings in the Manitoba School Case

Heard Before Her Majesty's Privy Council for Canada, February 26th to March 7th,

1895

Gerald F Brophy

Proceedings in the Manitoba School Case
Heard Before Her Majesty's Privy Council for Canada, February 26th to March 7th, 1895

ISBN/EAN: 9783337207588

Printed in Europe, USA, Canada, Australia, Japan

Cover: Foto ©ninafisch / pixelio.de

More available books at **www.hansebooks.com**

PROCEEDINGS

IN THE

MANITOBA SCHOOL CASE

HEARD BEFORE

HER MAJESTY'S PRIVY COUNCIL FOR CANADA

FEBRUARY 26TH TO MARCH 7TH, 1895

OTTAWA
GOVERNMENT PRINTING BUREAU
1895

TABLE OF CONTENTS.

	PAGE
Preliminary meeting *re* fixing date for hearing appeal.	1
Argument of Mr. Ewart.	4
Argument of Mr. McCarthy.	25
Reply of Mr. Ewart.	89

APPENDIX.

Exhibits A to Q.	112

IN HER MAJESTY'S PRIVY COUNCIL

FOR THE

DOMINION OF CANADA

ARGUMENT *RE* SCHOOLS IN MANITOBA

OTTAWA, 26th February, 1895.

The Privy Council met at 11 o'clock a. m.

Present:—Sir Mackenzie Bowell, Sir Adolphe Caron, Hon. Mr. Foster, Hon. Mr. Patterson, Hon. Mr. Haggart, Hon. Mr. Ouimet, Sir Charles Hibbert Tupper, Hon. Mr. Ives, Hon. Mr. Daly, Hon. Mr. Angers, Hon. Mr. Dickey, and Hon. Mr. Montague.

Sir MACKENZIE BOWELL.—We are prepared to hear the continuation of the argument of Mr. Ewart on this matter. It will be remembered that he spoke at a previous meeting of the Council, and he will now go on.

Mr. McCARTHY.—Mr. President and gentlemen of the Privy Council, I appear here for the province of Manitoba, and before the argument is entered upon, I desire to state on behalf of the Government of Manitoba that they have had no opportunity of making any preparation for this argument, that the notice of this meeting was only received by them by telegraph on Saturday week. As you know, the Provincial Government are now busily engaged in the work of conducting the session; under the circumstances they say that there is no possibility for them to prepare an argument, or to give that attention to the matter which its importance demands. I am desired, therefore by the Attorney General "to protest," to use his own language, "and most vigorously, against the absolutely short notice which has been given." I do that now respectfully, before the argument is entered upon, as of course it would not be fair to my learned friend, who appears for the minority, to allow him make his argument, and then for me to make this statement.

Mr. EWART.—On behalf of the Roman Catholic minority, we will not object to any reasonable postponement my learned friend may ask for the purpose of preparing his case.

1

But as he has not indicated the length of the postponement he desires, I am unable to say whether we will oppose his request or not. If it is a reasonably short postponement for the purpose of preparation, I will not object.

Sir MACKENZIE BOWELL.— I was going to ask you, Mr. McCarthy, what time would you require to prepare your argument?

Mr. McCARTHY.— It is not so much for myself I am speaking as for the Attorney General; and what I rather gathered from him, though he has not said so in words, was that he desired to have been here himself. It is a matter which involves the educational system of the province, a question which, of course, has attracted a great deal of attention in Manitoba, and has been a subject of discussion in more than one session. I think what he would like is such a postponement as would enable him to go on with the work of the session and to come here after the session. You are aware, of course, that Mr. Greenway, the First Minister, is ill, and the leadership of the House, I suppose, devolves upon Mr. Sifton, the Attorney General. He instructed me that he telegraphed to this effect on Saturday, to the Secretary of State.

Mr. EWART.—I would object most strenuously to any postponement over the present session of the legislature. You are aware that there has already been very great delay in reaching a solution of this case, and that the difficulties that the minority in Manitoba have been labouring under, have been almost insurmountable, extending so far as that they have been unable to maintain a great many of their schools, and consequently the children go without that education which my clients believe they ought to have. If the postponement goes over this session, it will be impossible to make much progress with the case until the local legislature meets again a year from now; because, as you are all aware, if this government decides, as I hope it will, to make a request to the Manitoba Government, the first step is to submit to them some law which it is proposed they should pass; for after that submission took place the Dominion Parliament could do nothing until a refusal came from the Local Government. The delay, therefore, which my learned friend asks for. is not merely for a few days or a few weeks, it is a delay for one year. I think, therefore, that the circumstances mentioned by my learned friend are not such as to recommend his proposition to you. Indeed, we have in the Queen's Speech, in opening the Local Legislature a few day ago, this statement:

"Whether or not a demand will be made by the Federal Government that that Act shall be modified, is not yet known to my government; but it is not the intention of my government in any way to recede from its determination to uphold the present public school system which, if left to its own operation, would in all probability, soon become universal throughout the province."

I think those who are responsible for that statement cannot urge as a reason for postponing this case twelve months, that they have not had time to consider their position, for they have had time to consider their position.

Mr. McCARTHY.— That is not our ground.

Mr. EWART.- Nor can they urge, I think, that it is necessary for a proper presentation of their case that the Attorney General should be here. They have told you in advance what they intend to do, and surely my learned friend need not repeat that. I do not think it can be urged that they have had no opportunity for preparation. It is extraordinary that they have had no time to prepare themselves when this question has been before them for the last four years; and my learned friend has certainly had plenty of time to consider it, for he has been instructing the people of Canada upon this subject for the last two years; he is therefore perfectly qualified, I should think, to make such an argument as can be made on behalf of the Manitoba Government.

Sir MACKENZIE BOWELL.—Have you any idea, Mr. McCarthy, as to the length of the session?

Mr. McCARTHY.—My learned friend can say better than I with regard to that.

Mr. EWART.—It is not expected to be very long this time.

Sir MACKENZIE BOWELL.—Have they intimated to you the probable length of the session?

Mr. McCARTHY.—No.

Sir MACKENZIE BOWELL.—If it is put off until after the session, it will delay action for a year, whatever that may be.

Mr. McCarthy.—That will undoubtedly be the effect of it. What I desire to say is that the Attorney General did not ask for any particular postponement, but the tenor of his letter is that he desires to present the case himself. He looks upon it as a matter of great importance—not exactly with the same view as my learned friend has presented. He does not want, of course, a conflict with the Dominion. Although is is plain enough that the province does not intend to obey any remedial order that may be made, at the same time it is desirable there should be no conflict, and consequently, in order that I may show to this Council, if possible, that the Council ought not to interfere, I require to have a minuter knowledge of the old school system and of the practical working of the present system, than I am able to afford now, and it was impossible for me, with the time at my disposal, to have mastered the subject. I am not going to answer the personal observations of my learned friend ; I hope personalities will be kept out of the contest. I appear here as counsel for the Manitoba Government, I do not appear as a public man ; and I desire to present the case without regard to any other considerations than those affecting the province. It is a matter affecting the province only, and I have not yet been able to acquaint myself sufficiently with the practical working of the late system as contrasted with the working of the present system.

Hon. Mr. Ives.—Might I ask, in case the adjournment is not made as you suggest, would a short adjournment be of any particular advantage? If not, you might as well go on now as to go on a week from now.

Mr. McCarthy.—The only advantage of a short adjournment would be to enable me to communicate with the Attorney General and get specific instructions on matters as to which I may say I have no information, and I do not know where I can get it. I only received a lot of papers on Saturday at mid-day ; and I find that by some oversight, papers which ought to have been included in the parcel were not included. The object of an adjournment would be to enable me to consult with the Manitoba Government. in other words, to receive instructions. I have got some instructions here, three or four sheets of paper, merely saying that they inclose me so many papers, and that they have not had time to make any special preparation for the argument.

Sir Mackenzie Bowell.—I may say that the Manitoba Government has had precisely the same notice as the minority, having been notified by telegraph, anxious as we were to be in a position to take action one way or the other. What length of time, the shortest time, would you think it necessary to enable you to have a consultation with the Attorney General of Manitoba?

Mr. McCarthy.—It seems to me it would probably be necessary for some person to come from there here, or for some person to go from here there, in case the Council thought fit to allow an adjournment of sufficient length. I may say that when I saw in the press this morning that there was a possibility that the matter might be postponed, I telegraphed at once to Mr. Sifton to know whether he would care for any shorter postponement than a postponement till after the session. I would be better able to answer when I get that reply.

Hon. Mr. Daly.—A letter leaving here to-morrow morning will reach Winnipeg at 10 o'clock on Friday.

Mr. McCarthy.—Mr. Ewart says two or three days. Then, of course, they would want two or three days for preparation, to get the papers together, and another two or three days for the papers to come back.

Sir Mackenzie Bowell.—I may say on behalf of the Council that we could not think for a moment of consenting to an adjournment till after the session. Any reasonable adjournment, such as Mr. Ewart has agreed to, we would be quite willing to accede to. The Council will consult upon the length of the adjournment, and give our decision at three o'clock this afternoon.

At 3 o'clock p.m. the Privy Council met again.

Sir MACKENZIE BOWELL.—Mr. McCarthy, will you kindly inform us of the nature of the reply you have received from the Manitoba Government?

Mr. McCARTHY.—I have received a communication from the Attorney General in which he says: "Postponement of sufficient length to be of assistance in the preparation of the argument, accepted. Otherwise, proceed." I think that, taking three days to communicate with them and three days to get a reply, allowing a day or two to spare, probably Thursday next would be a convenient time, a time that would be of some service. That would be eight days.

Sir MACKENZIE BOWELL.—Could you not telegraph them to send the Superintendent of Education down here, or any one connected with this matter?

Mr. McCARTHY.—I am not able to say as to that. In a draft communication I have prepared, I make the suggestion that some official from the Educational Department should come. The 7th would do in a sense, but some accident might occur to cause delay.

Mr. EWART.—I am afraid that would be too long. If we could be sure that the Legislature would remain in session a sufficient time after that to enable them to consider anything that might go to them from this Government, I would make no objection at all. But, as I was informed before I came away that the session would be extremely short, I am afraid that if there is a delay now of even a week, it will defeat our purpose. It seems to me my learned friend might act upon the suggestion of Sir Mackenzie Bowell, and send a telegram to bring down the Superintendent of Education with the papers required, and he could be here in three days. Then, giving Mr. McCarthy a day to consult with him, we might get on this week.

Hon. Mr. OUIMET.—Would not Monday next be a reasonable time?

Mr. McCARTHY.—It could not be earlier than Monday.

Sir MACKENZIE BOWELL.—Would Monday suit you?

Mr. McCARTHY.—I am not speaking personally at all. Of course, I want to meet the views of the Council as far as I possibly can.

Sir MACKENZIE BOWELL.—We will adjourn till Monday at 11 a.m.

OTTAWA, 4th March, 1895.

The Privy Council met at 11 o'clock a.m., in the Railway Committee Room of the House of Commons.

Present:—Sir Mackenzie Bowell, Sir Adolphe Caron, Hon. Mr. Costigan, Sir Charles Hibbert Tupper, Hon. Mr. Foster, Hon. Mr. Haggart, Hon. Mr. Ouimet, Hon. Mr. Daly, Hon. Mr. Angers, Hon. Mr. Ives, Hon. Mr. Dickey, and Hon. Mr. Montague.

Sir MACKENZIE BOWELL.—Mr. Ewart, we are ready to hear your argument.

Mr. EWART. Hon. gentlemen of the Privy Council: Prior to the union with Canada of Rupert's Land and the North-west Territories in 1870, there were in the vicinity of the Red River about 12,000 settlers, of whom half were Roman Catholics and the other half Protestants. These people and their fathers had for many years lived happily and contentedly together under the paternal control of the Hudson's Bay Company. This era was, however, to come to a close, and by union with Canada the territory was to undergo a complete transformation. Railways, immigration, and the doubtful blessings of a written constitution were to take the place of hunting, isolation and patriarchal government. It was a great and momentous change, and the settlers naturally desired to know beforehand what was to be the exact nature of it; what was to be their position with reference to the ownership of the land; what compensation was to be given to them for the extinction of the Indian title; what sort of government they were to have; and what constitutional guarantees were to be provided with reference to those subjects of legislation which both English and French, Protestant and Roman Catholic, had always thought it proper to provide safeguards. With almost inconceivable folly no satisfaction of any kind was given to the settlers, indeed no communication was had with them upon any of the subjects. In Colonel Wolseley's language : "No attempt was made by the Ottawa Government to conciliate their newly acquired subjects. * * No explanations were made as to what was to be the policy of Canada in its dealings with Rupert's Land. * * Unfortunately the arrangement entered into had an air of purchase about it, and a cry resounded throughout the North-west that its inhabitants were being bought and sold like so many cattle."

So far from conciliating the settlers or explaining matters to them, the Canadian Government sent forward surveyors to plot out the country into townships, and they and some other Canadians staked out farms for themselves, "which they declared they meant to claim as soon as the new Governor had arrived"—so Lord Wolseley tells us. This was more than the settlers could stand. They accordingly stopped the surveys, and proceeded in the most formal manner, and with the sanction of the Governor of the Hudson's Bay Company, to form a Legislative Assembly. This Assembly did not consist of a few illiterate half-breeds as has been so often said. One-half of it was composed of English-speaking settlers, and among them were some of the most notable men of the locality—the present Senator Sutherland was one of them.

Eventually retracing her steps, Canada sent to Red River three commissioners, who prevailed upon the people to send delegates to Ottawa, to negotiate as to the terms upon which the union should be accomplished. These delegates were Judge Black, Mr. Alfred Scott, and the Rev. Father Ritchot, and they took with them a list or bill of rights containing the demands of the people. The seventh clause of this bill of rights was as follows :—

"7. That the schools be separate, and that the public money for schools be distributed among the different religious denominations in proportion to their respective population according to the system of the province of Quebec."

This demand was made as much on behalf of the Protestants as of the Roman Catholics, for it was not then known which denomination would be in the majority in years to come. There was consequently no objection to it. After the negotiations had proceeded at Ottawa for a few days, the government prepared a draft of a bill framing a constitution for the new province, and sent a copy to each of the delegates for their comments. The nineteenth clause of this draft made provision for separate schools upon the lines of the British North America Act. This was quite satisfactory to the delegates, and the Rev. Father Ritchot wrote as his comment upon the clause (and sent it to the government) these words :—

"This clause being the same as the British North America Act confers, as I interpret it, as a fundamental principle, the privilege of separate schools to the fullest extent, and in that is in conformity with article 7 of our instructions."

The bill which was introduced into the House by Sir John A. Macdonald on the 2nd May, 1870, contained the same provisions as to education as are now found in the Statute. The only objection made to these provisions in the House (see Hansard of 1870, p. 1546) was that it appeared to give the minority more security than was accorded to the other provinces by the British North America Act. For that reason an amendment was proposed, having for its object to strike out the clauses; and thus to leave as applicable the provisions of the British North America Act only. This amendment was defeated by a vote of 81 to 34; and the greater safeguard provided by the bill was thus given, as it was thought, to the future minority.

The bill having been passed, and become the Manitoba Act, it was taken back to Red River by one of the delegates. After it had been read and explained to the Legislative Assembly the following resolution was, amid much cheering, unanimously passed :—

"That the Legislative Assembly of this country do now, in the name of the people, accept the Manitoba Act, and decide on entering the Dominion of Canada on the terms proposed in the Confederation Act."

This compact thus entered into was made under the express direction and authority of the Imperial authorities. The Canadian Government had applied for the assistance of the British troops to put down the outbreak, but were met with the repeated injunc-

tion to come to terms. On the 5th March Earl Granville telegraphed to the Governor General :--
"Her Majesty's Government will give proposed military assistance provided reasonable terms are granted to the Red River settlers."
On the 22nd of March Earl Granville directed that : "Troops should not be employed in forcing the sovereignty of Canada on the population of Red River, should they refuse to admit it."
On the 23rd of April Earl Granville again telegraphed :
"Canadian Government to accept decision of Her Majesty's Government on all portions of the settlers' bill of rights."
On the 3rd of May the Governor General was able to telegraph : "Negotiations with delegates closed satisfactorily."
And to this Earl Granville replied :—
"I take this opportunity of expressing the satisfaction with which I have learned from your telegram of the 3rd inst that the Canadian Government and the delegates have come to an understanding as to the terms on which the settlement on the Red River should be admitted into the Union."
Finally the Imperial Parliament by statute ratified and confirmed the compact so entered into and embodied in the Manitoba Act.
While the Imperial authorities were thus determined to see for themselves that reasonable terms were granted to the settlers, the Canadian Government and the Governor General were profuse in their promises of liberal treatment. By their instructions the Canadian commissioners who were sent to the Red River were directed to say :
" That no administration could confront the enlightened public sentiment of this country which attempted to act in the North-west upon principles more restricted and less liberal than those which are fairly established here.
" The people may rely upon it that respect and protection will be extended to the different religious denominations. In declaring the desire and determination of Her Majesty's Cabinet you may safely use the terms of the ancient formula ' Right shall be done in all cases.'"
About the same time the Governor General wrote to the Governor of the Hudson's Bay Company :—
" And the inhabitants of Rupert's Land, of all classes and persuasions, may rest assured that Her Majesty's Government has no intention of interfering with, or setting aside or allowing others to interfere with, the religion , the rights, or the franchises hitherto enjoyed, or to which they may hereafter prove themselves eq al."
The Canadian Secretary of State, too, wrote to Mr. McDougall :—"You will be in a position to assure the residents of the North-west Territories :—
" 1. That all their civil and religious liberties will be sacredly respected :—
" 7. That the country will be governed as in the past by British law, and according to the spirit of British justice."
In order that these assurances might have all the weight of the name of Her Majesty the Queen, the Governor General issued a proclamation (6th December, 1869) in which is the following :—
" By Her Majesty's authority I therefore assure you that on the union with Canada all your civil and religious rights and privileges will be respected, your properties secured to you ; and that your country will be governed as in the past under British laws, and in the spirit of British justice."
I have shown that in the belief of one of the negotiators (on the part of the settlers) of the Manitoba Act separate schools were provided for. I now desire to add proof that the chief negotiator on the part of the Dominion was of the same opinion, and thus that all parties so understood. From Mr. Pope's very interesting "Life of Sir John A. Macdonald " I extract the following :—
" In 1870 he secured, or thought he had secured, like privileges to the Roman Catholics of Manitoba. We are not left in doubt as to his view of what was intended by the operation of the Manitoba Act. In the very beginning of the present agitation

in that province, he thus addressed a member of the local legislature, who had applied to him for counsel :—

" 'You ask me for advice as to the course you should take upon the vexed question of separate schools in your province. There is, it seems to me, but one course open to you. By the Manitoba Act, the provisions of the British North America Act (sec. 93) respecting laws passed for the protection of minorities in educational matters are made applicable to Manitoba, and cannot be changed ; for by the Imperial Act confirming the establishment of the new provinces, 34 and 35 Vict., c. 33, sec. 6, it is provided that it shall not be competent for the Parliament of Canada to alter the provisions of the Manitoba Act in so far as it relates to the province of Manitoba. Obviously therefore the separate school system in Manitoba, is beyond the reach of the Legislature or of the Dominion Parliament.'

" It is true that the highest legal tribunal in the empire has put a different interpretation on the Manitoba Act. But with the merits of this question we are in no wise concerned here, my object is merely to show what were the views of him who had by far the greatest share in the framing of this piece of legislation, as to its scope and effects."

All the facts to which I have referred are undisputed, with the exception of the statement that the bill of rights contained a demand for separate schools. To my mind it is unimportant whether the suggestion of protection for the minority came from Red River or Ottawa ; for whichever be the case there is no room to doubt that the education clauses were agreed to by the negotiators, and formed part of the arrangement for the union with Canada, which was finally adopted both by the Dominion Parliament and by the Red River Legislative Assembly.

But for those who deem the point important, I am in a position to prove the fact that the separate schools provision emanated from the settlers. I produce now an affidavit made by one of the delegates—the Rev. Father Ritchot—which, not only because of the oath of the venerable priest, but because of the circumstances to which he refers, leaves no room for further doubt.

(Affidavit read. Exhibit A.)

It will be observed from this affidavit that the original bill of rights was filed in court upon the trial of Lepine. It has in some way been lost, but I am in position to prove a copy of it. In accordance with the usual practice in capital cases, the prothonotary of the court, immediately after the trial, sent to the Department of Justice a copy of all the proceedings, and among these a copy of the bill of rights. I now produce from the Department of Justice a certified copy of this document. (Copy produced. Exhibit B.)

The relation of these facts ought to be sufficient to prove that there was a solemn agreement entered into by the Dominion of Canada with the Red River settlers that the future minority should be entitled to separate schools. But for those who retain any doubt upon the question I quote the language of the recent judgment of the Imperial Privy Council :

" The terms upon which Manitoba was to become a province of the Dominion were matters of negotiation between representatives of the inhabitants of Manitoba and the Dominion Government.... Those who were stipulating for the provisions of section 22 as——

Mr. McCarthy.—That is not in the judgment.

Mr. Ewart.—I think you will find it there.

Hon. Mr. Ouimet.—If what you are quoting is to be found in the case as edited for the Canadian Government by the appellant's solicitors in London, will you please give us the page ?

Mr. Ewart.—What I am quoting will be found at the top of page 272.

"——a condition of the union, and those who gave their legislative assent to the Act by which it was brought about, had in view the perils then apprehended.... It was notorious that there were acute differences of opinion between the Catholics and Protestants in the education question prior to 1870. This is recognized and emphasized in almost every line of those enactments. There is no doubt either what the points of difference were, and it is in the light of these that the 22nd section of the Manitoba Act of 1870 which was in truth a parliamentary compact, must be read."

It may be argued that in their first judgment the Judicial Committee held that the Manitoba Act did not guarantee separate schools. I am aware of the language used, but its effect (as explained in the second judgment) is merely that the words which occur in the statute were not sufficient to accomplish the purpose intended—that is, that the drafting of the statute was defective. A perusal of the second judgment makes it clear that in their Lordships' opinion it was intended to guarantee separate schools, and that that guarantee was a matter of agreement and "compact" between the Dominion of Canada and the people of the Red River.

This then is my first argument: The people of Canada made a solemn agreement that in Manitoba the schools should be separate. If the minority there now were Protestant, and Catholics desired to ignore this agreement, we would hear much of the supposed Catholic principles of "No faith with heretics," "The end justifies the means," &c., but it is the Catholics that are in the minority, and what excuses do Protestants allege for breach of faith and violation of solemn pledges? The excuse of the vast majority, so far, may well be that they were not aware of the facts. I have placed these facts in the very forefront of my argument to-day, with the hope that they may be widely circulated by the press, and thus that no Protestant shall any longer be unaware of what is being done in his name in the province of Manitoba.

One of the guarantees afforded by the Manitoba Act for the preservation of the rights of the minority was the Provincial Senate. Six years' experience proved to Manitoba that, apart from its functions as a guarantee, the Senate was little more than an item of expense; and the Protestants then in the majority, and feeling confident of their own rectitude, proposed to abolish it. The Catholics naturally hesitated, but their apprehensions were removed by profuse promises. The premier (Mr. Davis) in the debate said :—

"It may be said that the Council is a safeguard to the minority. He could assure the minority that their rights would never be trampled upon in this province. There would always be sufficient English-speaking members in this House, who would insist on giving their French fellow subjects their rights, to protect them."

Mr. Luxton (then and still a very influential journalist) said :—

Hon. Mr. FOSTER.—Was Mr. Luxton a member of the legislature?

Mr. EWART.—Yes, and this was said in the course of debate :

"There were some questions of sentiment which lay close to the hearts of the French people ; and he could assure them that tne English-speaking members would not ruthlessly deal with these, if the French representatives were sufficiently patriotic to support the measure before the House. They would recognize their generosity and not forget it."

Mr. Frank Cornish (then a prominent lawyer) said he "believed the old settlers and the French would make common cause if their rights were infringed upon ; and he could assure them that when the Canadian (then the English speaking) party became the great majority it would not be found oppressive." In accepting these promises on the part of the French and Roman Catholics, Mr. Royal said :—

Hon. Mr. HAGGART.—Are you using that merely as a matter of history, or as bearing on the right that was acquired then?

Mr. EWART.—I am showing that these promises were made to the Roman Catholics at a very important juncture in the history of the province, and I am appealing to the Protestants who made these promises to see that they are carried out. Mr. Royal said : "But there was something else for himself, which had not been guaranteed by any act ; he found it yesterday in the remarks of the Hon. Messrs. Davis and Norquay, in the applause given by Mr. Brown to the sentiments of Mr. Luxton, and in the expressions of Mr. Cornish."

And Mr. McKay added :—

"He was very much pleased to hear the generous and just remarks of the Hon. Premier, the Hon. Prov. Secretary, and also that of the hon. member for Rockwood, which gave the minority in the House that confidence which the members of this House, and by their vote on this bill would express, the security they felt in the hands of that majority."

This is my second argument. My first was based upon an agreement entered into by the Dominion of Canada with the settlers at Red River. I now present the assurances of the Protestants of Manitoba to the Roman Catholics of Manitoba,- assurances that their " rights would never be trampled upon in this province ; " that the " Protestants would recognize their generosity and not forget it : " that " the great majority would not be found oppressive," etc. Again I say let the Protestants of Canada know what has been done in their name.

My third argument is based upon further promises, and this time the promises made by the Liberal party in Manitoba, which enabled them to defeat the Harrison Government, in St. François Xavier, and themselves to acquire power. The facts may best be stated by reading the following affidavits :—

Mr. Fisher, the President of the Liberal Association ; Mr. A. F. Martin, the Liberal Organizer in St. François Xavier, Mr. Francis, the Liberal candidate in St. François Xavier ; Mr. Burke, the Conservative candidate in St. François Xavier, and also those of Messrs. Joseph Hogue, William Hogue, J. P. McDougall, Francis Walsh, G. Todd and N. Todd, electors in St. François Xavier.

Mr. McCARTHY.—I suppose there is no object in making any objection ; I suppose that everything is regular.

Sir MACKENZIE BOWELL.—What would the nature of the objection be ?

Mr. McCARTHY.—I do not suppose that a promise given by an organizer or by a gentleman running as candidate in a constituency can be held as binding upon the province ?

Hon. Mr. ANGERS.—These may be witnesses to some promise made by persons in authority.

Mr. McCARTHY.—I suppose that everything is regular.

Hon. Mr. ANGERS.—We can hardly know what these affidavits are, until they are read.

(The affidavits were read by Hon. Senator Bernier, Exhibits C, D, E, F, G.)

Mr. EWART.—The affidavits of the other five electors are almost identical with the last read, and I suppose they may be taken as read.

(Affidavits put in, Exhibits H, I, J, K, L.)

My fourth argument is nearly allied to the third. It is based upon promises made by the Greenway Government (after its accession to office), to His Grace the Archbishop of St. Boniface and to various other persons, in order to enable him to obtain for his cabinet a representative of the Roman Catholics and to carry the general elections of 1888. In support of this I read the affidavits of the Reverend Vicar-General Allard, and Mr. W. F. Alloway. (Affidavits read by Hon. Senator Bernier—Exhibits M. and N.)

The promises proved by these affidavits, given at these four periods of the history of Manitoba have all been violated by the passage of the School Act of 1890. I have endeavoured to think of language which would fittingly characterise the utter degradation and complete abnegation of all truth and honour exhibited by the recital of the conduct which it has been my painful duty to lay before this Honourable Council, but I acknowledge myself utterly unable to find adequate expression. I do not suppose that it would be possible in the political record in any civilized country to find anything so utterly and indefensibly base, cowardly and heartless. My first four arguments, then, are founded upon agreements and promises :—First, the compact made by the Dominion of Canada ; second, the promises made by the Protestants of Manitoba ; third, the promises made by the Liberal party in Manitoba ; and fourth, the promises made by the Greenway Government. All these agreements and promises have been violated—those of the Greenway Government ; those of the branch of the Liberal party in Manitoba (and I say it with bowed head, for to that party I once belonged) : those of the Protestants of Manitoba (and I feel the shame of it, for in that faith was I born and nurtured) ; and those, too, of the people of Canada. For this violation, however, the Liberal party of Canada, the Protestants of Canada, and the people of Canada have not yet made themselves responsible ; and to them I lift my eyes with confidence, that when the facts are known, then that which has been done will by them be repudiated, and all injustice remedied. With a full sense of my responsibility for the statement, I add that in my humble judgment Canada would not be a fit place for an honest man to live in, were its inhabitants to remain unaroused to indignant action by the relation of such shamefully perfidious action.

I pass on now to argue, as a fifth point, that even had we no agreements or promises to urge, yet that relief should be given to us. But upon this subject I will not be expected to present all the arguments which may be advanced in favour of separate schools. I shall not do more than indicate the more salient of them.

First and ever first upon this subject must stand the principle of individual liberty. There are three kinds of schools :—The purely secular ; the secular, plus a little religious teaching ; and the secular plus some more religious teaching. Many of the supporters of the first urge that all religion must be excluded from all the schools ; but I need not stop to argue with them, because Manitobans will have none of such a system. Many of the supporters of secular schools plus a little religion want to have all the schools conducted according to their particular views. They argue to their own satisfaction that "Godless schools" are an abomination ; that a certain particular quantity of religion is the proper allowance for all schools ; and that any more than that is an interference with the principle of separation of church and state—something to be violently declaimed against. These gentlemen never stop to tell us why it is that if their modicum of religion may be admitted without breach of everlasting principle, some other person's modicum must be excluded because of the same principle. If we determine that the schools are to be in some sense religious, then the question arises : How much is there to be ? Now that question may be answered by Mr. Greenway and Mr. Martin and others, skilled in theology, by adopting some one or other of the thousand conflicting opinions which are held upon the subject. For example, they might adopt the opinion of one of the most influential of the Winnipeg Protestant theologians, and say that the "Being, character and moral government of God," but not the higher graces due to the operation of the Holy Ghost, should be taught—that the schools ought not to be Godless (it seems), but may very well be Ghostless—and these politicians might probably think it advisable to prepare a model lecture or two upon the subjects prescribed. But the better way, as it appears to me, to answer a question as to the amount of religion to be admitted in the schools, is to say that the people shall be permitted, so far as possible, to answer it for themselves—better to allow freedom of opinion upon a matter of that kind than resort to the old-fashioned method of endeavouring to make everyone think and act alike.

But I shall be told that such a course is not practicable—that Government must regulate the supply of religion in the schools, or we shall have no public schools at all. To such persons I say : Look around you. Broadly speaking, there are the three great divisions or opinions already referred to, and no difficulty has been felt in arranging so as to let all three have their own way. I do not say that there are not individuals who are not within any of three classes ; but I do say that no one of the three great classes is to be deprived of liberty because it is found impossible to give a like complete liberty to every individual. Extend liberty as widely as possible. That you cannot attain the ideal is no reason for not doing the best you can. Because you cannot convict all criminals, furnishes no argument for the abolition of the administration of justice. How then are we to give liberty of action in this matter to the three great classes in the community ? The answer is, that the system in force in Manitoba prior to 1890 secured that end. It gave to Protestants complete control of their schools, and that body (including as it does the first two classes of persons) could arrange for their religious modicums, and the absence from attendance of those who desired purely secular education, as they pleased. The third class of persons, forming the Roman Catholic body, were entrusted with the control of their schools, and they introduced into them the religious instructions which they thought proper. All classes, therefore, had their way, and were quite content till informed in 1890 that they were not.

Now what are the objections raised to that system ? The most usual one is that thereby public money is used to propagate denominational teaching. But this is a very easily answered mistake. In England public money is distributed among the denominational schools, but does the State pay the money for propagation of religious teaching ? Not at all. Upon the contrary it is specially provided (33 and 34 V., c. 65, s. 97) :—

"Such grants shall not be made in respect of any instruction of religious subjects" ; and no inspection takes place upon religious subjects.

The State pays for the secular work accomplished and does not prohibit people from teaching, or being taught religion : -that is all ; nor does it attempt to cut off a religious portion and prescribe that for every body. When the city of Toronto makes large grants to charitable institutions, many of them under denominational control, it pays nothing for propagating religious doctrines, but only for the good work done to the bodies of the needy. Surely, if the Government paid for certain road work done by Roman Catholics in industrial schools it could not be charged with propagating Roman Catholic doctrine ; and if it pays the same institution for educating in secular subjects some of its youthful citizens, how can a similar charge be made? It may be as well said that I paid money for extending the Roman Catholic religion did I send my washing to a Roman Catholic house of industry. I pay for the washing, not for the prayers which may be said over it, about the advantage of which I might have my own opinion.

The truth is that the general principle invoked by our opponents is, as so often happens, one made for the occasion. They are opposed to anything savouring of the Roman Catholic religion appearing in the schools, but are in favour of some portion of their own religion being there. They, therefore, have to manufacture a principle which fits their wishes, and then from such principle they triumphantly argue. They cannot assert that Church and State being separate, there ought to be no religion in the schools, for that would exclude their own, so the formula they hit upon is that there ought to be no kind of religion there which could be recognized as belonging particularly to anybody. They say to the Catholics : We both believe this much ; let therefore, this much be taught in the schools. The Catholics answer : Those items which you pick out, standing apart from other things, are Protestant and not Catholic. Protestants reply You can teach these other things on Sunday in your churches elsewhere. In fact to use a simile, Protestants say to Catholics we must eat together, and we both like porridge. The Catholics answer : Yes, but not without salt in it ; and Protestants with unanswerable logic, and without a shadow of a smile, reply : Very well, you can take the salt on Sundays, at home or elsewhere, as it pleases you.

A second objection to separate schools is, that when there is Roman Catholic religion in the schools, the children do not progress properly in their studies. Some people think that this is because God has so ord:red, others think that it is because of the encroachment upon the time of the children. To these latter I say, did you ever visit a Roman Catholic school ? If so, how much time did you find devoted to catechism ? But such persons never did visit a Catholic school, and they tell me it is not necessary to do so—that the results tell the tale. Let such persons be informed that the facts are not so clear as they may think them ; that in Winnipeg and many other places, Protestant children are sent to Catholic schools because the education is better there than in other schools ; and that if the results in some schools are otherwise it ought to be remembered that the Roman Catholic church in Ontario and Manitoba is not the church of the elite, but of the poor, and that results in every department of life are largely governed by the material employed.

This leads us to discuss the facts with reference to the character of the schools now in Manitoba. I do not at all concede that if the schools can be shown to be non-sectarian our right to relief is any the less strong. That Catholics are prevented from teaching their own religion is the complaint, and it is no answer to that, that others are likewise so prevented. Many minds may, however, be influenced by the settlement of the fact and for them I shall now answer the question, Are the schools unsectarian or Protestant ? The answer is not difficult : and it forms my sixth argument.

Prior to 1890 there were two sets of schools in Manitoba—Protestant and Roman Catholic. The Protestant schools were fashioned and conducted by Protestants, without either Catholic or State interference ; and the Catholic schools were fashioned and conducted by Catholics without either Protestant or State interference. We are in a position therefore to ascertain exactly what Protestant schools are—what kind of schools, and how much religion Protestants would have if left to themselves to regulate it. This system commenced in 1871 and in that same year the Protestant Board " determined to exclude all distinctive religious teachings from its schools, but enjoined the reading of the Holy Scriptures and the prayers as published in the by-laws and regulations, at the opening and closing of the schools." (*See* Report 1871, p. 8.)

The regulations of the Protestant board which were in force immediately prior to the Act of 1890 provided as follows :—

"The Bible shall be used as a text book in the Protestant schools of Manitoba. A supply for use in each school may be obtained by the trustees, otherwise each pupil from standard three upwards shall be required to provide himself with a Bible in addition to his other text books.

"The selections for reading shall always include one or more of the lessons in the authorized list given herewith ; but any other selection from Scripture may, in the discretion of the teacher, be read in connection with them.

"The Scripture lesson in each school shall follow the opening prayer, and shall occupy not more than fifteen minutes daily. Until notes and questions are provided under the authority of the Board, the readings shall not be accompanied by comment or explanation."

No notes and questions ever were provided, so that the Bible reading was without "comment or explanation." A form of prayer was also prescribed. The regulations adopted immediately after the Act of 1890 provided :—

"(a.) The reading without note or comment of the following selections from the authorized English version of the Bible or the Douay version of the Bible.

"(b.) The use of the following forms of prayer."

The Bible selections after 1890 are not so numerous as those prior to that year, but so far as they go they are the passages selected by the Protestant board, and the forms of prayer are identical with those previously used by Protestants. It will thus be seen that the religious exercises prescribed by Protestants for purely Protestant schools are substantially identical with those for the non-sectarian schools. Catholic services are of course wholly different. The non-sectarian exercises were, therefore, constructed to meet Protestant and not Catholic ideas, and so may well be said to be Protestant. But they are sectarian not only in Roman Catholic view, but in the estimation of Jews, Unitarians and others. It will not be possible for any Jew or Unitarian to join in the prayer prescribed.

I now turn to the religious instruction prior and subsequent to 1890. Prior to 1890 the regulations were as follows :—

"It shall be the duty of the teacher of each school to instruct his pupils from standard three and upwards in the Ten Commandments and the Apostles' Creed, so that they may be able to repeat them from memory ; and to devote one-half hour weekly to this exercise ; and to the giving of such instruction in manners and morals as he may find practicable."

Since 1890 the following regulations prevail :—

"To establish the habit of right doing, instruction in moral principles must be accompanied by training in moral practices. The teacher's influence and example, current incidents, stories, memory gems, sentiments in the school lessons, examination of motives that prompt to action, didactic talks, teaching the Ten Commandments, &c., are means to be employed."

The only difference then between Protestant religious teaching prior to the Act, and non-sectarian teaching after the Act, is that the latter is a little more specific than the former. I cannot imagine that any wider instructions could be given for the conduct of a Sunday school than are contained in this "non-sectarian" programme. As one reads them one feels that the atmosphere becomes distinctly sabbatic. One sees the "memory gems" upon the wall—"There is no other mediator, &c."; the teacher becomes the superintendent ; he tells of "the motives that prompt to action," observing that superstitions are not sufficient foundation for a system of ethics, and recounting, as Mr. Heath recently did in British Columbia, the contempt which he personally displayed towards the Holy Wafer by putting it in his pocket instead of in his mouth ; he calls upon his class to recite the fifth commandment, and when some of the children commence with the Protestant fifth and others with the Catholic fifth, he explains which has the right of the matter; and he finishes with a "didactic talk," which may very well be a Presbyterian sermon. It may be said that the "didactic talks," the "memory gems," &c., must be all of a non-sectarian character. But this can only be properly accomplished when you have a supply of non-sectarian teachers. It would be impossible for a Presbyterian or a Roman Catholic conscientiously to conduct a Sunday school without disclosing his distinctive characteristics. But if a teacher can successfully conceal his real belief under general language when talking in didactic fashion, what is the poor non-sectarian teacher to do when he is set to teach the Ten Commandments? What reason is he to give why the Protestants divide the Catholics' first commandment into two, making up for it by adding their ninth and tenth together. When he is teaching the Protestants' second commandment, is he to state that it is a special commandment aimed at Roman Catholics' images and relics? or is he to explain "Thou shalt not make unto them any graven image" as the Catholics explain that language? And when he comes to the Protestants' fourth commandment enjoining the keeping of Sunday, shall he inculcate Protestant or Catholic belief as to the lawfulness of recreations, and works of liberal and artistic character? Let Protestants tell me that they are willing to have their children taught the Ten Commandments by Roman Catholics, and I shall then, but not till then, acknowledge, that the present schools are unsectarian.

I have with me the Presbyterian and the Roman Catholic methods of teaching the decalogue. According to the former, one of the sins forbidden by the first commandment is "Praying.....to saints, making men lords of our faith and conscience," &c. ; one of the sins forbidden by the second is "the making of any representation of God, of all or of any of the three persons, either inwardly in our mind or outwardly in any kind of image, or likeness of any creature whatsoever ; all worshipping of it, or God in it, or by it," &c. : one of the sins forbidden by the third is "the maintaining of false doctrines," &c. ; one of the sins prohibited by the fourth is "all profaning the day by....recreations"; and so on. Does any one tell me that this is not sectarian, or that it is possible for a Presbyterian believing that these are sins, and that they are prohibited by the Ten Commandments, to teach the decalogue and say nothing about them? I need not stay to contrast the lessons drawn by the Roman Catholics from the same Commandments. Suffice it to say that they are such as are anathematized by all Protestants.

I have now shown that the religious exercises and the religious instruction are essentially sectarian. The same vice (or virtue) invades even the programme of studies prescribed for "non-sectarian" schools. I shall in this connection mention but one of the objections which Roman Catholics urge against this programme : but it is directed to a subject so palpably sectarian, and of such clearly controversial, if not explosive, character that Protestants will at once recognize the validity of the objection. Among the subjects prescribed for Grade VII., there is the following :—

"History—(a) English—Religious movements—(Henry VIII. and Mary)."

Now I should think it extremely difficult for anyone to teach at all adequately the history of religious movements, without leaving himself open to criticism by one of the parties interested. But of all periods, I know of none more difficult to treat in this fashion than the two selected for our non-sectarian schools. To Protestants, Henry VIII. was the one who released the English Church from the "thraldom of Rome," and threw off for ever the yoke of the "foreign potentate." To Catholics, he was the great schismatic, the disrupter of God's Church, and the confiscater and plunderer of her heritage. For Protestants, the religious movement under "Bloody Mary" were principally movements from homes and hiding places to scaffold and faggot fires. To Catholics, Mary's reign was a period of rehabilitation, and of return from the sin of schism to the bosom of the true church. It is not possible for Protestant or Catholic, if he be earnest, to teach these subjects without offending the other, and the poor non-sectarian, struggling to please both, would most certainly be condemned by both.

I cannot leave this part of my argument without quoting from an address delivered before the Winnipeg Liberal Club on the 20th February, 1894, by the author of the School Act of 1890—Mr. Joseph Martin—in which he himself argues against the religion in the schools as being unfair to the Catholics. He said that :—

"He was himself not satisfied with the School Act and had never been so. He had made a strong effort to have the public schools, controlled by the Government, really made national schools with religion obliterated ; and he was now more convinced than ever that was the only school which could be justified as constitutional. They said that the

State had no right to interfere with the different denominations, but had the right to interfere in the matter of religion; but he contended that they would not do the one without the other. It had been urged by satisfied supporters of the Act that none could complain of the devotional element introduced, as it was of the broadest nature. But they found that the Roman Catholics had the very greatest objections to this provision of the Act, and he was himself dissatisfied with it, and was glad many Protestants shared his objections.... The Roman Catholics had honestly stated that in their belief the two forms of education should go together. The Protestants admitted on the other hand that it was impossible to have religious training in the schools, and only asked that it be recognized—insisting, however, on imposing their views on others in that respect; rather than that small amount of religious training should be done away with in the schools, the Protestants said they would prefer the old state of affairs. He would leave it to his audience to determine which was the more honest stand of the two."

If, in the opinion of the author of the Acts (although for reasons other than those, which would be urged by Roman Catholics) their practical working has proved that their continuance is an imposition of Protestant opinions upon Roman Catholics, in a matter almost indifferent to Protestants, but affecting in a vital point the faith of the Catholics, to such an extent that the very honesty of the Protestants may thereby be impeachable, I say that if that is the opinion of the author of the Acts, I have to go no further for arguments, as to their unfairness.

One other suggestion as to the character of the public schools in Manitoba. Speaking very generally the Roman Catholic religion includes the Protestant religion, and the distinctions are found in its additional features. Protestants desire, so they say, to have taught in the schools that which is held in common. Catholics say that if you separate what is common from the rest that is Protestantism. Suppose a vegetarian asks me to dine with him, and I stipulate that the dinner is not to be of a vegetarian character, ought I to feel aggrieved if I got nothing but vegetables? My host would say that the dinner was not vegetarian, that I believed in the vegetables as much as he did, and that this was, therefore, a common and universally approved dinner—one to which all alike could come. Nevertheless, I think that I would be right in calling it a vegetarian dinner. In the same way I may say that the schools are distinctively Protestant—by the very omission of an ingredient (the very salt of the matter as is thought) the schools are rendered obnoxious to Catholics, and represent the Protestant and not the Catholic teaching of religion.

And why should not Catholics have salt in their porridge if they want it? They do not ask anyone else to have it in theirs. They are willing to accord to the non-salt eaters full liberty of action. Why should not the same liberty be returned to them? For what is there involved in the separate school question? Why this, and nothing more, whether Catholics are to be permitted to have in schools, attended by nobody but Catholics, a somewhat different kind of religion from that taught in the other schools, and, probably, a little more of it—they want salt in their porridge. They do not ask that their church should in any way control the schools. They are perfectly willing to work up to any state-prescribed standard of secular instruction, to be subjected to inspection, and to use school books not at variance with their religious doctrines. They do not seek to displace the Protestant schools or to change in any way the teaching in them. Protestants may have it without salt if they please. All that is desired is the same liberty as the Protestants, by their numbers, compelled the Greenway government in 1890 to give to them the same liberty which is willingly given by Roman Catholics to Protestants in the province of Quebec.

I feel certain that the settled belief of the people of Canada is that such liberty ought to be accorded to Roman Catholics everywhere throughout the Dominion. This forms my seventh argument. In Ontario an experience of very many years has made that matter so clear that now very few are left who complain, and these are usually those whose antipathy to Roman Catholics would carry them to the exclusion of their fellow-countrymen from public employment because of their faith. In Quebec there is no complaint. There the majority is Roman Catholic, and Dr. Robbins, Principal of the McGill Normal School, has testified: "We are of the minority of this province, but we know that we are not regarded as a factious or insignificant minority. Our susceptibilities are considered, our educational rights are maintained by the majority." Something of a lesson there, I think, for some Protestants in the virtues of tolerance and good fellowship. In New Brunswick and Nova Scotia, although there is no law permitting it, yet, by common consent, the Catholics are permitted exclusively to occupy certain of the public schools and there to teach their children such parts of their doctrine as they think fitted for the schools. I am informed that a similar custom prevails in Prince Edward Island.

This tolerance and freedom is also spreading in the United States, notwithstanding the fact that, as the law stands, the whole community must wink in common at it, or it would be stopped. At Poushkeepsie, at Rondout, at Savannah, New Haven, Lima and many other places, the people are more liberal than their laws, and Catholics enjoy no small measure of the liberty they so eagerly desire.

Returning to Canada, I can point to the unvarying support which the separate school principle has always received in the Dominion Parliament. In 1872, in the New Brunswick school case, by a majority of 117 to 52 the House of Commons regretted the passage of the Statute which was complained of, and by a majority of 114 to 73, passed an address asking Her Majesty " to use her influence with the Legislature of New Brunswick to secure such a modification of the said Act as shall remove such ground of discontent." The figures which I have given do not represent properly the overwhelming number of the majority that was in favour of the Catholics in New Brunswick, for upon both occasions, there were many in the minority who voted as they did, because the resolutions were not sufficiently strong. If the resolutions had been stronger, they would have had much additional support.

Afterwards, in 1878, the Dominion Parliament provided for separate schools in the North-west Territories without hardly a dissentient voice. When in 1894, Mr. McCarthy wished to amend the statute and leave the subject in the hands of the people of the North-west Territories, he was defeated by 114 to 21 ; and Major Hughes, who wished to prohibit directly all sectarian teaching in the North-west schools, by 131 to 2.

It has been urged that the matters in question here should be left to the disposition of the province of Manitoba. This argument emanates, of course, from the majority —leave it to the province, they say—that is leave it to us. Now, why was an appeal provided for by the constitution at a time when parties were about equally divided? Was it for the purpose of being acted upon, or was it inserted merely as something ornamental? Was it to be used if the Protestants were in the minority, but not if the Catholics were the injured ones? What was it put there for? I say that it was placed there as one out of many constitutional guarantees which Protestants and Catholics alike enjoy under Canadian constitution—a guarantee which it was hoped would remain unused, like a life-preserver, but which was to be resorted to in case of need.

Let me quote the language of the Privy Council upon this point :—" Bearing in mind the circumstances which existed in 1870, it does not appear to their Lordships an extravagant notion that in creating a legislature for the province with limited power, it should have been thought expedient, in case either Catholics or Protestants became preponderant, and rights which had come into existence under different circumstances were interfered with, to give the Dominion Parliament power to legislate upon matters of education as far as was necessary to protect the Protestant or Catholic minority, as the case may be."

I wonder what our opponents would say about Dominion interference with provincial rights, were Quebec to interfere with the Protestant privileges there. It would not be provincial, but " Protestant rights " then that we would hear of—" solemnly guarded and guaranteed by the constitution ;" and so I urge that it is Catholic rights and not provincial rights that are being interfered with ; that it is a provincial wrong, and not a provincial right that we have to deal with. The appeal is given so, that provincial wrongs may be made into rights.

Such considerations are, however, not properly up for discussion before this Council, for, as I have formerly contended and now repeat (as my eighth argument, and with all proper deference and respect), not only has His Excellency in Council a power of appeal, but it is his bounden duty to hear the appeal, and to adjudicate thereon, as its merits may require.

The Council adjourned until 2.30 p.m.

AFTER RECESS.

The Council resumed at 2.30 p.m.

Mr. EWART.—I argue that the constitution has given to the Catholic minority of the Queen's subjects in Manitoba, as a right, an appeal from Acts of the Legislative Assembly; that His Excellency in Council cannot decline to hear such an appeal, and cannot refuse, whether out of regard for the Legislature or for any other reason, to deliver a judgment upon the merits of the case, when brought before him. It is a well-known rule for the construction of statutes that where functions of a public nature are bestowed upon individuals, such persons have no right to refuse to exercise their powers. The rule includes cases in which jurisdiction of a judicial character is given. Even when the language of the statute is permissive—the judge may do so and so, "may" is always held to mean that if a proper case is made out he *shall* do so and so. Allow me to quote a passage from Maxwell on Statutes (pages 295-6):

"It is a legal or rather a constitutional principle that powers given to public functionaries, or others for public purposes, or the public benefit, were always to be exercised when the occasion arises." And again: "But as regards the imperative character of the duty, it was laid down by the King's Bench (R. v. Hastings, 1 D. & R., 48), that words of permission in an Act of Parliament, when tending to promote the general benefit, are always held to be compulsory; and as regards courts and judicial functionaries who act only when appealed to, the same rule was in substance, re-stated by the Common Pleas in laying down that whenever a statute confers an authority to do a judicial act (the word 'judicial' being used evidently in its widest sense) in a certain case, *it is imperative* on those so authorized to exercise the authority when a case arises, and its exercise is duly applied for by a party interested, and having a right to make the application; and that the exercise depends, not on the discretion of the courts or judges, but upon proof of the particular case out of which the power arises."

Our Supreme Court Act provides that "an appeal shall lie to the Supreme Court from all final judgments" of provincial courts. The Manitoba Act in similar terms, provides that "an appeal shall lie to the Governor General in Council from any act or decision of the Legislature of the province." What would we say of the Supreme Court did it refuse to hear an appeal, or to deal with it as justice required, merely because the case involved some political, or otherwise troublesome, question? With all proper respect and for identical reasons, I say that His Excellency in Council cannot decline to exercise the important powers by the Manitoba Act conferred upon him for the protection of the Roman Catholic minority in that province, and I humbly claim, as a right, that the petitions shall be disposed of upon their merits and without regard to the feelings of the body appealed from. A further consideration which emphasises the duty of the Council in this particular case, is the fact that rights, vested rights, which the Catholics had in Manitoba, prior to the Act of 1890, have been taken away from them. The Legislature of Manitoba voluntarily conferred those rights upon the Catholics, and I urge that Parliament ought, by an order to be made by this Council, be given the jurisdiction to deal with the matter, and, if it thinks proper, to restore to us the rights of which we have been deprived. In other words, I contend that this Council ought not to refuse to allow the matter to be taken before Parliament.

As to the measure of relief asked for by the Roman Catholic minority in Manitoba, I have prepared and now submit (without prejudice to any other claims which we may have) a draft of such a statute as we would propose the Legislative Assembly of Manitoba should be asked to pass. (Exhibit P.)

I may say that it is taken very closely from the old statutes, and it is one under which we would seek to get relief.

Hon. Mr. IVES.—Might I ask if it is an amendment of the law of 1890, or if it replaces the law of 1890?

Mr. EWART.—Neither, accurately. It is drafted upon the lines of the Ontario Statute. It is neither strictly an amendment of the Act of 1890 nor does it replace it. The Act of 1890 is left to its operation, and this will be a further Act. We have given it the title of "The Separate Schools Act," taking the title from the Ontario Statute.

It would then be in Manitoba, as in Ontario, a Public Schools Act and a Separate Schools Act.

Hon. Mr. Curran.—Do you go beyond the rights and privileges they had before?

Mr. Ewart.—No. We have been very careful not to go one step beyond, but we have given up some things we had before, as I shall now explain.

Prior to 1890 additional matters were confided to a board of education composed of twelve Protestants and nine Catholics. This board was divided into a Protestant and a Catholic section, each having care of its own schools. The Board, as a whole, had certain jurisdiction, and the respective sections had what remained. The Act of 1890 abolished the Board of Education and provided for a Department of Education, composed of the Executive Council, or a committee thereof. We do not propose to re-establish the old Board. If the Legislature would rather have a Department of Education than a Board of Education, we have nothing to say. But we do ask that those powers which, before 1890, were exercised by the Roman Catholic section of the Board, should again be entrusted to a similar body. The jurisdiction formerly exercised, not by the Catholic section of the Board, but by the whole Board, we are satisfied should for the future, be relegated to the Department of Education; although that will remove from Catholics all share in the settlement of such matters. The reconstituted body of Catholics will, I presume, and as I have provided, have to be appointed by Government, for that was the provision prior to 1890. We ask, too, that we should be relieved from taxation for the support of the present Protestant schools, and of any schools which are non-Catholic; that we should have power to organize our own schools and tax ourselves as formerly; and that we should have our share of all public moneys voted for the maintenance of schools.

So much for the future. With regard to the past some things that have been done ought to be undone. The effect of the Act of 1890 was to transfer the ownership of all Catholic school property to the Protestant schools. We think that this should be given back to us. As part of the property which was confiscated by the Act of 1890, I may mention the sum of $13,879.47, which the Catholic section of the School Board had at its credit in 1890. The circumstances connected with the confiscation of this amount of money (a large sum for Manitoba Catholics) can best be related by reading the affidavit of the Honourable Senator Bernier (Exhibit O). We think that we cannot be deemed unreasonable if we ask that this money, filched by Act of Parliament, should be restored to us.

The remedy which we seek we are content to obtain in the method pointed out by the judgment of the Privy Council, in which it is said : " It is certainly not essential that the Statutes repealed by the Act of 1890 should be re-enacted, or that the precise provisions of these Statutes should again be made the law. The system of education embodied in the Act of 1890, no doubt commends itself to and adequately supplies the wants of the great majority of the inhabitants of the province. All legitimate ground of complaint would be removed if that system were supplanted by provisions which would remove the grievance upon which the appeal is founded, and were modified so far as might be necessary to give effect to these provisions." By supplement and modification, then we are satisfied to obtain the relief which we ask.

There are various points regarding details upon which we would be very willing to make some compromise or agreement with the Manitoba Government, but we are at present in this difficulty, that we are not in a position to ask that any compromise, however fair, should be enacted by the Dominion Government, without the assent to it of the local legislature. We can ask only for that which we had before, and must be careful not even by concessions to change in any material respect the position which we formerly occupied. If we did, any statute that the Dominion might pass might be *ultra vires*.

I hear it frequently said that the Protestant portion of the province of Manitoba is almost a unit in its opposition to separate schools; that Manitoba will refuse to comply with any law passed by the Dominion Parliament; that Manitoba will defy the law laid down by the Judicial Committee of the Privy Council and refuse to be bound by the terms of her own constitution. But it is only when I come to Ontario that I hear those things; even as one had to go to that province to hear of the frightful wrongs imposed upon the downtrodden Protestants in Quebec, by the passage of the Jesuit Estates Act. The Manitoba School Act of 1890 is well known to have originated with one man, and to have been imposed by him upon the Government, of which he was the only strong member, much against the will of his chief; and to be maintained now purely for political purposes, and by the local representations of but one political party. The strategic uses to which the question is put, may well be seen when we observe that although it is the Liberals who conjure with it in Manitoba, it is the Conservatives who endeavour to make capital out of it in Ontario. I say that it is in Ontario alone that we hear of an intending rebellion in Manitoba. The local Government no doubt, has asserted that it will resist to the extent of its power, but outside of Ontario, there has been no hint of reconstitutional action, no suggestion that the loyal people of the Prairie Province had any idea of setting themselves against, or above, the law of their own constitution. The Conservatives in Manitoba are almost to a man in favour of liberty to my clients; and so too are many of the Liberals.

In closing my argument, I cannot do better than adopt (with the exception of a single expression) the concluding language of an address delivered by Dr. J. H. Morrison, before the Junior Liberal-Conservative Association of St. John, N.B. :—

He said :—" Anticipating the appearance of this question in the arena of federal politics, Mr. McCarthy and his Protestant Protective Association have launched out upon a campaign of open hostility to the Roman Catholic Church upon general principles. They hope to enlist the great army of loyal Orangemen upon their side, when they have to face this question. I am proud to be a member of the Orange Society. It is a noble institution and I wish its aims, principles and precepts were better understood by the public at large. But no part of an Orangeman's obligation, permits much less requires, him to oppose a Roman Catholic fellow citizen, merely because he is a Roman Catholic, and he is bound by his obligation to resist the encroachments of the Church of Rome only by just and legitimate means. Is it just and legitimate to break solemn pledges, to violate solemn compacts, to insult, despoil and trample under foot a weak minority, simply because that minority is Roman Catholic?"

Should the Legislature of Quebec abolish the Protestant separate schools of that province, what a cry would go up from all the Protestant newspapers all over Canada? The very men who now cry " let the majority rule," would then enter the lists to see that the minority should have protection ; and you would find Mr. Dalton McCarthy in the vanguard of those who would be ready to unsheathe their swords for the defence of separate Protestant schools. And if the helpless Protestant minority in Quebec should appeal to the Parliament of Canada for protection, wou'd not the entire country endorse and support the Government which would restore them to their present favoured position? Who would then cry "let the provincial majority rule." Can we afford to withhold from the Catholic minority in Manitoba the same justice which we would readily grant to the Protestants in Quebec? Can we make flesh of the one, and fish of the other, and still maintain our own self-respect? Will it be just for us to ratify the wiping out of the separate schools of Manitoba, simply because we are on general principles opposed to separate schools, without taking into consideration the circumstances which surround the case? We cannot afford to adopt the Jesuitical (I object to that word) doctrine, that the end justifies the means, we cannot afford to do wrong that good may come. We cannot afford to be unjust.

" Nearly 1900 years ago, there was delivered to the world a law, which has been the greatest of all forces, in the revolution of religion, civilization and society. It was the law," Do unto others as you would that they should do unto you." Actuated by the spirit of that law, President Cleveland decided to restore to her throne the deposed Hawaiian Queen. Should party jealousy, or Republican hatred of monarchical institution, thwart his beneficent purposes the finger of scorn will be turned upon the United States by the nations of the world. Let not the finger of scorn be turned upon Canada, because she shall refuse to be as just and generous as the President of the Great Republic.

" Again I say, that when this question comes before us, as it must come, if the Government of Canada find it their duty to interfere, let our motto be " Let justice be done though the Heavens fall."

Sir CHARLES TUPPER.—You have submitted a bill. Is your construction of the British North America Act or of the Manitoba Act—I refer to the clause having to do with this matter in each case—is it your construction that the Governor in Council, if they decide to act, are bound to submit a bill to the Legislature of Manitoba?

Mr. EWART.—I am inclined to think so. I am not perfectly clear about it, but I am so much of that opinion that I would be afraid to adopt any other course.

Sir CHARLES TUPPER.—Then what is your construction of that clause 4 in the first Act, and of clause 3 in the other, where, in one case, they use the expression 'provincial authority'? I desire to call your attention to this point, and to ask whether, in the clause to which I refer, the Legislature contemplated an alternative answer, that is to say, whether the Governor in Council, in the first part of the paragraph, should intimate to the Legislature what is requisite, and in the alternative, whether it would be sufficient for the Governor in Council to make a decision in general terms?

Mr. EWART.—I am inclined to think that it applies to different cases, that the first of these alternatives applies to the case of a law, and the second, to some administrative proceeding taken by some provincial authority.

Sir CHARLES TUPPER.—Other than the Legislature?

Mr. EWART.—I am inclined to think so. I admit the clause is not free from doubt. There are so many different opinions about it that one must admit that it is not free from doubt.

Hon. Mr. ANGERS.—Do I understand that the bill you have presented is suggestive and not an injunction?

Mr. EWART.—Suggestive merely.

Sir CHARLES TUPPER.—As the widest measure of relief, I suppose.

Mr. EWART.—Not as the widest measure of relief, but what we are willing to ask and accept.

Hon. Mr. ANGERS.—One that would satisfy your clients?

Mr. EWART.—Yes.

Hon. Mr. IVES.—In your previous address, you say that you appreciate the fact that the Government have no power except to confer jurisdiction upon the Parliament of Canada. I suppose you still adhere to that view?

Mr. EWART.—Yes.

Hon. Mr. OUIMET.—That the Government has no legislative authority.

Mr. EWART.—None whatever.

Hon. Mr. OUIMET.—What is suggested in your bill would give you a full remedy of all the grievances you now have to complain of.

Mr. EWART.—Yes, except as to some matters such as this, for instance, a share of the legislative grant during the last four years, we have not got any of that. We have had to maintain our own schools out of our own pockets in the meantime, and we have had to pay taxes for the support of Protestant schools, but we have not had any share of that. There are one or two other matters. I cannot say that by this bill we would be put in anything like the position we would have been in had there been no interference, or as a matter of broad equity, we should be in.

Hon. Mr. HAGGART.—I suppose you intend to produce evidence to show how the Acts of 1890 interfered with rights and privileges that you acquired

Mr. EWART.—That is established sufficiently by the judgment. That must be taken as conclusive upon that point.

Mr. McCARTHY.—Mr. President and gentlemen of the Privy Council: Before proceeding, I desire to state that Mr. John O'Donohue, a public school trustee of the city of Winnipeg, has come here on behalf of himself and that portion of the Roman Catholics in the province that he believes to be in sympathy with his views, and I would ask that you hear him before I commence my argument.

Sir MACKENZIE BOWELL.—Mr. O'Donohue may proceed.

Mr. O'DONOHUE (reading a statement).—I am a resident of Winnipeg, a public school trustee for Ward 3, and a member of the Catholic Church and a regular communicant. I desire to appear before you to present my views on the public school question on behalf of myself and a large number of Catholics of the province of Manitoba, whom I represent.

When I first arrived in Manitoba in 1882, my business for the first five or six years brought me into contact with the people all over the province, more particularly the French settlements. From the first I took considerable interest in the schools, and it was clear to me from the first that the French schools and the Catholic schools generally were not in the progressive state that the Protestant schools were. My reason for coming to this conclusion was on account of the class of teachers generally employed, and the wretched shape of the schools, both as to grounds, buildings and furniture, notwithstanding that in most of the school districts, the school taxes should be sufficient to maintain the schools in a much better shape as to comfort and efficiency. Seldom did I find a French teacher that could teach or even speak English. I called on His Grace the Archbishop, and asked him if there could not be some improvement. He said that he was looking forward to a better state of affairs, but at that time he was not prepared to make much change, as the class of teachers necessary was not easily procured, and if they were, the accommodation they would require was not procurable. So matters went on as of old from year to year. In the year of, I think, 1886, I spoke to the Hon. John Norquay and asked him if he could not do something to improve the French and Catholic schools so as to put them on a level with the Protestant schools of Kildonan and St. Andrews, and other country Protestant schools. Mr. Norquay's answer was that the Catholic School Board had the matter entirely in their own hands, and he saw no reason why their schools should not be as efficient as the Protestant schools. I may here say that I don't think that 25 per cent of the French youths can write their names, while I think I am safe in saying that 75 of the Protestant natives can read and write.

When the present Provincial Government came into power, or soon after, I called on Mr. Martin and asked him if he would take up the school system of Manitoba and remodel it in some way that would improve them, and in particular the Catholic schools. He, Mr. Martin, said then that he did not think it was within the jurisdiction of the Provincial Government to do so, but it rested with the Federal House, but he promised me to give the matter his consideration. I afterwards spoke to Mr. Smart, Minister of Public Works, in that strain. He also said he would think the matter over. So when the present School Act of 1890 was spoken of, and after its adoption, I gave it my humble and strongest support, and have no reason to regret the course I took, but am more convinced than ever that it is the best for the country and for the Catholics in particular, that they would be the greatest gainers, and would accept the School Act if the French clergy would allow them to do so.

Another grievance many Catholics complain of is that our school property, instead of being held by the Catholic trustees, for the people, is held in fee simple by the Superintendent General, or head of the Oblate Fathers in France, and although in Winnipeg, all the cash invested belongs to the people, the Oblate Fathers always charged a good rent for the Catholic schools. I may also state that about three years ago I canvassed some of the members of our City School Board to find out if there might not be a compromise effected as regards our city schools. My idea was to try and introduce something known as the Faribault system, as then and now in force in Minnesota, that is, our Catholic friends would engage Catholic teachers qualified as the law requires, if our City School Board would provide funds for their payment. I received reasonable encouragement from the City School Board, and then waited on our clergy and made the suggestion as above. The idea was heartily received by Father McCarthy for himself, and on behalf of the parish priest, then Father Fox. The former asked me to wait on the Bishop and lay the matter before him, and said he had no doubt but His Grace would think favourably of the scheme. I said I would not go alone, but if the priests would nominate two other parishioners to go with me, I would see what could be done on the lines mentioned above. The two gentlemen named by the priest, and myself, visited His Grace, and to my surprise were told that it was useless to suggest any compromise, and the interview was cut short, His Grace adding that he was advised by his eastern friends to accept nothing short of the repeal of the 1890 School Act, as he honestly considered the constitution and bill of rights entitled him to on behalf of his people.

There were several letters passed between His Grace and myself, all on the lines as described, but in the most courteous and friendly way. Soon after this, the English-speaking people were granted what His Grace said, was a special favour to them, calling from Boston, Mass., a very clever young Irish priest named Father Maloney. He was not long in Winnipeg till he became very popular, even with the French people. The schools of the city soon received his attention, and he visited them, both Protestant and Catholic, and came to the conclusion at once that the Catholic people would have to do one of two things, either greatly improve their own schoo's or send their children to the public schools. These independent opinions brought down on him the wrath of the powers that then existed, and he had to leave us in a hurry, not, however, before a public meeting of the parishioners was called and a committee named and appointed to call on His Grace and remonstrate, and ask for Father Maloney's retention, but His Grace advanced other and stronger reasons, from his standpoint, why Father Maloney should be let go. I may here say that I was one of the committee above mentioned.

About 18 months ago there was a public meeting of Catholic school supporters called by the trustees, I believe of a school district in the parish of St. Norbert, I think all French people ; and at that, or a subsequent meeting, a resolution was carried that the school districts should come under the late School Act. This, notwithstanding the protest of the parish priest, would have been carried out but for the influence of His Grace being brought to bear on the trustees and people, in fact there is scarcely a day that there are not Catholics calling on me and expressing their wish that matters should shape themselves so that they could send their children to the public schools. Of course, they do not like to express themselves publicly lest coming into contact with the clergy.

Mr. McCarthy.—You said a moment ago that a resolution was carried in the parish of St. Norbert, that the school district should come under the late School Act.

Mr. O'Donohue.—I meant to say the present School Act.

Hon. Mr. Ouimet.—How does it read in your statement ?

Mr. O'Donohue.—I read it, the late School Act.

Hon. Mr. Ouimet.—Was it written by you ?

Mr. O'Donohue.—Yes, sir.

Hon. Mr. Ouimet.—And it reads that way now ?

Mr. O'Donohue.—It reads that way now. My intention was to say the Act of 1890. It was written since I left home.

Hon. Mr. Ouimet.—Could you produce that resolution that you referred to passed by that School Board ?

Mr. O'Donohue.—I do not know, the proceedings appeared in the Winnipeg papers at the time. The resolution was carried at a school meeting.

Sir Mackenzie Bowell.—The Winnipeg papers are in the Library, perhaps you could find it there.

Mr. O'Donohue.—It was a year ago last summer, as near as I can remember it now.

Sir Adolphe Caron.—That is close enough to find out.

Mr. O'Donohue.—The school matter dragged on a long time much as stated above, till Father Langevin, now Bishop elect, became parish priest, when he took hold of the matter in a much more vigorous manner. Every Sunday we were treated to a dose of school matter from his standpoint, in the shape of petitions and processions to the Government, &c. In his warm remarks from the pulpit he would call the Government thieves and scoundrels, those of his congregation that did not fall in with his views, blackguards, &c. I may here say that during my candidature for school trustee last December, Father Langevin opposed me strongly, and canvassed one of the Catholics that signed my nomination papers to withdraw his support from me. Notwithstanding all this, 90 per cent of the Catholics in my ward voted for me, many of them taking out their vehicles to help my election. I consider this very strong evidence that the bulk of the Catholics are ready to accept the present School Act if left to act for themselves. You will remember the election referred to was by ballot.

I may also say that two of my daughters have taught in the public schools of Winnipeg and at present there is one teaching there. They both are, I think, good practical Catholics, and would resist any religious exercises offensive to the Catholic

Church, and they always reported to me that they neither saw or heard anything offensive to Catholics. In closing my remarks I wish to be understood as not referring to the convent schools, which I have good reason for saying are all even more efficient than they are represented to be, and very many of our Protestant friends take advantage of their usefulness for the education of their daughters.

By Mr. Ewart:

Q. Do you speak French?—A. No, sir.

Q And you judge of the efficiency of separate schools when you do not understand what is going on in them?—A. Yes. It is not very hard to pass an opinion on the majority of the country schools.

By Sir Adolphe Caron:

Q. Did you write that out yourself?—A. I wrote it out. I wrote it out yesterday in the Queen's Hotel, and got it typewritten. Mr. McCarthy told me I had better write it out. I did not know what I would be asked to say. That is just how it was done, it was written yesterday and typewritten to-day.

By Sir Charles Tupper:

Q. I would like to ask you how many schools you personally inspected before that conversation you referred to?—A. I was in the great bulk of the schools along the river.

Q. Can you tell us any of the schools you had particularly in mind when you discussed them with Mr. Norquay in 1886?—A. Yes, I was in a school about four or five miles east of Ste. Anne, a French school.

Q. Who was the teacher?—A. I could not tell you that now. I was in two schools in the parish of St. Norbert.

Q. Can you give the names of the teachers in any of the schools?—A. I can give one of them, for the teacher came to my house several times. She felt that there ought to be something done for the schools, and she knew what it was, for she lived, and cooked, and slept in the school-house. That was done in more schools than one. Her name was Miss Richot.

Q. What year was that?—A. That would be about 1887 or 1888.

Q. I was referring to the schools that you had been in personally before 1886?—A. I was in her school, and I was in a school at Oak Point.

Q. Was that a French school?—A. Yes. Very seldom I found any teachers that could talk English. My business led me a good deal through the country. Mr. Daly knows my business. I was on the board all the time I have been there.

Q. Then, as to the percentages. When you speak of the percentage of French who can read and write, and the percentage of English who can read and write, how do you make out that calculation?—A. I will tell you how I come to that. I have been in the agricultural implement business since I came to that country; I take a great many notes, and in addition to that, I have collected a lot of notes for persons in Ontario; and from the class of notes, and from the way they were signed, I came to that conclusion.

Q. Did you reduce that calculation to paper? For instance, did you add up the number of people who could speak French?—A. No, I did not, I compared my notes.

Q. Then practically it was a guess from your experience?- A. I went over the notes in my possession.

By Hon. Mr. Ives:

Q. The notes were given by elderly people, I suppose, rather than by children?—A. There were a good many young people.

Q. They were not given by school children?—A. No.

By Sir Charles Tupper:

Q. Can you tell us to-day about how many people you came across in selling these goods, who could not read or write—within ten or twenty?—A. No, I do not think I could.

Q. You did not keep a record?—A. I have had several hundred notes in my possession, but I have not got so many just now.

Q. And it was from your experience gained in that way that you made this estimate?—A. Yes.

By Hon. Mr. Montague :

Q. Was this true in the case of English people, a great majority of whom had attended school in the provinces from which they had emigrated to Manitoba?—A. I am talking of the natives only, I am talking of the half-breeds.

Q. Do you remember what was the percentage of the French?—A. About 25 per cent of the French half-breeds and 75 per cent of the Scotch half-breeds, in a rough way. I might be wrong a little, one way or the other, I cannot vouch for the accuracy of it at all. Of course, I am speaking altogether of the natives.

Mr. McCarthy.—Before discussing this matter, I desire to say that I think you ought in fairness to allow me an opportunity of answering the affidavits which have been filed here to-day. There was no ground at all to suspect, and no notice was given of any intention to use affidavits ; and if this matter is to be determined upon affidavit evidence, it is manifest, if there is to be fair-play, that there must be an opportunity for answering those affidavits, and no such opportunity has been afforded. On the contrary, my learned friend who has used those affidavits in support of no less than four arguments, and as to three of them they are based solely upon affidavits, gave formal notice to the Attorney General, and that formal notice was taken from the forms which are used in the courts. He winds up by saying :—

"Take notice, that in default of anyone appearing at this time to speak on behalf of the Government of Manitoba, then His Excellency the Governor General in Council may proceed to hear such appeals in support."

Now, my learned friend knows perfectly well that if affidavits are to be used, a notice must be given that they are to be used, and opportunity must be afforded of seeing them and answering them. The affidavits to be used are always mentioned in the notice, and I hold in my hand the formal notice which was served upon the Attorney General. I think you will see the fairness of my claim. I am quite prepared, of course, to discuss the matter from the historical standpoint, from a knowledge that has come to us all, and from a legal standpoint ; but to meet a case upon affidavits, those affidavits having been carefully kept in my learned friend's possession until the last moment, without a hint being given that they would be used, would be so gross a perversion of justice that I do not see how I can be forced into an argument until an opportunity is afforded me of meeting those affidavits.

Hon. Mr. Ouimet.—What is the conclusion of your argument? Do you ask for something?

Mr. McCarthy.—The conclusion of my argument is that I want an opportunity of answering these affidavits. That is my application. My learned friend made nine arguments, four of these are based partly upon affidavits, three of them altogether upon affidavits. Now, it never entered into my head that this matter could be determined upon affidavits. If it is to be determined upon affidavits, they cannot be produced upon one side only, and of course an opportunity must be afforded me of answering these affidavits by others.

Mr. Ewart.—My learned friend's objection, if there is anything in it, comes entirely too late. If he was going to object to these documents being read, the time for him to take objection was when I put in the first one, if he wanted time to answer them. Not until he heard our whole argument does he ask for an adjournment for the purpose of answering these affidavits. My learned friend, however, has done exactly what I have done, he has gone upon the same lines of procedure. We have brought such evidence here as we thought proper : he did not tell me what his evidence was going to be, nor did I tell him what mine was going to be. If the notice had been a little longer, I would have sent my learned friend copies of the affidavits, out of courtesy merely, but as the notice was short, I was unable to get the affidavits completed until after I had arrived at Ottawa. My learned friend has got Mr. O'Donohue here, and he has given testimony. He gave it orally, we have put in our testimony by affidavit. I could have got all these gentlemen here no doubt, at great expense and asked them to make speeches and they could have had all their testimony type-written upon foolscap, and read it off. I will merely mention that Mr. O'Donohue has come here, not as a witness for me at all, but on his own behalf and on behalf of those whom he says he represents. I think there is little doubt that Mr. O'Donohue comes here at the instance of the Local Government: I do not think it is at all probable that Mr. O'Donohue is paying his own expenses here to make the statement he has done. I do not think I am at all wrong in suggesting that Mr. O'Donohue is here for the purpose of giving testimony for the Provincial Government. Therefore, I say that my learned friend has been procee ling upon the same lines, and he has no more right to ask for an adjournment to answer my affidavits than I would have to ask for an adjournment to answer the statements of his witness. If he makes a distinction, saying mine are affidavits, and his are statements, I am content to take mine as statements and not affidavits : I am content to say that so far as this court is concerned, they should be regarded simply as statements and not as sworn documents.

Sir MACKENZIE BOWELL.—Of course, Mr. Ewart must remember that Mr. McCarthy objected in the first place, not very strenuously, I admit, to the reading of these affidavits. He must be permitted, however, to answer them.

Mr. EWART.—My learned friend hardly objected, he rather presumed that he could not object.

Hon. Mr. MONTAGUE.—I think Mr. McCarthy offered his objection at the time.

Mr. MCCARTHY.—I certainly do not think I had any right to do more than to point out as I did that it was irregular. I do not know anything about what this Council will do. It seems to me if the matter was to be discussed upon public grounds, as provided by Mr. Blake's Act to which reference was made, in any question of fact to be tried, the reference should have been made under that Act. Without reading the affidavits, I do not know how anybody can determine the matter.

Sir MACKENZIE BOWELL.—It has been suggested that we should adjourn four or five minutes to consider this question.

Hon. Mr. OUIMET.—Suppose, Mr. McCarthy, that you go on with your argument. I presume you are very well cognizant of the facts upon which you are going to base that argument, and at the end of your argument, permission might be given to you to file affidavits.

Mr. MCCARTHY.—It would be very inconvenient to do that. If I am to be of any service at all upon this case, I must base my arguments upon facts and not upon mere suppositions. I do not know what is to be said of this intimation of bad faith in the three arguments which have been adduced. I want to see what reply can be made, and, of course, I cannot argue that upon any assumption which I do not know and which I have not before me.

Hon. Mr. OUIMET.—These facts have been before the public for several years.

Mr. MCCARTHY.—Never did I hear of them, and I know nothing about them.

Hon. Mr. OUIMET.—They were discussed in the Manitoba Legislature, and they were discussed here, and several times within your hearing.

Mr. MCCARTHY.—All I can say is that I know nothing about these facts, and never supposed any claim was to be based on them.

Hon. Mr. OUIMET.—I never suspected you were ignorant of all these facts.

Mr. MCCARTHY.—There are a good many other things that you never suspected.

Sir MACKENZIE BOWELL.—I think I have read some of those affidavits before.

Hon. Mr. MONTAGUE.—Some of them were in Mr. Ewart's speech.

The Privy Council retired for ten minutes to consult together, and returned.

Sir MACKENZIE BOWELL.—The Council has decided to request Mr. McCarthy to proceed with his argument upon points of law, and upon such points of historical interest as he may desire to submit : but they will give reasonable time afterwards to produce affidavits in reply to those produced by Mr. Ewart. But no affidavits of any new matter can be produced. Mr. Ewart can be heard upon them upon a subsequent day, to be fixed at the end of the argument.

Mr. EWART.—Allow me to say that that would throw the matter over so late that it would be impossible that anything could be done this year; and rather than that should happen, I would withdraw the affidavits and rest the case upon the other material.

Mr. McCARTHY.—I can not object to that course.

Sir CHARLES TUPPER.—Then we will consider them withdrawn.

Hon. Mr. OUIMET.—Do you not wish to answer that statement of Mr. O'Donohue?

Mr. EWART.—In my argument I shall say something about it.

Hon. Mr. OUIMET.—Then there is nothing in the way of arguing the case to-morrow morning.

The Privy Council adjourned until 11 o'clock a.m. on Tuesday morning.

Affidavits referred to in Mr. EWART's opening argument and filed as Exhibits A, B, C, D, E, F, G, H, J, J, K, L, M, N and O, were subsequently withdrawn.

OTTAWA, 5th March, 1895.

The Privy Council met at 11 o'clock a. m.

Present:—Sir Mackenzie Bowell, Sir Adolphe Caron, Hon. Mr. Costigan, Sir Charles Tupper, Hon. Mr. Foster, Hon. Mr. Haggart, Hon. Mr. Daly, Hon. Mr. Ouimet, Hon. Mr. Ives, Hon. Mr. Dickey, and Hon. Mr. Montague.

Mr. McCARTHY.—Mr. President and Gentlemen of the Privy Council: Before commencing my statement, perhaps you will allow me to read something in confirmation of Mr. O'Donohue's statement made yesterday. Some of the members of the Council asked for reference to a statement which Mr. O'Donohue said had been published, he thought, in the summer of 1893. Dr. Blakely has discovered the article referred to in searching the paper. I refer you to the Winnipeg Daily *Tribune* of the 29th June, 1893, from which I now read:—

"A member of St. Mary's Church complained to a *Tribune* man that for five consecutive Sundays the only discourse from the pulpit of said church has been exclusively devoted to the school question, and a large number of the congregation think it is about time to change the subject to some discussion not quite so stale and unprofitable. He expressed the hope that Father Drummond, who is announced to take the pulpit next Sunday, will preach to them on something more instructive and acceptable to the congregation. Last Sunday, the 25th inst., Rev. Father O'Dwyer, during his remarks on ' Candid Catholic,' said, ' He had the proof, or could prove, that Protestantism was taught in the city schools, and that the Catholic teachers in some schools were not allowed the privilege of knowing anything about such teachings.'

"Our informant said that all Catholic teachers in the city know the untruthfulness of Rev. Father O'Dwyer's remark. He also stated that on the Saturday, the 24th inst., a meeting of the ratepayers of St. Norbert Schools (Ritchot) was held for the purpose of considering the present condition of their schools, and after a full discussion of its position, came to the conclusion to elect a board of trustees under the present school law, accept the Government grant, and hire a qualified teacher, etc. Father Ritchot, parish priest of St. Norbert, being alarmed at the apparent independence of the ratepayers, despatched a messenger to inform His Grace at St. Boniface of their move for freedom, and on Sunday, the 25th inst., another meeting was called, at which the Bishop's message was delivered, which was that no change was the order of the church ; and hence there was nothing done. But the people have become so thoroughly aroused to the necessity of a change in school matters, that they have called another meeting for this (Thursday) evening and the advocates of public schools are bound, if possible, to come under the Government school system, and in the future to give their children the benefit of the school tax which they have never enjoyed up to the present."

I may say, at the outset, and for reasons which I will give before I close, that I do not come here at all on behalf of the Provincial Government recognizing this tribunal as sitting in a judicial capacity. I quite concede that the judgment of the Privy Council in the late case determines that the Governor General in Council has jurisdiction to make a remedial order, and that that remedial order being made and disobeyed, the Parliament of this country will have authority or jurisdiction to carry that remedial order into effect by legislation. But I will endeavour to show that this tribunal is not sitting in a judicial capacity, and I desire, at the outset, to have it clearly understood that the province which I represent here does not recognize the Council sitting in this matter as being any more than the Council sitting in any other matter, namely, as advisers of His Excellency the Governor General. Of course I need not say to the members of the Council who have had more experience than I have had in such matters, that it is not an unknown thing—I will not say that it is a common thing, but it is not unknown—for Council to hear arguments on matters which they have thereafter to determine, matters relating to private affairs and sometimes, public questions. I myself have appeared twice, as I recall, and perhaps oftener, before the Council to argue such questions; once with reference to a public matter, and once with reference to a private matter, which afterwards became a public question, I appearing on behalf of a private individual. Having said so much in a preliminary way, I think it will be more convenient if I deal first with the argument of my learned friend Mr. Ewart, who appeared here on behalf of a section of the Roman Catholic population of Manitoba—because, as I am instructed, my learned friend does not represent the Roman Catholic minority in any concrete or organized form. I am not at all disputing his right to appear, but I want to draw your attention to the fact that, as I am instructed, and as I think I shall be able to show, Mr. Ewart appears only for a section of the Roman Catholic minority, and that no means have been taken to ascertain the views of that minority as a body, that there is nothing to show even that he represents the majority of that body, though it might be found that he spoke according to their views if a poll or census of that minority had been taken. My learned friend, in the first place, dealt with what he called the historical question, that is to say the bargain or treaty or compact that was made between the government of this country and the inhabitants of the prairie country prior to the passage of the Manitoba Act. My own view is—and I put it before you with great deference—that you have nothing at all to do with the negotiations which led up to the passage of the Manitoba Act, but the Manitoba Act must speak for itself and that you have to find within the four corners of section 22 of that Act all the powers that are conferred upon the Governor in Council or upon the Parliament of Canada. But in one sense possibly it may be pertinent to the argument, because, as I have already been pointing out, you are not sitting here in a judicial capacity, and therefore are not bound by the same strict rules of construction as a court of law would be. It may therefore be pertinent, with a view to establishing a certain line of policy as advisable to be adopted, to endeavour to show as my learned friend has done, that some arrangement had been made between the people of the province and the Government of Canada prior to the passage of the Manitoba Act, prior to the union of that territory with the Dominion of Canada. I am sorry to say that my investigation has not led me to the same conclusion by any means upon the historical matter of fact as that which my learned friend has stated he has arrived at. On the contrary, I think it can be demonstrated, and I desire, therefore, to make it as clear as I can, that the only arrangement that was made so far as the inhabitants of that country were concerned, was based upon lists of rights or bills of rights, whichever they may be called, in which no reference whatever was made to the question of public schools. Now I caution the Council, the members of which have no doubt had the opportunity of perusing the book compiled and edited by my learned friend Mr. Ewart, not to rely wholly upon the statements made in that publication. I am not at all imputing to my learned friend bad faith, I am not imputing a desire to misrepresent; but he has been so long bound up with the advocacy of this question that it is hardly reasonable to expect that he should be always in the judicial frame of mind one ought to be in who purposes to write an impartial history of events. He states in his books and he has argued here before you that there were four bills of rights prepared, and in that book you will find two if not three of these bills of rights given—if my memory serves me right the number is two. My learned friend's argument is that it was the fourth bill or list of rights that was handed to the delegates who were invited to visit Ottawa, and who did, in point of fact, visit Ottawa for the purpose of making terms with reference to the entrance of that part of the present Dominion of Canada into confederation. Now I take issue with my learned friend with regard to what is called the fourth list or bill of rights as being the document that was entrusted to these delegates. On the contrary, I think I shall be able to satisfy you by the clearest possible testimony—so far as one can have testimony upon a matter of that kind, the testimony of history—that the bills of rights that were prepared, so far as we know or so far as we can learn, by persons who professed to be the representatives of the people, did not contain any reference whatever to the question of separate schools, contained no demand that the school system should be in any way protected or in any way guarded by the Government or by the authority of the Act which was to take this province into the Dominion. Now just let me give you the history of this subject and let me fortify my statement with regard to it as far as I possibly can do so by the public documents ; because, of course, I am not going to rely in the slightest degree upon anything that is not common to us all, such as written histories and public documents, etc., such as the members of the Council would have a right to look at in forming their opinion on this question. I speak with submission, and I speak subject to correction, when I say that the first that was heard of this fourth bill of rights was in 1890 in a letter published in the Winnipeg *Free Press* by the late Archbishop Taché; that the publication of that so-called fourth bill of rights which His Grace alleged had been given to the delegates when they visited Ottawa was followed immediately by a letter from Mr. Taylor controverting the statement, Mr. Taylor professing to know the facts of the case. Following Mr. Taylor's first letter a controversy raged between Mr. Taylor on one part, and another gentleman, I think Mr. Hay, on the other, and His Grace the Archbishop, and that controversy I do not know ever to have been settled to the mutual satisfaction of these contending parties. But, up to that time, nothing at all had been heard, so far as I know, of this fourth bill of rights. Let me call your attention to what did take place, according to the historical records, with reference to this matter. There was a body elected in November, 1869, and in Mr. Ewart's book,—and I think that is not an inconvenient term—this body is called the Council of November. This Council consisted of 24 members. It prepared a list of rights which is dated 16th, December, 1869. I think my learned friend will agree with me and save me the trouble and you the delay of my referring to it, that there was no claim of separate schools made in that bill of rights.

Mr. EWART.—Yes.

Mr. McCARTHY.—You will find that bill of rights at page 333. I think it was on the 4th of that month that delegates were sent from Ottawa to the Red River country, these delegates being the Very Rev. Grand Vicar Thibault, Col. de Salaberry and Mr. (now Sir) Donald A. Smith. Those delegates reached the Red River settlement. Sir Donald Smith seems to have taken the principal part in the negotiations which ensued. Now that council of 24—it is not important to state to you how or why—were superseded by a council which is called the Council of Forty. You will find it stated in Mr. Ewart's book, at page 349, that this council of forty also prepared a bill of rights, and that bill of rights was submitted to Sir Donald Smith. Sir Donald Smith made comments upon, reported upon, that bill of rights upon his return here to the capital. That bill of rights is to be found in the Sessional Papers of 1870. I think it is not to be found in Mr. Ewart's book, but is included as an appendix to Sir Donald Smith's report. You will find it in the Sessional Papers of 1870, No. 12 of vol. 5. Sir Donald Smith states the fact of his having met this council of 40, and of the council having submitted to him this bill of rights which he dealt with. At page 3 of the report I have mentioned, you will find the following :—

" As is generally known the result of the meeting was the appointment of forty delegates, twenty from either side to meet on 25th January, 'with the object of considering the subject of Mr. Smith's commission, and to decide what would be the best for the welfare of the country,' the English as a body, and a large number of the French declaring their entire satisfaction with the explanations given, and their earnest desire for union with Canada. "

He gives details of how that body was elected and continues (page 4):

" The delegates met on the 25th and continued in session till the 10th February. On the 26th, I handed to their chairman, Judge Black, the documents read at the meetings of the 19th and 20th January, and, on the 27th attended the convention by appointment. I was received with much cordiality, by all the delegates, explained to them the views of the Canadian government, and gave assurances that on entering Confederation, they would be secured in the possession of all rights, privileges and immunities enjoyed by British subjects in other parts of the Dominion ; but, on being requested by Mr. Riel to give an opinion regarding a certain 'list of rights,' prepared by his party in December last, I declined to do so, thinking it better that the present convention should place in my hands a paper, stating their wishes, to which I should ' be happy to give such answers as I believed would be in accordance with the views of the Canadian Government.' The convention then set about the task of preparing a 'list of rights' embodying the provisions upon which they would be willing to enter the confederation. While the discussion regarding this list was going on, Mr. Riel called on me and asked if the Canadian Goverment would consent to receive another province. "

I pass on, for this part is not pertinent to the matter I am now dealing with. On page 5, the report continues :—

"The proceedings of the convention, as reported in the *New Nation* newspaper, on the 11th and 18th February, copies of which I have had the honour of addressing to you, are sufficiently exact and render it unnecessary for me here to enter into details ; suffice it to say that a large majority of the delegates expressed entire satisfaction with the answers to their 'list of rights,' and profess confidence in the Canadian Government, to which I invited them to send delegates, with the view of effecting a speedy transfer of the territory to the Dominion, an invitation received with acclamation and unanimously accepted, as will appear by resolution hereto annexed, along with the list of rights and my answer to the same. The delegates named were John Black, Esq., recorder, the Rev. Mr. Ritchot, and Mr. Alfred H. Scott—a good deal of opposition having been offered to the election of the last named of the three.

"The proceedings of the convention came to a close on the 10th February by nomination of a provisional government, in the formation of which several delegates declined to take any part. Governor MacTavish, Dr. Cowan, and two or three other persons were then released, and the Hudson's Bay Company's officers again allowed to come and go at pleasure, but I was still confined to the fort : Riel, as he expressly stated to Judge Black, being apprehensive of my influence with the people in the approaching election."

All I am quoting for is to show you the nature of the appendix, the list of rights. That document contains nineteen articles, but amongst them is not to be found any reference to the question of separate schools, though I think there is some reference to the question of education. There is one article to which I may draw your attention and which provides "that there should be no interference by the Dominion Parliament, in the local affairs of this territory other than is allowed in any of the provinces in the confederation ; and that this territory shall have and enjoy in all respects, the same privileges, advances, and aids in meeting the public expenses of this territory as the confederated provinces have and enjoy."

The only reference that is made to education is in paragraph 9.

"That while the North-west remains a territory, the sum of $25,000 (twenty-five thousand dollars) a year be appropriated for schools, roads and bridges.

Now, shortly after, the unfortunate incident——
Hon. Mr. OUIMET.—Did you state who had sent Sir Donald Smith to the territory ?
Mr. McCARTHY.—Yes. The Government here at Ottawa. He was sent with Col. de Salaberry and the Very Rev. Grand Vicar Thibault ; but the others do not seem to have taken part in the negotiations and did not make reports. Sir Donald Smith seems to have borne the burden of the negotiations then carried on with those who, at the time, represented the Red River Settlement. Now that meeting with Sir Donald Smith is referred to in Mr. Begg's recent history, from which I find my learned friend has quoted in his work. You will find it referred to at page 59 of the first volume, but it does not add anything to what I have stated. Of course I have quoted from the original document as published in the Sessional Papers, and the history is, of course, based upon—or purports to be—that original document. These delegates were to have left on 10th February, but, unfortunately, the murder of Thomas Scott intervened, and affairs were in a dreadful condition as we can easily imagine, and the delegates did not leave at the time intended.
Hon. Mr. DICKEY.—Did these transactions take place before the murder ?
Mr. McCARTHY.—The murder took place upon the 4th of March. The Council was disbanded and a new election took place on the 26th February, so now we have three different bodies—the Council of November which met in December : the Council of 40, which met Sir Donald Smith, and the Council elected on the 26th February. On the 4th March the unhappy incident took place to which I have referred, and this assembly which was elected, met on 4th March and continued to 26th March.
Mr. EWART.—There were twenty-four members in that body.
Mr. McCARTHY.—I am prepared to accept my learned friend's statement as regard to that. What appears in Mr. Ewart's book is that the list of rights shown to Sir Donald Smith was not the list of rights which was sent to Ottawa and formed the basis of the negotiations here. It was intended that that list of rights should be taken by the delegates who were then appointed to come to Ottawa, but my learned friend's argument, and the statement in his books is that they did not leave for Ottawa—as I believe the fact to be—on 10th February as intended, that they did not leave until after the meeting of the new elected body of twenty-four ; that it was not until about the end of the month—the 26th or 27th—that they left. So you will see that upon the main facts we are agreed. Now, upon the 26th or 27th March the main bill of rights was prepared, and it appears from the history—though I do not find the record of it anywhere else than in this only history we have of it, that it was this third bill of rights which was handed to the delegates who came here to Ottawa, and which formed the sole instructions from the provisional council—because by this time Riel had organized a so-called government and provisional council. You will find that His Excellency the Governor General at the time, as well as his responsible advisers, refused to recognize this provisional government—refused to read or look at, formally or officially, this third bill of rights which the delegates brought. It also appears in some of the statements, at all events from the report made by the Rev. Mr. Ritchot, upon his return to the territories, that they were told that they might advocate what was stated in this bill of rights, but the Dominion Government could not recognize the authority of the provisional government and look at this bill of rights. This bill of rights—which, as I say, contained no reference to separate schools—is the one which Mr. Ewart in his book calls bill of rights No. 3, and you will find it set out at page 365, where it appears in parallel column with the one which is called bill of rights No. 4. Now it was bill of rights No. 3 that was taken as stated by the historian Begg—whose fairness I do not think my learned friend impugns and you will find it in volume one at page 476. This was handed to the delegates with the following letter :—

"SIR,—The President of the Provisional Government of Assiniboia, (formerly Rupert's Land and the North-west), in council, do hereby authorize and delegate you to proceed to the city of Ottawa, and lay before the Dominion Government the accompanying list of propositions and conditions as the terms upon which the people of Assiniboia will consent to enter confederation with the other provinces of the Dominion. You will also herewith receive a letter of instructions, which will be your guide in the execution of this commission.

"Signed this twenty-second day of March in the year of our Lord one thousand eight hundred and seventy.

By order,

"THOMAS BUNN,
"Secretary of State."

Nothing could be more formal than this. And here is the letter of instruction accompanying the same :

"SIR,—Inclosed with this letter you will receive your commission and also a copy of the conditions and terms upon which the people of this country will consent to enter into the Confederation of Canada. You will please proceed with convenient speed to the city of Ottawa, Canada, and on arriving there you will in company with the other delegates, put yourself immediately in communication with the Dominion Government on the subject of your commission. You will please observe with regard to the articles numbered 1, 2, 3, 4, 6, 7, 15, 17, 19 and 20, you are left at liberty in concert with your fellow commissioners to exercise your discretion ; but bear in mind that, as you carry with you the full confidence of this people, it is expected that in the exercise of this liberty, you will do your utmost to secure their rights and privileges, which have hitherto been ignored.

"With reference to the remaining articles, I am directed to inform you that they are peremptory. I have further to inform you that you are not empowered to conclude finally any arrangements with the Canadian Government, but that any negotiations entered into between you and the said government must first have the approval of and be ratified by the Provisional Government before Assiniboia will become a province of confederation."

Then follows the list of rights which is called No. 3, and which does not contain any reference to separate schools. The paragraph referring to separate schools is to be found in the document called bill of rights No. 4, the seventh section or paragraph. So, I think, I establish, so far as anything of that kind can be established, by historical reference, that, up to this time at all events, no documents had been sent by the people of the territories making any demand with regard to separate schools. Now the delegates came to Ottawa. If you want to follow the question further you will find the facts in the evidence included in the Journals of 1874. I dare say the President (Sir Mackenzie Bowell) will remember—I think he was in public life at the time—the inquiry brought out by reason of the assertion that was made that there had been an agreement for amnesty. I think that was the primary cause of this commission, and the evidence collected will be found in the Journals of 1874, Vol. 8. Sir John Macdonald's evidence to which I shall briefly refer you is at page 103, though I do not refer to it altogether. He says :—

"Sir George Cartier and I had been appointed, I think, by Order in Council, to represent the government in dealing with these delegates.

"Judge Black and Father Ritchot met Sir George and myself in Sir George's house. Mr. Scott was absent from some accidental cause. They presented themselves as delegates appointed at a meeting of the people at Winnipeg. They presented a resolution or resolutions passed at that meeting.

"Judge Black took me aside and stated that they had received and brought with them an authority from Riel as chief of the Provisional Government to act on behalf of that Provisional Government, and also a certain claim or bill of rights, prepared by that government. He asked me what was to be done with the authority and the 'bill of rights.' I told him they had better not be produced as the Governor General could not recognize the legal existence of the Provisional Government and would not treat with them as such. I stated, however, that the claims asserted in the last mentioned bill of rights could be pressed by the delegates, and would be considered on their own merits."

This is still dealing with the bill of rights No. 3. I think I am right in my statement that these were the only lists or bills of rights heard of until 1890—and I was not pretending to be very familiar with the history of Manitoba, for the history has not been very detailed, and I can only state that that is the conclusion I have arrived at from what I have seen, and leave it to the better judgment of the Council to say whether I am right or wrong. Then, in 1890, when an attempt was made to abolish the separate schools, and only then, was the claims set up that there was a fourth bill of rights, that being the bill of rights which appears in Mr. Ewart's book as bill of rights No. 4, which was stated to have been changed or altered, not by the Council, as I understand the Archbishop's letter, not by this body of twenty-four people who prepared bill of rights No. 3———

Mr. EWART.—No.

Mr. McCARTHY.—In what do you wish to correct me?

Mr. EWART.—The Assembly of twenty-four did not prepare bill of rights No. 3.

Mr. McCARTHY.—Who did?

Mr. EWART.—The Executive Council did.

Mr. McCARTHY.—It may be so. I do not know and I do not care. But I say that what is claimed is that this bill of rights, before it was handed to these delegates, was changed or altered by some person, we do not know how, at least I have not seen any satisfactory statement, and it depends very much upon Father Ritchot's statement, in contradiction of the official documents of the time and all we know with regard to it officially. Now I have here a letter that was written on the 17th January, 1890, by Mr. James Taylor, and perhaps my learned friend can tell better than I can who Mr. Taylor is. I believe he had the custody of some document in relation to this matter.

Mr. EWART.—I never heard of that.

Mr. McCARTHY.—Mr. Taylor first wrote a letter on this subject, but unfortunately those issues of the Winnipeg paper containing it are not on the file which commences with the 13th of January instead of 1st January. But you will find first a letter from His Grace the Archbishop and subsequently a letter from Mr. Taylor to His Grace and from that the correspondence goes on. I will read you—and it is sufficient for the purpose I have in hand—the letter of the 17th January, 1890, and copied from the newspaper, I think, of the 18th of that month ——

"To His Grace Archbishop Taché, of St. Boniface.

"REVEREND AND DEAR SIR,—Your letter of the 13th inst., addressed to me through the columns of the *Free Press*, has been read with very deep interest.

"Referring again to our bill of rights, I have to say that the copies in my possession are not essays that were prepared and afterwards rejected by the Provisional Government, but they are authentic copies of the bill of rights that was handed by Mr. Bunn to the delegates and carried by them to Ottawa in March, 1870."

That is what Mr. Begg accepts as the true copy.

"Your Grace kindly states that the 'Executives of Government—legal or illegal—do not always publish their actions, and it is very seldom that the instructions to delegates are made public.' It happens that in this case the bill of rights was published and was issued from Government House, Fort Garry, in March, 1870. And it is the very same bill of rights that was handed by Mr. Bunn to the delegates. It differs, however, from your Grace's bill in the clauses already noticed. I may state that the late Hon. A. G. B. Bannatyne, who was a member of the Provisional Government, showed me on one occasion a printed copy of the bill handed to the delegates, which was exactly the same as the one filed away by Mr. Bunn."

Mr. Bunn was at this time dead, I understand, but these documents were found among his papers.

"I may also state that Mr. Bannatyne directed the Hon. John Norquay as to where he would find the authentic copy of the bill of rights that had been handed to the delegates. Mr. Norquay was so thoroughly convinced of the authenticity of the document that before making his memorable budget speech of 1884 he wrote to me as follows:—

"'March 19, 1884.

"'MY DEAR TAYLOR,—Will you kindly send me the old bill of rights, or a copy, as presented by Black, Scott and Ritchot? I want to refer to it this afternoon in my speech.

"'Yours truly,
"'JOHN NORQUAY.'

"In his budget speech of 1884, Mr. Norquay dwelt particularly upon clauses one (1) and eleven (11) in our bill of rights, and also quoted from other records that were furnished to him from our archives. Allow me to say—and I do so with all respect—that Your Grace did not condemn the language of the documents used by Mr. Norquay on that occasion. I admit that Mr. Bunn may have said : 'I do not know where the record of the proceedings of the Provisional Government is,' but Mr. Bunn could also have added with truthfulness that the record was somewhere in the parishes of St. Clement's and St. Andrew's.

"Now with regard to the capacity in which the delegates were received at Ottawa, Your Grace states that 'the delegates insisted upon a written acknowledgment of their official position, and that objections were made, but on the 26th of March, 1870, the promised letter was given to the delegates by the ministers.' Your Grace must be aware that upon this occasion the delegates were not received as the delegates from the president of the Provisional Government, but, on the contrary, were received as delegates from the people of the North-west. The following is a copy of the letter showing in what capacity they were received by the Federal Government :"—

This letter is among the public documents.

"'OTTAWA, 26th April, 1870.

"'GENTLEMEN,—I have to acknowledge the receipt of your letter of the 22nd instant, stating that as delegates from the North-west to the Government of the Dominion of Canada you are desirous of having an early audience with the Government, and am to inform in reply that the Hon. Sir John A. Macdonald and Sir George E. Cartier have been authorized by the government to confer with you on the subject of your mission and will be ready to receive you at 11 o'clock.

"'I have the honour to be, gentlemen,
"'Your most obedient servant,
"'JOSEPH HOWE.

"'To the Rev. N. RITCHOT, Ptre.,
"'J. BLACK, Esq.,
"'ALFRED SCOTT, Esq.'

"Your Grace does not state why the delegates did not report from time to time the arrangements they were making with the Federal Government. That not done, I maintain they were not loyal to our cause. I further maintain that they were unfaithful to the people of the North-west, when they allowed our bill of rights to be altered at Ottawa without our knowledge and consent?"

That is the charge—that the bill of rights was altered and amended here. The bill of rights they were sent with was bill of rights No. 3. It was altered here, as this gentleman states, and you will see the reason why :—

"They were solemnly warned that they were carrying with them the terms upon which the people of this country would enter the Confederation, and were told not to conclude finally any arrangements with the Canadian Government without first referring any conclusions arrived at to the Provisional Government. They concluded arrangements at Ottawa that have never been satisfactory to the people of Manitoba and the North-west, and the Federal Government, after taking advantage of us through our delegates to Ottawa in 1870, have treated us during the last twenty years more like serfs than like British subjects. They claim at the Dominion capital that on account of the arrangements entered into in 1870 (not with our consent) that we have been very fairly treated. I must say, however, that the Rev. Father Ritchot was not altogether silent. He told the Provisional Government of his presence at Ottawa—of the progress he was making, and of the idea of sending an expedition to this country. The last telegram sent was to Mr. Lepine, and read as follows :—

"'OTTAWA, 10th May, 1870.
"'To Mr. MAXIME LEPINE.
"'Our affairs settled, and satisfactory. Will start next Tuesday.
"'N. J. RITCHOT.'

" I hold the copy of Mr. Bunn's letter of the 23rd June, 1870, sent to Rev. Father Ritchot, asking him to report the result of his mission to Canada, and find it to be correct. He was the only delegate who made a report to the Provisional Government. The quotations published by Your Grace from the *New Nation*, bearing date the 24th June, 1870, are only the views that were held at the time by the editor of that journal. "The report of Rev. Father Ritchot was made after the following manner : —"

This you will find in the paper, the *New Nation*, which was in the Library. I saw it, but I did not think it worth while to bring it up. The report was a verbal one, and appeared to be addressed by Father Ritchot to the Assembly. Riel being in the chair. Mr. Taylor's letter goes on :

" In the Legislative Assembly of Assiniboia, on the 24th June, 1870, Mr. Riel, the president, took the chair at 4 o'clock p.m. Rev. Mr. Ritchot then addressed the House in French, which was translated into English by the president. The report is a lengthy one, and I will only give those portions of it that refer to the capacity in which the delegates were received at Ottawa, and how our bill of rights was tampered with there."

The evidence of it being tampered with first appears in this statement of Father Ritchot.

" Rev. Father Ritchot said : ' We were received as delegates from the North-west, and privately, when we had to treat with the Canadian ministry, due respect was paid to the commission given us by the provisional government, &c.'

"' As soon as we were recognized as delegates the ministry at Ottawa made out a list themselves which they proposed to place before parliament, and submitted it to the delegates. But we said we will have nothing to do with your list. You are not to propose the terms of treaty to us. We are sent here with certain instructions and you must hear us. We produced our list of rights, but they told us that as ministers they could not take the responsibility of introducing a bill into parliament; which would embrace all the articles specified in the list. They then drew up another list, quite different from that sent by the people of the North-west. They did it on their own responsibility, and for this reason, that if our list had been presented to parliament it would have been lost, and what would have been the issue as far as we were concerned ? It would be hard to tell. The list drawn up by the ministry was submitted to us as delegates and the Governor General asked us if some arrangement might not be come to by which instead of having two lists there would be but one— and said that if it were impossible to make the two lists agree it would be necessary for him to receive and treat with the delegation in the name of England. Again we found provision made that even if we could not come to an understanding with the Governor General, a special agent had been sent out by the English Government to treat with us. I refer to Sir Clinton Murdock. In reply to the Governor General we said that we would not then decide finally, but hoped that an agreement might be made between ministers and delegates which would bring the ministerial list nearer to that of the people of the North-west and enable both parties to agree on it. This was done. An understanding was arrived at and another list was formed from the two first named. We put that list into the hands of competent men—lawyers—in order to get a thoroughly reliable opinion concerning its merits. We desired to be clear as to whether the proposed measure was one which we could reasonably accept and which Canada could reasonably offer. Those who submitted the measure to were men from different provinces of the Dominion—men who sympathized with us—and they agreed that it would be to our advantage to accept it.'"

3

I think that is all I need trouble you with, though the whole letter is here. However, I may quote a part of Mr. Taylor's letter in which he said :—

"Your Grace will, I am sure, agree with me when I say that when delegates from the people of the North-west found that upon their arrival at Ottawa ministers were not inclined to deal with them according to our wishes—they should have reported the facts to the people of Red River. If the Governor General who informed them of his intention to deal with them in the name of England, had also shown a disposition to be unfair, then the delegates, before leaving Ottawa, would have been perfectly justified in inviting the British Ambassador, Sir Clinton Murdoch, to come to Fort Garry, where the people of Red River would have been pleased to deal with him.

"If this course had been pursued by the delegates, then the desire of Sir F. Rogers, the Under Secretary of the Colonies, would have been fulfilled, viz., 'That troops should not be employed in forcing the sovereignty of Canada on the population of Red River should they refuse to admit it.'"

I will just add one further statement and then I am done with that part; and that is, that I think, if I may be pardoned for saying so, that you will do wisely to adopt the advice of the Privy Council and to pay attention merely to what is to be found in the Act of Parliament. Lord Her chel in delivering the judgment of that body at pages 272 and 273 states emphatically that the terms agreed upon, so far as education is concerned, must be taken to be embodied in the 22nd section of the Act of 1870. Further on he uses these words :

"It is true that the construction put by this board upon the 1st subsection reduced within very narrow limits the protection afforded by the subsection in respect of denominational schools. It may be that those who were acting on behalf of the Roman Catholic community in Manitoba, and those who either framed or assented to the wording of that enactment were under the impression that its scope was wider and that it afforded protection greater than their Lordships held to be the case. But such considerations cannot properly influence the judgment of those who have judicially to interpret a statute. The question is not what might be supposed to have been intended, but what has been said. More complete effect might in some cases be given to the intentions of the legislature if violence were done to the language in which their legislation has taken shape, but such a course would on the whole be quite as likely to defeat as to further the object which was in view."

So that I submit that what you have to deal with is the language of the section by which the jurisdiction is conferred, and that travelling outside of that and being influenced by considerations of what took place, after this lapse of time, would be to tread upon very dangerous ground indeed.

Sir CHARLES HIBBERT TUPPER.—Would not that argument be stronger if your position was that we were acting in a judicial capacity?

Mr. McCARTHY.—I said so. I said that it would be a matter binding upon a court of law, but as you were acting not in a judicial capacity, it is a matter of policy which it has been for my learned friend to urge and for me to meet. Dealing with it in that way the question of fact must arise as to whether bill of rights No. 4 was ever brought here or not, and there being no trial of that question of fact, you will plainly see how difficult it would be to come to a conclusion with regard to it either one way or another. On that question all the official papers seem to be one way and the statement of the Rev. Father Ritchot in the other direction. Now that brings me naturally enough—because I think it would be fitting for me if I follow the events chronologically—to the abolition of the Senate, which is a matter of history. But as that happened some years after the passage of the Act it may be fitting if I inquire as to the manner in which, and the principles upon which this question is to be determined by the Council of His Excellency the Governor General. There are, as I understand it, two views and perhaps three, presented with regard to that matter. One is that you are sitting as a court of law and that the matter is to be determined as a question of law would be determined in a court. Another is that the question has been disposed of by the judgment of the Privy Council and that you are only here to obey the mandate of the highest tribunal of the Empire. The third view is that you are to deal with the matter upon its merits and that is a view, I am very glad to say, which was pressed upon you yesterday by my learned friend, Mr. Ewart. It is upon the merits that he invokes your interference and it is upon the merits that I propose to ask you to leave matters as they are. Now I utterly deny, in the first place, that there is a word to be found in the judgment, or that there could by any possibility be anything found in the judgment which could be treated as having dealt with and disposed of this matter. What the Privy Council were asked to do was to say—(which was undoubtedly a matter of constitutional law)—whether the Governor in Council had the jurisdiction to entertain the complaint of the minority, which, in the section, is called the appeal. What the Privy Council has to determine is that there is a jurisdiction to entertain that complaint; but you are to deal with it as a matter which the Privy Council was not asked to determine and which, as I would point out, some of the Lords of the Privy Council said very emphatically they would not advise upon because it was not a matter for them to consider, so that the matter must be dealt with by this Council upon its responsibility in its ordinary capacity. Now let me draw your attention to the questions which arose in the case before the Judicial Committee of the Privy Council. What we have to deal with is subsection 2 of section 22 of the Act of 1870. That has been held to be a substantive section. May I summarize what the Privy Council have determined? They have determined that the corresponding clause of the British North America Act, section 93, has nothing to do with it. They have determined that in this matter of education you have to look for a statement of the constitutional rights of the province to clause 22 of the Manitoba Act. They have determined that subsection 2 of that section is not ancillary, is not for the purpose of giving effect to the prohibition contained in subsection 1, but is a substantive clause, which gives a right in no sense dependent upon the preceding subsection 1. Now this subsection 2 provides :—

"An appeal shall lie to the Governor General in Council from any act or decision of the legislature of the province....affecting any right or privilege of the Protestant or Roman Catholic minority of the Queen's subjects in relation to education."

These are the words which confer the jurisdiction. The Judicial Committee has determined that the circumstances which exist in this case do give the right to the Roman Catholic minority of the Queen's subjects to appeal to the Governor General in Council against the Act of 1890, passed by the Legislature of Manitoba. I refer you to the record of the questions which you will find more conveniently perhaps in the commencement of the judgment of the Lord Chancellor, at page 268. The first question is as follows :—

"Is the appeal referred to in the said memorials and petitions and asserted thereby such an appeal as is admissible by subsection 3 of section 93 of the British North America Act of 1867, or by subsection 2 of section 22 of Manitoba Act, 33 Vic. (1870), chap. 3, Canada ?"

The answer to that question is that this is an appeal permitted by the Manitoba Act, but not by the British North America Act. The second question is :—

"Are the grounds set forth in the petitions and memorials such as may be the subject of appeal under the authority of the subsections already referred to or either of them ?"

The answer to that is : Yes ; they are. The third question is :—

"Does the decision of the Judicial Committee of the Privy Council in the cases of Barrett v. the City of Winnipeg, and Logan v. the City of Winnipeg, dispose of or conclude the application for redress based on the contention that the rights of the Roman Catholic minority, which accrued to them after the union under the statutes of the province have been interfered with by the two statutes of 1890 complained of in the said petitions and memorials ?"

The answer is that those judgments do not conclude the application. The fourth question is :—

"Does subsection 3 of section 93 of the British North America Act of 1867 apply to Manitoba ?"

That is already included in question 1, and of course the answer is: No. The next question is:—

"Has His Excellency the Governor General in Council power to make the declarations or remedial orders which are asked for in the said memorials and petitions, assuming the material facts to be as stated therein, or has His Excellency the Governor General in Council any other jurisdiction in the premises ?"

I will just for a moment pass over and return to it again. The next question is—

"(6.) Did the Act of Manitoba relating to education passed prior to the session of 1890 confer on or continue to the minority 'a right or privilege in relation to education' within the meaning of subsection 2 of section 22 of the Manitoba Act, or establish a system of separate or dissentient schools 'within the meaning of subsection 3 of section 93 of the British North America Act of 1867,' if said section 93 be found applicable to Manitoba; and if so, did the two Acts of 1890 complained of, or either of them, affect any right or privilege of the minority in such a manner that an appeal will lie thereunder to the Governor General in Council ?"

The answer to that question is: Yes. In other words the question was whether the rights acquired subsequent to the union by virtue of the Separate School Act passed in 1871, and continued in force until 1890, had been interfered with so as to give cause of complaint or appeal, and their Lordships held that they had. Here the majority of the Supreme Court of Canada held that there could not be any legal complaint as to rights and privileges being taken away by competent legislative tribunal, in other words, that the legislature which had the power to confer the right had the power to take it away, and that if it were taken away complaint could not be made in the ordinary way. Instances of this are familiar. For example, if a law was passed depriving municipalities of the power of issuing liquor licenses, it would be looked upon as a very grievous matter by the present license holders, but they could not get redress except by agitation or the repeal of the law. If the present system of protection were done away with those who now enjoy the benefits of that system would be injured, but they would have no right to redress except by way of agitation to get the law restored. The Supreme Court held that the Separate School Law of 1871, being a matter which the legislature had the right to pass, they had the right to repeal it. That was held in the Barrett case, but it was also held neverthelesss by the Privy Council, that the taking away, in 1890, of the rights given in 1871, did constitute a grievance which gave the minority the right to seek redress in the way that they are now doing ? What I am coming to, and what I hold is, that it is perfectly plain that the course which is to be taken by this Council has not been determined by the judgment; that you are not sitting here obeying the mandate of the court; that you may hear the appeal or not, that no court has directed that you must hear the appeal, and that hearing it, no court can direct what course his Excellency the Governor General should take in the matter.

Hon. Mr. DICKEY.—Do I understand you to contend that it would have been constitutionally open to this Council to have refused to hear the appeal ?

Mr. McCARTHY.— Yes; and I am going to give you the best authority on that subject, an authority which will be accepted by this body above every other, that of Sir John Macdonald. You will remember the introduction of Mr. Blake's resolution on the subject of referring such questions as are here involved to the courts. The terms of Mr. Blake's resolutions were as follows :—

"It is expedient to provide means whereby on solemn occasions touching the exercise of the power of disallowance, or of the appellate power as to educational legislation, important questions of law or fact may be referred by the executive to a high judicial tribunal for hearing and consideration in such mode that the authorities and parties interested may be represented, and that a reasoned opinion may be obtained for the information of the executive."

This was moved by Mr. Blake on going into the Committee of Supply and was accepted by the whole House, and the following year the Government brought down a bill embodying the object of the resolution. Mr. Blake made a careful speech explaining what he desired to effect by means of his resolution. I gather that the object was, in certain cases, instead of asking the Minister of Justice what the law upon the subject was—as his opinion might be open to question of being influenced by party consideration—the Council should have the power to have the opinion of a high court of law on the subject, and therefore be in a position to act upon it without danger of their proceeding being criticized upon this ground. In speaking on the subject, Sir John Macdonald said :—

"When I first read the hon. gentleman's resolution, it occurred to me, as I daresay it occurred to many hon. gentlemen who hear me now, that it was an advance towards the American system, and proposed to transfer the responsibility of the ministry of the day to a judicial tribunal ; but on scanning the resolution in its carefully prepared terms that impression was dissipated, and I saw that the principal object of the resolution, as I read it, is that the question submitted by the Executive to the judicial tribunal should be enforced, sustained and presented to parliament, to the public and to the crown, by the fact of this legal decision having been given * * Of course my hon. friend in his resolution has guarded against the supposition that such a decision is binding on the executive. It is expressly stated that such a decision is only for the information of the government. The executive is not relieved from any responsibility because of any answer being given by the tribunal. If the executive were to be relieved of any responsibility I should consider that a fatal block in the proposition of my hon. friend. I believe in responsible government ; I believe in the responsibility of the executive. But the answer of the tribunal will be simply for the information of the government. The government may dissent from that decision, and it may be their duty to do so, if they differ from the conclusion to which the court has come * * I do not think that there can be any doubt as to the meaning of the motion of my hon. friend. I think it is so explicit in its terms that no questions can arise as to what its meaning is, and if there were any doubts as to its meaning—there are none in my own mind—those doubts would be removed by the illusive speech of my hon. friend."

Hon. Mr. FOSTER.—What are you quoting from ?

Mr. MCCARTHY.—From Hansard. Now that is going, of course, a very long way. But, undoubtedly, it is sound constitutional law.

Hon. Mr. DICKEY.—You would say that this decision does decide that there is a right of appeal, but not that that appeal must be heard ? The point that struck me was that the decision gives an absolute right to somebody.

Mr. MCCARTHY.—Yes, but the question is as to working it out under our constitutional system. If this Council decides not to hear the appeal how are they to be forced to do so ?

Hon. Mr. DICKEY.—Of course there is no means of forcing that action, but there is still an absolute right on the part of somebody to appeal.

Mr. MCCARTHY.—Of course.

Hon. Mr. DICKEY.—I understand you to say that there is no correlative duty on our part to hear the appeal ?

Mr. MCCARTHY.—Yes. Somebody has the right to appeal, but we have not the duty to enforce it. I say that is going a long way, because they have obtained a solemn decision of the highest tribunal, but there is a constitutional power with this Council to say, notwithstanding the decision of a court of law upon this point, that they will not act upon that opinion. And in favour of that view, we have the opinion of Sir John Macdonald, than whom no higher authority can be quoted.

Sir CHAS. H. TUPPER.—Was not more said as to the object of the legislation providing for the reference ? Besides the object of getting advice for the Executive was there not the purpose of removing these troublesome questions from the arena of politics as much as possible ? That is the impression remaining upon my mind.

Mr. MCCARTHY.—Speaking from memory I think what Mr. Blake was driving at was that these questions were very troublesome and that whatever decision was come to with regard to them, some of those interested would say that the decision was influenced by partisan motives. That might be overcome to a greater or less extent by a reference to a judicial tribunal as to whether there was power of interference or not. If it had not been for Sir John Macdonald's speech, I should have thought that more was intended. But no doubt it was contemplated that if reference was made and answer was given that the Council had the power to grant redress, in 99 cases out of 100 they would hardly have set up their own views against it. But I am saying that the responsibility rests here; that whatever you do you are responsible in your ordinary capacity. But that, of course, is only one question. The hearing of the application is one thing; the disposal of it is another. Now no other question was asked of the Privy Council than those I read; but there was one as to the power of the government to grant this remedial legislation, the answer to which I did not read. There may be a power and still you may decide—and I trust and believe that looking at this question in a statesmanlike manner you will decide—to leave this matter as it is. I desire to show that the decision leaves the matter for you to exercise your power without deciding the way in which you are to exercise it. Let me read what was said by their Lordships of the Privy Council in the course of the argument. You will find some pretty strong expressions used in favour of the view I present to you. In the first place, Mr. Blake, in the course of his argument—page 62 —is addressed by the Lord Chancellor:—

"The question seems to me to be this : If you are right in saying that the abolition of a system of denominational educa'ion, which was created by a post-union legislation is within the 2nd section of the Manitoba act and the 3rd subsection of the other if it apply, then you say there is a case for the jurisdiction of the Governor General, and that is all we have to decide."

And Mr. Blake replies :—

"That is all your Lordships have to decide. What remedy he shall purpose to apply is quite a different thing."

Then Mr. Ewart at page 183, says :—

"Before closing I would like to say a word or two as to what we are seeking. As it has already been remarked, we are not asking for any declaration as to the extent of the relief to be given by the Governor General. We merely ask that it should be held that he has jurisdiction to hear our prayer, and to grant us some relief if he thinks proper to do so."

I do not at all mean to say that Mr. Ewart is saying now to the contrary. He put it fairly upon the grounds of his clients' rights, that is upon the manner in which you think to dispose of it in accordance with the principles which regulate our system of government. I would refer you also to Lord Watson's statement at page 180. This is in the course of Mr. Ewart's argument :

"The power given of appeal to the Government, and upon request of the Governor to the Legislature of Canada, seems to be wholly discretionary in both.

"Mr. EWART.—No doubt.

"Lord WATSON.—Both in the Governor and in the Legislature.

"Mr. EWART.—Yes."

Again at page 192, when the other side is arguing. I may explain that the point they were making, Mr. Cozens-Hardy speaking, was that subsection 2 of section 22 of the Manitoba Act had reference to subsection 1, and that it was in reference to rights in subsection 1 that the appeal was given in subsection 2, the protection given by subsection 1 being protected against infringement not only by act of Parliament but by any provincial authority, so that if the advisory school board did something regarded as objectionable there would be an appeal from the advisory board to the Governor General in Council. But their Lordships held that this was not what was meant in the section, but that subsection 2 is a substantive section. It is with reference to that that Lord Watson makes the remark :—

"It does not seem very probable *prima facie* that there should be a reference given to the Governor whether an act which this statute declares to be *ultra vires* shall be retained on the statute-book or shall be modified."

What he means is to ask how he is to declare in favour of there being any discretion if the act is *ultra vires* under subsection 1. At page 193 Lord Watson says :

"I apprehend that the appeal to the Governor is an appeal to the Governor's discretion. It is a political administrative appeal, and not a judicial appeal in any proper sense of the term, and in the same way after he has decided the same latitude of discretion is given to the Dominion Parliament. They may legislate or not as they think fit."

Could any words be more definite or precise?

Hon. Mr. DICKEY.—Lord Watson is drawing a distinction between a judicial appeal on the question of *ultra vires* and an appeal on the other ground.

Mr. McCARTHY.—At page 258, in the course of Mr. Haldane's argument on the same point, he says:—

"I do not think it is any more technical or unsubstantial than the functions of your Lordship, who often have to declare that an act is *ultra vires*. The Governor General would give his decision.

"LORD McNAGHTEN. —We are a judicial body and he is not sitting as a judicial body."

Then at page 121, Lord Watson, speaking of the principles upon which the Governor General in Council is to decide, speaks as you will see in the following quotation:—

"Mr. HALDANE.—All we say is that your Lordships must look at the kind of Act which is complained of in order to see whether the conditions of the appeal to the Governor General have arisen.

"LORD WATSON.—I am prepared to advise the Governor General and decide on the meaning of this clause, but I am not prepared to relieve him of the duty of considering how far he ought to interfere."

Sir CHARLES HIBBERT TUPPER.—But as a matter of fact the Privy Council did go a little further than Lord Watson said he was prepared to go.

Mr. McCARTHY.—In what way?

S r C. H. TUPPER.—May it not be argued that they did consider how far we might interfere and suggested how we might remove these grievances by pursuing a certain course?

Mr. McCARTHY.—I will not close my argument without referring to that point. In the first place it would be inoperative, and, in any case, taken altogether, I think it does not bear that meaning. There is another part in which Lord Macnaghten says that the suggestion that the Governor General in Council should be a court of appeal on matters of law is a startling one, but I do not know that I can find it at the moment.

Hon. Mr. DICKEY.—I think at page 221 you will find it.

Mr. McCARTHY.—That is what I refer to, thank you. I will read the passage:—

"The Lord CHANCELLOR.—What the judge did would be the interpretation of the law *intra vires*.

"Mr. HALDANE.—Yes.

"The Lord CHANCELLOR.—Then was the Governor General in Council to decide that the judge had misinterpreted the law?

"Mr. HALDANE. —Yes.

"The Lord CHANCELLOR.—That is rather startling?

"Lord McNAGHTEN.—A court of appeal on matters of law from the decision of a competent judge?

"Mr. HALDANE.—A court of appeal from a decision of a provincial court, which was the only court which could give judgment.

"Lord McNAGHTEN. —It is a most startling suggestion."

Now let me give you a clause to which the Minister of Justice referred a minute ago. It is at the foot of page 285. Having decided the main question, the Lord Chancellor goes on :

"For the reasons we have given their Lordships are of opinion that the 2nd subsection of section 22 of the Manitoba Act is the governing enactment and that the appeal to the Governor General in Council was admissible by virtue of that enactment, on the grounds set forth in the memorials and petitions, inasmuch as the Act of 1890 affected rights or privileges of the Roman Catholic minority in relation to education within the meaning of that subsection."

Now we come to the point the Minister of Justice referred to :—

"The further question is submitted whether the Governor General in Council has the power to make the declarations or remedial orders asked for in the memorials or petitions, or has any other jurisdiction in the premises. Their Lordships had decided that the Governor General in Council has jurisdiction and that the appeal is well founded, but the particular course to be pursued must be determined by the authorities to whom it must be committed by the statute. It is not for this tribunal to intimate the precise steps to be taken."

He then goes on to say :—

"It is certainly not essential—

Sir CHAS. H. TUPPER.—That is what I referred to.

Mr. McCARTHY.—" It is certainly not essential that the statutes repealed by the Act of 1890 should be re-enacted, or that the precise provisions of these statutes should again be made law. The system of education embodied in the Act of 1890 no doubt commends itself to, and adequately supplies, the wants of the great majority of the inhabitants of the province. All legitimate ground of complaint would be removed if that system were supplemented by provisions which would remove the grievance upon which the appeal is founded, and were modified as far as it might be necessary to give effect to these provisions."

No doubt it would, but the judgment does not say that you are to do it.

Hon. Mr. DICKEY.—They contemplated some action.

Mr. McCARTHY.—But it is an *obiter*.

Sir CHAS. H. TUPPER.—I did not mention the point to refute your position as to whether we had the absolute duty to perform, but merely to point out that Lord Watson's position was not acted upon when he said that he would not give a suggestion. There is a very marked suggestion there as to what we could do, and, perhaps, as some would argue a suggestion as to what we should do.

Mr. McCARTHY.—Possibly that observation is warranted by what Lord Herschell has said. But the question was not asked what you should do, but whether you have jurisdiction. The Privy Council, if they venture to instruct this body, were stepping beyond their jurisdiction.

Hon. Mr. CURRAN.—They said the rights of the minority had been affected?

Mr. McCARTHY.—Yes; that is the ground of appeal; that I am not seeking to deny. The question is how it is to be redressed if redressed at all? I do not know if it is necessary to fortify my ground any further, but I will call attention to one point. If this were a judicial body I should expect to see His Excellency here. If, on the contrary, this is an ordinary matter of administration, I would not expect His Excellency to be present. In other words the Privy Council here is the same as the Cabinet in England, and in England the Cabinet sits apart from the Queen, but advises her in matters of policy. But in England when the Privy Council sits Her Majesty is present, and in the same way, if this Council is sitting as a judicial body the Governor General should be present in person. Another question is as to how remedial action is to be carried out. You will make a remedial order. I do not quite agree with my learned friend that you are to frame an Act of Parliament for the Legislature of Manitoba. Your duty would be well performed, in case remedial action was to be taken, if you passed the remedial order and left the Legislature of Manitoba to put that in the form they saw fit. That order would be an Order in Council upon the report, I suppose, of a committee or of the whole Council and approved of by the Governor General in Council in the ordinary way. Now, under our system, for such an action there must be Ministerial responsibility. With reference to that matter I would refer to Sir William R. Anson's work, "Law and Custom of the Constitution," page 43 of part 2. Then if you would look at Mr. Todd's work you would find the subject of ministerial responsibility dealt with. I refer to the work "Parliamentary Government in the British Colonies," 2nd edition prepared by Mr. Todd's son, he says :—

"The responsibility of the local administration, for all acts of Government is absolute and unqualified. But it is essentially a responsibility to the legislature, and especially to the popular chamber thereof,—whilst the responsibility of the Governor is solely to the crown. It is indispensable to the welfare and good government of the colonies that these separate responsibilities should never be allowed to clash, and the best guarantee against the occurrence of such an event is to be found in the continued existence of the most cordial and unreserved harmony and co-operation between the Governor and his advisers."

I would cite from the same book at page 128 :

"Ministers cannot relieve themselves from the responsibility of advising as executive councillors ; nor is a Governor free to act without or against ministerial advice, in cases not involving the rights or prerogatives of the crown or imperial interests."

At page 814, he summarizes as follows :—

"The general conclusions arrived at in the preceding chapter, after a careful investigation of the several questions therein discussed, may be briefly epitomized as follows :—

"1. The position of a governor in a colony possessing representative institutions, with 'responsible government' is that of a local constitutional sovereign. Whatever other powers may be conferred upon him by the law of the particular colony, he is by virtue of his commission and instructions from the crown, the representative of the Queen in this part of her dominions, who is herself the source of all executive authority therein. He has his responsible ministers, who advise him upon all acts of executive government and in all legislative matters. The identity of aim and the mutual co-operation in endeavour which must invariably subsist between the representative of the crown and his constitutional advisers is a pledge and assurance to the people that they enjoy the full benefit and security which the monarchical system is capable of affording in our colonial system, combined with the advantages of ministerial control and responsibility."

Sir MACKENZIE BOWELL.—Your object in reading that is to show that we should be responsible politically as an executive ?

Mr. McCARTHY.—Yes.

Sir MACKENZIE BOWELL.—We do not deny that.

Mr. McCARTHY.—Then I need not take up further time. My object is to show that you cannot be acting judicially. If you were, it would be a monstrous thing to hold you responsible for an error in judgment. We know that judges are not and that they commit errors in judgment, otherwise there would not be the reversal of their decisions in appeal.

Sir CHARLES HIBBERT TUPPER.—You claim that we are still a political body ?

Mr. McCARTHY.—Yes : and it is upon political considerations the matter must be determined. After what the president has said, I need not go on with my argument by which I had intended to show that all judicial functions had been withdrawn from the crown under our system, and properly withdrawn, thus taking away a prerogative which the crown claimed to exercise. The exception to that rule is the Judicial Committee of the Privy Council. If you care to see how that was brought about you will see it referred to in the work I have mentioned, "Law and Custom of the Constitution," pages 442 and 443.

"When the Long Parliament, the Court of Star Chamber, had restrained the jurisdiction of the council, it did no more than take away the powers conferred by the statute of Henry VII., and forbid the action of council, which had extended to matters cognizable by the Courts of Common Law.

"But the King in Council was still the resort of the suitor who could not obtain justice in one of the dependencies, and the act which took away the original jurisdiction of the King in Council at home did not touch petitions from the adjacent island or the plantation."

Appeals were thus allowed from the colonies to the crown, which were dealt with by an open committee of the Privy Council, which advised the crown as to the order to be made in each case. But the Act of 1833 conferred judicial powers upon a certain portion of the Privy Council in England, and it is upon that act that the authority of the Judicial Committee of the Privy Council rests.

Sir CHARLES HIBBERT TUPPER.—Take the case of the Railway Committee of the Privy Council, that is governed by special statute and often in connection with these cases there are thrown upon us from time to time what you would call *quasi* judicial duties, which we have to perform very much as judges would have to do, except that we are politically responsible for all the conclusions at which we arrive.

Mr. MCCARTHY. I think that in the Railway Committee the powers are partly judicial and partly administrative and that you would not be responsible as ministers for the conclusions reached. If you were to trace that back, as I have had occasion to do, you will find that the difficulty arose in England that the judicial bodies were found utterly incompetent to adjudicate in railway disputes. The jurisdiction was first, you will remember, in the Common Pleas in England, and that was found so unsatisfactory that the jurisdiction was taken away and vested in a body and called the railway commissioners. In this country when the trouble first arose in a small way between railway companies and their customers, or between railway companies themselves, it was not thought advisable to establish a new body to deal with these matters; but the jurisdiction was not conferred upon the courts, but a committee of the Privy Council was appointed, whose jurisdiction has been from time to time enlarged, and finally, in the last Railway Act of 1889, I think——

Hon. Mr. DALY.—1888.

Mr. MCCARTHY,—these powers were much enlarged. It was thought better to enlarge the powers of the committee than to appoint railway commissioners. I should think it unfair to hold that a minister was responsible to Parliament for his decisions in that committee. There is another matter that has a bearing on this—the Minister of Agriculture had certain powers under the law relating to patents. I believe that the courts have held that the Minister of Agriculture in these matters is not acting judicially, but he exercises a *quasi* judicial function.

Hon. Mr. ANGERS.—That is transferred now to the Exchequer Court.

Mr. MCCARTHY.—I am speaking of the matter as it used to be.

Sir MACKENZIE BOWELL.—Such functions are certainly exercised in the Customs Department.

Hon. Mr. DICKEY.—How about the pardoning power?

Mr. MCCARTHY.—That is a prerogative of the Crown and must be exercised upon the responsibility of the ministers.

Hon. Mr. DICKEY.—But the function is purely judicial.

Mr. MCCARTHY.—Not purely. Take, for instance, the case of the Irish prisoners in England, for whose release many are pressing. They have been found guilty over and over again, and the Home Secretary says that they were properly convicted. But he is still urged to pardon them, upon grounds for which he will be held responsible.

Hon. Mr. DICKEY.—Would it not be difficult to make a definition of the word "judicial," which would not include such functions as that exercised by the Minister of Justice in relation to the release of prisoners? I am quite willing to accept the responsibility, but I think we should all understand that the act we perform is a judicial one.

Mr. MCCARTHY.—I think there would be the difficulty pointed out. But, in the case of the Minister of Justice, after the law has decided there still remains the question of policy which it is for him to decide.

Sir CHAS. HIBBERT TUPPER.—Would you go so far as to say that the main consideration in a matter of this kind should be the political effect of our action and not the actual merits and rights of it?

Mr. MCCARTHY.—That is undoubtedly my position. That is a duty you have to exercise. Let me crystalize it. The Privy Council have determined that there is a grievance; they have determined that there is jurisdiction in the Governor General to pass a remedial order. If that order is to be passed, *ex debito justitiæ*, there is an end of the matter. Why all this ceremony, why all this talk?

Hon. Mr. CURRAN.—It may be necessary to hear why justice should not be done. But there is a grievance.

Mr. McCarthy.—I am not going to say that there is not a grievance; I am precluded from that by the judgment.

Sir Chas. Hibbert Tupper.—The question that occurs to me right or wrong, is this :—Granting all you say as to our political responsibility and as to our power to do one thing or another, does not the Act, in its nature contemplate that we shall approach the question, not as a political or party body, not that we shall merely go through the form of an inquiry on the appeal made to us, but that we shall, to the best of our ability, deal with the merits of the case, being responsible, to Parliament, nevertheless, for our action on the merits.

Mr. McCarthy.—The moment you do that, you have to see to it that you have the confidence of a party majority, for we are governed under the party system. But I have a good deal to say about that and I do not want to anticipate that part of my argument. I hope to show that you are to deal with it as a matter of policy, but not at all to say that you have not jurisdiction.

Sir Charles Hibbert Tupper.—Under your contention, we should call a party caucus when this appeal is made and see whether it would be wise to grant a remedial order or refuse it?

Mr. McCarthy.—I will answer you in another way. Would it be said to be a matter to be dealt with judicially when one of the Council, by no means an uninfluential member, has already pledged himself that this remedy shall be granted or he will resign his seat?

Hon. Mr. Ouimet.—Perhaps I may change my opinion, if you are going to give me a proper definition of what is political conscience and what is individual conscience.

Mr. McCarthy.—You are recorded, and that in a government organ, to have said :

" Will the Federal Government have a session or will they have a general election? He could not give them a definite reply at this time, and he could tell them that there were many important questions under consideration and especially the question which interested all true patriots, I refer to the Manitoba school question. It was a duty that the Government owed to the electors to say what they would do in the presence of such an important question. They could not say as yet exactly what would be done. It was a constitutional question, and there had been a difficulty. Mr. Ouimet said that the Conservative leaders had been perfectly sincere in the line of conduct they had followed in the question, and it was also in conformity with the resolution as submitted to the House of Commons in 1890 by Mr. Blake himself. Mr. Ouimet said he was one of those who had demanded that justice should be given to the minority. They had taken the appeal to England at their own expense——"

I understand that he was one of the parties who subscribed money to take the appeal to England. If so his acting now in a judicial capacity would be an anomaly. My clients would be compelled to come for a decision before one who was interested in the matter.

Hon. Mr. Ouimet.—We wanted to find out what the law was. That it would not be useless according to your opinion, surely, for you have said we did not know much law.

Mr. McCarthy :—

" They had taken the appeal to England at their own expense and they have been successful. The appeal of the minority had not only been maintained, but had been solemnly confirmed. The judgment had once for all decided that not only had the majority in Manitoba the right to have schools of their own choice, but that nobody had the right to deprive the majority of their schools."

I have endeavoured to show that it did not decide anything of the kind

"The course now open to the minority was to demand the re-establishment of the separate schools which they formerly enjoyed. Mr. Ouimet said that there was unanimity amongst the members of the Government on this question."

That was before the argument.

Hon. Mr. Ouimet.—Unanimity in what ?—in a determination to do justice.

Mr. McCarthy.— "A time had been fixed for the advocate of the minority to plead their wants and to show what remedial legislation should be passed. The Cabinet would be called upon to act in accordance with the judgment of the Privy Council. As soon as the case was heard a decision will be rendered, and Mr. Ouimet added, that if that decision was not in accordance with the constitution, there would be but one thing for them to do, and that was for them to retire from the Government."
I do not know what that means.
Sir CHARLES HIBBERT TUPPER.—You would not want him to remain in a government that had taken unconstitutional action ?
Mr. McCarthy.—He says further :
"The Government was not afraid to make known its policy and there would be no alternative before its policy would be defined. The government would go before the electors with a definite programme, and if he was a member of the government that programme would mean the perfect execution of the judgment rendered by the Privy Council."
Hon. Mr. OUIMET—That is right.

The Council adjourned until 2.30 p.m.

AFTER RECESS.

The Council resumed at 2.30 p.m.

Mr. McCarthy.—Referring, and as I trust only for a short time longer, to the point that was still under discussion when the adjournment took place, I want to point out what the position must necessarily be upon any action being taken by the Council. If the Council has no discretion at all—as to that I have said all I propose to say—of course there is no necessity of any argument or of any inquiry ; the order goes as of right. If the Council has discretion, then I take it that that discretion is one which would not be justly implemented by the simple passage of a remedial order. If the Council come to the conclusion to advise His Excellency to pass a remedial order, they do in effect say to their followers, and say to the country, that they are prepared to advise Parliament to carry out that remedial order if necessary, and to support it through Parliament. That I think demonstrates that the order being made, and a party government pledges its party to its adoption by such party, so far as the party can be bound by the act of the Government—the Government is bound in honour and bound in justice to the minority who are claiming it, to see that that order is afterwards carried into law in case the province declines to obey it. Now, the moment that is done, it enters the field, indeed it has already entered the field, of Dominion politics. It has become a question as to whether it ought or ought not to be done. If it is not done, the Government take the responsibility of saying, we won't interfere ; and they antagonize a certain section of the community, not merely the minority in Manitoba, but a very large and important section of the community in the Dominion. If the Government say there ought to be a remedial order passed, then they antagonize another section who differ from them ; and therefore it appears to me it becomes, in every sense in which it can be viewed, a question of politics, and a question of moment to the Dominion at large, into which field of politics it has entered. I do not know that I can better put what I mean than in the language of the Hon. Mr. Pelletier, who delivered a very carefully prepared speech on this question, and who, I think, has put it, from his standpoint, in a very fair manner. He commences by saying :—

"It is time, however, for us to ask if this question should not be decided before rather than after the elections. If the elections take place before the question is settled, or before tangible measures are taken to guarantee us the settlement, the question presents itself, namely, what attitude those should take who hold before and above all that justice should prevail, and that the question of finance, administration, protection, or of free trade should be subordinate to the great cause we have at heart. Two political parties will ask your support. What, therefore, is the position of each party on this question ?"

Then he goes on to criticize the conduct and the course of the leader of the opposition. He points out that Mr. Laurier declares that he would only settle the school question in case the schools were Protestant ; that if he is entrusted with power by the electorate he will grant remedial orders ; and he draws from that the conclusion, whether rightly or wrongly, that if the schools are neutral, then Mr. Laurier would not interfere.

But he comes now to the powers that be, and he says :—

"We will see now what is to be thought of the present Ottawa Government. Let me tell you, in the first place, that if Mr. Laurier is obliged to have a policy clear and defined on this question, the Government has likewise obligations and elementary responsibilities. Mr. Laurier is obliged to speak, and the Government is obliged to act, and if the Government does not do its duty, it must not be relieved of the consequences which such want of action would entail."

Further on he says :

"We, however, have not come to this in the province of Quebec, this classic land of true liberty and real grandeur ; but if, on the one side, we are just, if we wish to continue to be so, we have the right to ask the same measure of justice and equity for the sections of country where our peop'e are in the minority, and we are obliged to insist on this point independently of all political attachment and of all party interest. The Federal Government has no right to be frightened by the hydra of fanaticism ; and even if it were to succumb for not having done its duty, the Ministry should not flinch before the possibility of a defeat, which would be surrounded by a veritable halo which would be more glorious than a victory obtained by trampling under foot the most sacred rights.

"Therefore, let us consider the duty of the present hour. If the Federal elections are brought on before the settlement of the school question, or before the Government gives tangible proof that the question is going to be settled, they will do no more than Mr. Laurier . they will go no further than he in thus hiding themselves behind a culpable ostentation. I am not one of those who believe that this question is one that can be settled at the wink of an eye. I am aware that there is a regular procedure to follow. I am aware that it is necessary that the interested party should plead their appeal before the Executive Council. I know that the Greenway Government must be placed *en demeure* to act, and that the Federal Government can only take action after this is done ; but that which we have a right to ask is that if the dissolution of the House is to take place, it should be preceded by an effective action, engaging the Government in a formal manner. The Ministers cannot make, each in their own provinces, contradictory declarations necessitated by the exigencies of the situation. I have, however, confidence in the promises and engagements of our Ministers. I cannot forget that at a moment when, after the last decision of the Supreme Court, everybody believed the grand cause for ever lost, it was they who united on one document the names of twenty persons who undertook to pay the judicial expenses in order to take the case before the Privy Council. I know also that they paid their own money for this good cause. I know also that the twenty persons whose names are upon this historic document have paid out up to the present time the sum of $9,000, in order that the grievances of the Manitoba minority might be taken to the foot of the throne. I know that upon this document there are the names of men who expect no political reward, the names of venerable priests who have affixed their names through a religious spirit and in the public interests. I have also confidence that Ministers who have such a splendid act as this to their credit will not come before us with false electoral promises. Individual promises, however, are not always possible to execute. What the Catholics wish is that the question may be settled by a law, if there be a session, and if there is no session, by an Order in Council, sanctioned by the representative of Her Majesty, and consequently binding on all the Ministers and on the party, and submitting the question directly to the people. If the Government takes this course it will merit the entire confidence of the public, and if not it will be unworthy of it."

Now, I do not think that at all an unfair view from the standpoint from which Mr. Pelletier spoke. He, of course, is desirous of seeing this remedial order made, and he puts it to the Government that they should be compelled to take a stand upon the subject and declare themselves in a tangible manner before the election, and to commit themselves and their party to the passage, not merely of a remedial order, but to subsequent legislation which might follow upon it and without which, of course, it would be mere waste paper. You are not, sir, unmindful of the fact that a considerable portion of the press of the province of Quebec are clamouring for a session : they are insisting not merely that a remedial order shall be passed, but that by this present Parliament legislation should be passed. All that goes to show that this question has entered the field of politics, and can only be dealt with as any other matter of politics is to be dealt with. Let me add to my quotation from the judgment, a reference which had escaped me, and which a friend has been kind enough to point out, and which, perhaps, is even more pertinent than any I have read before. I quote from page 32 of the Order in Council under which the reference was made :—

"The remedy, therefore, which is sought is against Acts which are *intra vires* of the Provincial Legislature. His argument is also that the appeal does not ask your Excellency to interfere with any rights or powers of the legislature of Manitoba, inasmuch as the power to legislate on the subject of education has only been conferred on that legislature with the distinct reservation that your Excellency in Council shall have power to make remedial orders against any such legislation which infringes on rights acquired after the union by any Protestant or Roman Catholic minority in relation to separate or dissentient schools. Upon the various questions which arise on those petitions, the sub-committee do not feel called upon to express an opinion."

That was your own sub-committee, composed of the late Sir John Thompson, and, I think, of the Minister of the Interior and yourself, and Mr. Chapleau.

"And so far as they are aware no opinion has been expressed on any previous occasion in this case, or any other of a like kind by your Excellency's Government, or any other government of Canada. Indeed, no application of a parallel character has been made since the establishment of the Dominion. The application comes before your Excellency in a manner differing from applications which are ordinarily made under the constitution to your Excellency in Council."

Now this is the point that was criticized.

"In the opinion of the sub-committee the application is not to be dealt with at present as a matter of political character or involving political action on the part of your Excellency's advisers."

That was the opinion of the sub-committee. Then, Mr. Blake criticized that as follows :—

"Your Lordships will observe the phrase ' at present,' on the preliminary question which is a question whether there are grounds to entertain an appeal, the committee thought they were going to act judicially, but very properly they added the words ' at present ' because it is quite obvious that when they enter upon the sphere of action of entertaining an appeal, their functions must be political, of expediency and of discretion, just as much as the functions which in the last resort upon their recommendation are assigned to the Parliament of Canada itself, of course a political body.

"If the recommendation of His Excellency in Council is not obeyed by the local authorities, there devolves upon the Parliament of Canada the right to legislate to the extent that is necessary to achieve redress, warranted by the recommendation of his Excellency in Council. Both these transactions, the prior substantive transaction of deciding on the action of the Governor in Council, and the action of the Parliament in Canada, are, of course, not judicial but political."

Then there is another passage at page 26 :

"THE LORD CHANCELLOR.—It is not before us what should be declared, is it ?

"Mr. BLAKE.—No, what is before your Lordships is whether there is a case for appeal.

"THE LORD CHANCELLOR.—What is before us is the functions of the Governor General.

"Mr. BLAKE.—Yes, and not the methods in which he shall exercise them—not the discretion which he shall use, but whether a case has arisen on these facts on which he has jurisdiction to intervene. That is all that is before your Lordships."

Now there is a well known rule that if a court of law goes beyond what is necessary for the decision of a case, the decision is not binding, it is what is called *obiter*. They have no more right to affect the interests or rights of parties by going beyond the question itself, than a mere stranger has. The court is limited in its decision, and this has a binding character only so long as it is confined to the questions which were submitted. For these reasons, therefore, I submit with confidence, that this question does not come before you as one settled and determined by anything the Privy Council has said ; that this question does not come before you to be dealt with judicially, and you are not sitting here judicially : that this question does not come before you to be disposed of as any other question which comes before the Council, and on which the Council has to advise the Governor, upon the responsibility of the Council, as the ministers of the Government, and upon their responsibility to Parliament and to the people whom Parliament represents. Now that being so—as I will assume, for the sake of my further argument, that it is so—what is the question ? Perhaps, however, before I come to that, I might as well clear up those other small matters which have been introduced into the argument, and then I will not have to interrupt the course of the discussion by any irrelevant observations further on. I refer to the suggestion—the argument, as my learned friend calls it— that when the Legislative Council was abolished in Manitoba the minority in that province had the pledge of the majority that their rights would not be interfered with. Now let us see what took place. My learned friend has referred you to two or three passages to be found in his book from speeches made by Mr. Davis, who was then premier, by Mr. Norquay, and I think by Mr. Luxton. I may have to say a word about these speeches, though I hardly think they are of sufficient consequence to justify me in taking up your time, but I want to point out to you the account we get of the abolition of the Legislative Council in Mr. Begg's volume. From that book I gather that Mr. Davis came to power, pledged to the abolition of the Legislative Council, that he first attempted to carry that out, and a bill passed through the Lower Chamber, but in the Upper Chamber it was rejected, the Legislative Council refusing to be a party to its own abolition.

Hon. Mr. MONTAGUE—There is no record of that.

Mr. McCARTHY—I find that here on page 197 of the second volume of Begg's history. What I have not seen is the statement that he pledged himself, but I assume that he gave a pledge. Then the history goes on to state :—

"About this time also, at the request of Hon. Alexander Mackenzie, a delegation from the Local Government, composed of Hon. R. A. Davis and Hon. Joseph Royal, visited Ottawa in reference to obtaining better terms for the province. The result of this mission was a readjustment of the financial relations between the Dominion and the province, by which the subsidy of the latter was increased, until 1881, to $90,000, per annum ; and in addition, a number of accounts standing between the Federal and Provincial Governments were satisfactorily adjusted, practically wiping out a debt of $120,000, which Manitoba owed the Dominion, and leaving the province with a clean sheet to continue anew on its increased subsidy."

I refer to that because I noticed with surprise that Mr. Blake said in his argument before the Privy Council that he had to do with the abolition of the Senate. Mr. Haldane, not having known of the change, was speaking of the two Houses, and Mr. Blake said, one House ; and then, upon some conversation taking place, he said he had to do with the abolition.

Sir MACKENZIE BOWELL.—It was on the advice of Mr. Mackenzie and his government. ,

Mr. McCARTHY.—Yes. Then the book goes on to say :—

"On January 18th, 1876, the second session of the second Parliament of Manitoba was opened, and the most important measure passed was the abolition of the Legislative Council. The bill, as it will be remembered, had been defeated at the previous session by the casting vote of the Speaker, Hon. J. H. O'Donell, but on the present occasion the government prepared for an emergency of this kind, by arranging beforehand with a majority of the members comprising the Council to vote themselves out of office. The vote in the Council for abolition stood as follows: Hon. Messrs. MacKay, Inkster, Gunn, and Ogletree voted for it, and Hon. Messrs. Hamelin, Dauphinais and O'Donell against it."

So the whole number voted either for or against, the French members voting against it, and the four gentlemen bearing English and Scotch names, having been provided for in advance, voted for the abolition of the Legislative Council. It is not pretended that there was any bargain or arrangement made by any person who had authority, that on account of that vote, or notwithstanding that, the rights guaranteed to the French minority should be preserved. But I will only use this argument: Is it possible for any gentleman, even for the First Minister, or for any other member, to pledge a legislative body, and if so, for how long? They may speak for themselves, but they have no right to pledge posterity. They have no right to speak for anybody else but themselves, and they have no power to bind the legislature in any way. But, I think, if you read the language which has been cited to you by my learned friend, of Mr. Davis, Mr. Luxton and Mr. Norquay, you will find that what they were speaking of and thinking of, was not the separate school question at all, but it was the French language. I think it was a year later when the question arose as to the abolition of the separate school system, and so far as I know, and so far as I can gather from my investigation of history, there had been nothing said at all after this, nothing said in the press about changing the school system. So I submit that, looking at the facts as I could get them, the province wanted to get an increased indemnity, and the Dominion authorities said, Before we give you more money we want to see that you are not going to waste it on this legislative council. Under these circumstances, it would be carrying any statement that might be made by these gentlemen, a great length, to pretend that they could bind either Protestants, or Catholics, or anybody else. They had no mandate to make any promise as to what they might do, either on behalf of that Parliament or any subsequent Parliament. Then, I am instructed to-day by the Attorney General, and that is all I propose to say about it—that the alleged agreement between Mr. Greenway and the Archbishop has been repeatedly denied. I am not denying it now, but it has been repeatedly denied, and I gather from the statement read yesterday that it had been denied. Then, as to these statements that are alleged to have been made at St. François Xavier by Mr. Joseph Martin,—I do not know whether they have been denied or not—but if Mr. Joseph Martin or any other member of the Manitoba Legislature made any such statements, they had no authority to bind the Liberal party. The Liberal party at that time had a platform in which there was nothing said one way or the other as to the question of schools, or the question of language; and if these gentlemen did in that constituency make any such statement, they could only speak for themselves. They were not authorized or justified in any way to speak on behalf of the Liberal party of whom they were representatives on that occasion. I think Mr. Greenway's statement was denied, and the other statements, if made, were certainly not statements which the party felt that they were bound by in the slightest degree. Now, then, coming to the question of abolition. Without troubling you with extracts from the book of the Privy Council, let me summarize the views of their Lordships, which I fully adopt for the purposes of my argument. It was stated over and over again to the counsel who were arguing, and I think admitted by them, and it seems to me to be the only possible view that can be taken of this jurisdiction, that the power to deal with schools was given to the provinces: that power is said to be exclusive in the first section :—

"In and for the provinces the legislature may exclusively make laws in relation to education."

That, if stated alone, would give them absolute and unqualified power. But it does not stand alone ; it says :—

" Subject and according to the following provisions : "—

The first limitation of that power is to be found in that subsection which the Privy Council have determined has no meaning, because there were no facts to which it was to be applied. Then, they were not to make any school law which would prejudicially affect any rights or privileges with respect to denominational schools which any class of persons, not mereley Roman Catholics, or Protestants, but any class of persons, Church of England. Methodists or Presbyterians, had at the time of union. It has been found now, as a fact, and announced as a settled judgment of law, that there were no rights or privileges which any class of persons enjoyed prior to the union, and therefore, that might as well be written out of the section. It cannot be of any application so far as one can see at present, but it has been held. and this is a further limitation, that if a right or privilege which the minority enjoyed after the union is taken away by the acts of the legislature. there may be, under these circumstances, jurisdiction in the Parliament of Canada to pass a law to remedy that grievance : so that in that event the power is for a time concurrent in both legislatures. Up to the time of the complaint being made to the Governor in Council, the power is absolute and unlimited, section one being eliminated, in the legislature of the province. From the time that the jurisdiction of the Governor in Council is invoked and the time the remedial order is passed, the province still has the power, and still remains with the power from the time that order is disobeyed. If that event should happen, and we have reason to know from what was said at the opening the other day that that event is likely to happen, then there would be concurrent legislative powers until the Parliament of Canada exercised its legislative power. I think Sir John Thompson spoke of it in his speech as parallel legislative power. I do not know whether my expression or his is the happier, but I think you understand what I mean ; in other words, the legislature of Manitoba might, this session, refuse to pass remedial legislation, and then there would be authority, in the Parliament of Canada to pass it, and until the Parliament of Canada passes it, there would still be power in the legislature to pass it. They might repent and pass it the next session if they please, or even the same session. They might not deal with the matter until this Parliament dealt with it. So that this power and authority, which I understand you may, under certain circumstances, exercise, is a power and authority which, under the events which have happened, may arise, and if it does arise, it is a legislative authority to be exercised like any of the other legislative authorities conferred by section 91 of the B. N. A. Act. Speaking generally with regard to the scope of the constitution, we know that the powers conferred by the legislation are absolute and sovereign, that is, when they act within their jurisdiction, and subject, of course, to the veto, which we are all subject to. The legislative acts by the Governor General in Council and the Parliamentary Acts of this Parliament. are only subject to the Queen in Council, and subject to that, their authority is absolute. There is no over-lapping. The single exception, I think, is in the matter of agriculture. There in an absolute jurisdiction in the one or in the other, and where they act within their jurisdiction, they are sovereign. But this jurisdiction may be, as I pointed out, for a time concurrent ; but the moment the Canadian Parliament act. the authority passes away from the local for all time ; and as I pointed out to you, the Dominion authority have an opportunity of repealing its own legislation. What I want now to point out is this : that this being a legislative power, conferred under these circumstances, and existing under these circumstances in the Parliament of Canada, it has to be exercised just as any other power would be. The Government are now bound, for instance, to come down with a bill ; the Government, in matters of this moment, would be bound, after passing a remedial order, to come down with a bill and carry that order into effect. What I ask now is, there being with regard to this province, under these circumstances, a right in this Government —because if the Government refuses to act, and thinks it is wiser to leave the province to manage her own affairs, then, of course, the question can never arise—but there being the right in this Government to set this jurisdiction in motion,

4

what considerations should actuate the Government, before they come to an affirmative conclusion and grant the prayer of the petition which has been presented here? What are you asked to do? It is impossible to disguise it from ourselves after the draft bill which has been submitted to you as the demand of the minority—you are asked to pass a separate school law for the province of Manitoba. You are asked to repeal their Public School Act to that extent. The two cannot stand together; and with all deference be it said, it shows how little the Lord Chancellor understood the question when he seemed to think that an act to supplement an act of this kind, might be passed without interfering with the Public School Act. This Public School Act, of course, stands now as a general law throughout the province. The proposed legislation would enable a neighbourhood of Roman Catholics to take themselves out from under the control of the public school law, and to bring themselves within the control of the separate school enactment. The Parliament of Canada, at the instance of the Government of Canada, is to be asked, and is now being asked, to change the school law of the province and to establish a system of separate schools in that province.

Hon. Mr. HAGGART.—Are we for ever invested with that authority? Could we repeal that?

Mr. MCCARTHY.—I think not. I think this is legislation *ad hoc*. The moment you exercise this power, you have nothing more to do with it in Parliament, except in case you have made a mistake and have not gone far enough. But as for repealing it, I think it is gone.

Sir ADOLPHE CARON.—You could not restrict the power, but you could extend it.

Mr. MCCARTHY.—I do not think you can go further. The Governor sanctions whatever remedial order he thinks Parliament can carry out. But suppose Parliament fails to carry out to the full extent the remedial order at one session, they might the next session, so as to make effective the Governor General's order. But once they do that, so far as I have been able to understand the Act, there would be no power to repeal, certainly not in the local, certainly not in the Dominion, because it is legislation *ad hoc* for that purpose, and that is what we call the execution of a power. Now, I say with all earnestness, that this is a matter that must be carefully considered. Here you act in this hasty manner. I do not intend to make any disrespectful allusion, but the judgment had hardly reached the province of Manitoba, before the Ministers of that province have had time to consider its effects and to weigh the arguments which are to be found in it, and the new position which is created by it, when they are called upon to appear here, as it were to defend their system, which, when you have heard this history, you will find has not been hastily adopted by them, but has been deliberately adopted, and still more deliberately adhered to. Now, the Parliament of Canada has no right to interfere in schools, in educational matters, which, of all others, it will be admitted, are purely local concerns. There is an observation of one of the law lords that education is a purely local concern. At page 218 Lord Watson says:—" It is a matter purely local." In that matter purely local, you are called upon now, not merely to override, but to coerce a great province of the Dominion, in respect to a system which this province has in its wisdom adopted; and if I were seized, as I ought to be, as fully as the Attorney General is, who has charge of this matter in the province, of the merits, and all the arguments, and the reason which induced the Government to adopt, and which induced the people to support, the public school system, I think I would be able to give you a very good reason why the people thought fit to abolish separate schools and to adopt the public school system. Let me point out to you in the first place that you have to determine, and according to my learned friend's view, you have got to determine it as an abstract proposition, that the separate school system is to be preferred to the public school system. In my learned friend's whole contention there is not one circumstance that he has given you as to the condition of the province when the public school system was adopted. He tells us that there is a minority, as there are in all the provinces, of either Catholics or Protestants, and that there is a jurisdiction, which is not now in question. He has told you what the separate system of schools is, he has given you arguments in favour of that system. I join issue with him at once, and I ask you to look at it as he presents it. He says that because the separate school system is to be preferred, you should pass this remedial order.

I say that the separate school system is not to be preferred, that you should not therefore pass this remedial order. I say that that would be a proper conclusion to come to if the matter were open and unembarrassed by the decision that the province has arrived at ; but it is still more impossible to arrive at that conclusion, when you are sitting in appeal upon an act of the legislature, unless you have more than the simple fact that one is separate and one is public. Now there is not a gentleman sitting in the Council who has not made up his mind on the merits of the two systems. The question is not new to us here. I do not think there is a man in public life that has not a definite view upon that question. Therefore, it does appear to me to be a waste of your valuable time for me to argue in favour of the public school system as against the separate school system. I should never convince those who believe in separate schools as the proper system, and I do not need to convince those who do not. I believe there are men sitting at that board, who, if they have not changed their opinion lately, are as firmly convinced that separate schools are against the interests of the people of this country, as the humble individual who now addresses you. So that it is not necessary for me to go into that question, and to tell you that separate schools are contrary to our system in this country, where no religion is recognized by the law, where we have no state religion, if you except the province of Quebec, where there is a *quasi* state church—where we have no state religion, and where all religions are open, and free, and equal before the law. I say that under these circumstances it is not necessary to repeat the stale and hackneyed argument which has been presented so frequently, and which you all know so well, that the state ought not to lend its assistance to the propagation of the dogmas of any particular religion or of any particular church. According to our theory, the state owes to its people the gift of elementary education. Those who have no children have to bear their taxes as well as those who have. Those who choose to send their children to a private school have nevertheless to bear their taxes, although they get no benefit therefrom. The state itself, in the interests of the public at large, has decided that the children of the people should be educated, and to enforce their education and insist upon it, they not merely provide means, but they make attendance at school compulsory. Now, if the system of separate schools is to be preferred, and if this Council concludes that it is better to adopt that as its view, I do not think that any argument I can present will affect that result. I am only here to protest in the name of the Government of Manitoba against the adoption of that principle. But I think I can point out to this Honourable Council that no affirmative decision can be arrived at in this case, without this Council laying down the proposition that of the two systems, the separate and national, they prefer the separate system. Now, in this matter, you are legislating not for this Dominion. This will be a local law. You remember that in the old days laws were frequently passed to affect merely Upper or Lower Canada. We had two systems of jurisdiction, as it were, although the Parliament was one. This is a law which will affect merely the province of Manitoba, and affect it in a matter of purely local concern. It can only be passed, I submit, by the Council after having arrived at the conclusion that as between the separate school system and the public or national system, the separate school system is preferable ; and not only that, but you restore the separate system which has been abolished. I say there are no circumstances affecting Manitoba which make it an exception to the general rule. A man might say : Well, speaking generally, the separate school system is not to be preferred, the public school system is better, but looking at the peculiar circumstances of the province of Manitoba, that forms an exception. But I think I shall be able to establish, by facts which you have not yet heard, that there are no exceptional circumstances which require that the school system should be separate.

Hon. Mr. Ouimet.—Would it be asking too much of you to give us a definition of what constitutes national or public schools, and separate schools, in your opinion ?

Mr. McCarthy.—I intended to do that.

Sir Mackenzie Bowell.—Do you mean in your argument to say that if a man refused to vote for the abolition of separate schools, he would necessarily approve of separate schools ?

Mr. McCarthy.—You have no power to abolish them in Ontario, and there is no use in voting if you have not the power.

Sir MACKENZIE BOWELL.—We know they have not the power, but the question has been raised.

Mr. McCARTHY.—Yes, I think I was one of those who raised it, but in view of petitioning the Imperial Parliament, and only in that sense. No person ever dreamed of attempting to vote for the repeal of separate schools in Ontario at present.

Sir MACKENZIE BOWELL.—Do you mean that any person refusing to sign that petition, would prefer separate schools?

Mr. McCARTHY. A law affecting any of our provinces ought not to be interfered with unless the legislative body of that province has asked for its repeal, and consequently, unless this Parliament has concurred; in other words, the Imperial Parliament would not interfere with the British North America Act, unless, for instance, the Ontario Legislature asked for the repeal of the clause which imposed separate schools upon that province, and the Parliament of Canada coincided with that request. The only question that arises here is, is it wise, is it proper, to set on foot an agitation with a view of electing gentlemen to the Legislative Assembly who would adopt that petition?

Sir MACKENZIE BOWELL.—Then those who would vote against that proposition would affirm the principle of separate schools, according to your argument.

Mr. McCARTHY.—Not necessarily. I leave things as they are. We have got the public school system in Manitoba, and the question is, is this Council going to re-establish separate schools? My argument is that they cannot re-establish separate schools unless they are convinced that the separate school system is preferable to the public school system, or a national school system, as to which I promised the Minister of Public Works that I would give a definition before I am done.

Sir CHARLES H. TUPPER.—The Privy Council make a reference to what was actually contemplated by this Parliament at the time of the passage of that Act, that is to say, they take it that it was practically certain there would be a separate school system there, as the parties were equally balanced, as they put it.

Mr. McCARTHY.—That is what gave rise to the jurisdiction.

Sir CHARLES H. TUPPER.—I would say that is a declaration on the part of the Canadian Parliament providing for that contingency, and in favour of that system of separate schools.

Mr. McCARTHY.—What the Canadian Parliament has provided for is what the Canadian Parliament has said. But what they said was that if they intended to accomplish anything by the first section, they utterly failed to do so.

Sir MACKENZIE BOWELL.—It often occurs that the intention of Parliament is not carried out by the wording of the Act.

Mr. McCARTHY.—Lord Herschel has expressed the same opinion. I think the draughtsman who drew up this particular legislation was not very well versed in the business.

Sir CHARLES H. TUPPER.—The parliament who originally passed that Act contemplated and endorsed a system of separate schools for Manitoba, just as we would be doing by a remedial order of this kind, for protecting that system would be endorsing it.

Mr. McCARTHY.—That may or may not be so. It is quite evident, I think, from the absence of a provision as to separate schools, that parliament did not think fit at the time to say that there should be separate schools. Nothing would have been simpler than for parliament to have enacted that in the province of Manitoba there shall be separate schools, just as this parliament has more than once provided with regard to the North-west. That could have been done, and that would have been simple.

Sir MACKENZIE BOWELL.—There is no declaration in the British North America Act, because at that time the province of Manitoba did not exist.

Hon. Mr. IVES.—If your view as to our declaring in favour of separate schools, if this remedial order is given, is correct, then you would hold that the question upon which the appeal is based, is this: the Catholics say common schools or national schools are the law, but we think separate schools would be preferable, and we ask you to give us separate schools. Now, I do not understand that to be the petition at all. They say: We have a right to separate schools, we have been deprived of that right, and we want them restored.

Mr. McCarthy.—I understand that, but I am done with part of the question. I pointed out that they are saying they have a right to the separate schools.

Hon. Mr. Ives.—I understood you to say that anybody who favoured referring the matter to Parliament, must necessarily declare in favour of separate schools.

Mr. McCarthy.—No, I say this Council cannot come to the conclusion to give this remedial order for separate schools without putting as your major premise that you approve of separate schools as against national schools.

Sir Mackenzie Bowell.—It is to that declaration that I take objection.

Mr. McCarthy.—I am not asking you to give judgment in my favour on the spot. All I am asking you to do is to listen to me.

Sir Mackenzie Bowell.—I will endeavour to do so.

Mr. McCarthy.—I do not mean to say that you have not a perfect right to object to it.

Sir Charles H. Tupper.—Do you object to my interposing the question with reference to the decision, to which I wished to call your attention, at the time the Manitoba Act was passed. On page 276, in the judgment of the Privy Council, I read this —

"Those who were stipulating for the provisions of section 22 as a condition of the union, and those who gave their legislative assent to the act by which it was brought about, had in view the perils then apprehended. The immediate adoption by the legislature of an educational system obnoxious either to Catholics or Protestants, would not be contemplated as possible. As has been already stated, the Roman Catholics in the province were about equal in number. It was impossible at that time for either party to obtain legislative sanction to a scheme of education obnoxious to the other. The establishment of a system of public education in which both parties would concur was probably then in immediate prospect. The legislature of Manitoba first met on 15th March, 1871. On the 3rd of May following, the Educational Act of 1871 received the royal assent, but the future was uncertain. Either Roman Catholics or Protestants might become the preponderating power in the legislature, and it might be under such conditions for the minority to prevent the creation of the public cost of schools which though acceptable to the majority could only be taken advantage of by the minority of the terms of sacrificing their cherished convictions. The change to a Roman Catholic system of public schools would have been regarded with as much distaste by the Protestants of the province as the change to an unsectarian system was by the Catholics."

Mr. McCarthy.—That, of course, is not law, it is merely a historical reference. Of course, that is an endeavour on the part of the Lord Chancellor to find a reason for this extraordinary legislation. It may be I am wrong, but it does not bind anybody.

Hon. Mr. Dickey.—I understand you to say that in your view that section of the Manitoba Act should not, under any circumstances, be given effect to.

Mr. McCarthy.—That is my view, speaking here on behalf of the province of Manitoba. Speaking elsewhere, I should say it should never have been invoked in any province at all. Circumstances, of course, change very much, and what might have been thought feasible in 1871 is impossible in 1895. It does not follow that because there is power, it ought to be exercised, any more than because there is power to expend public money, it should be expended. Now, let me draw your attention to the fact that every province of the Dominion that has been free, has deliberately adopted the public school system. This is a circumstance that is not lightly to be disregarded in view of this appeal to the central body. We know that in New Brunswick the public school system has been adopted. Early after confederation the province passed a public school law, and you are all familiar with the struggle that was made against that law, and the attempt that was made to induce the central body here to veto it. But the New Brunswick law remains to this day a public school act. I do not know whether Nova Scotia preceded or followed New Brunswick in her legislation in this respect, but she, too, has a public school act. Prince Edward Island followed, and there again there was a struggle. Petitions were presented, questions debated, and the future rendered dismal by the possibilities that were conjured up if the law was not repealed. Let me quote the language in the report of the Executive Council of Prince Edward Island :—

"The great principle that the public money was not to be appropriated for the purpose of teaching sectarian dogma or creeds, is one which a large majority of the people of this province value very highly, and which they will not surrender without a struggle commensurate to the importance they attach to the principle itself."

Then we have British Columbia adopting a public school system. Now, all of us who come from Ontario, know that there is a great deal of unrest by reason of the limited authority that the legislature of that great province has to deal with the subject of schools; and I venture to say, as a proof of the evil of that kind of interference, that there is more disquietude, there is more heart-burning, there is more bitterness in the province to-day on account of the restriction on the legislature in that respect, and the compulsory adoption of separate schools in the constitution, than there is in any other province in the Dominion. In the provinces that are free, we are told, and it is the best possible argument that can be urged, that so tolerant are the majority, so willing are they to yield rights which could not be legally claimed, that, to adopt the language of my learned friend, we wink at infractions of the public school law so that it becomes almost a separate school system. And they do it willingly. But it is one thing to compel people to do a thing, and it is another thing to leave it to their free choice. It is a strong argument in favour of allowing the people of Manitoba to work out their own salvation without interference.

Hon. Mr. Costigan.—You speak of excitement in Ontario about their being compelled to retain separate schools. Would that apply to Quebec also, as the same condition of things exists there?

Mr. McCarthy.—I am not so familiar with the politics of Quebec, therefore I am not speaking of it. I was comparing Ontario with the other English provinces of which I have more knowledge. I do not desire to include the province of Quebec in that category. On this question I am disposed to adopt the arguments of Dr. J. M. King, in a lecture which I find reproduced in Mr. Ewart's compilation. It is only a repetition of what has been said in favour of a national school system as against a separate school system, and giving objections to the latter system. If you will look at pages 189 to 193 in Mr. Ewart's book on the Manitoba school question, you will find Dr. King's arguments reproduced. I will read a summary of them:—

"First, it is in direct violation of the principle of the separation of church and state. It is unnecessary, indeed it would be quite irrelevant to argue this principle here. It is that on which, rightly or wrongly, the state with us is constituted. I do not understand it to mean that the state may not have regard to religious considerations, such as it shows when it enforces the observance of the Sabbath rest, or that it may not employ religious considerations, such as it shows when it enforces the observance of the Sabbath rest, or that it may not employ religious sanctions, as it does when, in its courts of law, it administers an oath in the name of God ; but I do understand it to mean that the state is neither to give material aid to the operations of the church in any of its branches, nor to interfere with its liberties."

Mr. Dickey.—That would include exemptions from taxation.

Mr. McCarthy.—Yes, it does. The Baptists have gone the length of saying that they are willing to give up exemptions. Then he points out what, of course, we know :—

"Now, when the right of taxation, and in addition, grants of money are given by the state to schools, in which distinctive doctrines and rites of any church, whether Protestant or Catholic, are taught, schools which, while giving instruction in secular branches are used at the same time to extend the influence, if not to increase the membership of that church, then the principle of the separation of church and state is violated almost as much as if the officiating minister or priest were taken into the pay of the state, and the violation (I say it with all frankness, but without any feeling of hostility to any class), is not more easily borne, than it is mainly in the interest of a single section of the church. The public school is surely meant to be the school of the state by which it is supported. It does not exist to initiate the youth of the province into the details of Christian doctrine, or to prepare them for communion. Its main, if not indeed its sole aim is to make good citizens ; intelligent, capable, law-abiding citizens. But under our present system, schools exist and are maintained by the state which are church schools in everything but in name, which are in fact, proselytising agencies. Their establishment in the early history of the province is an inconsistency which is not, perhaps, difficult to explain, but their perpetuation can scarcely fail to be felt by the majority of the inhabitants as a misappropriation of public funds and an injustice to a large section of the community."

Then, he argues next that the system of separate or sectarian schools operates injuriously on the well-being of the state, and that argument I have endeavoured to adopt in the strongest possible way. I do not think anything can be more mischievous to that community, in which we all ought to be interested, than the perpetuation from its early history of a system dividing the people into antagonistic and positively hostile bands, on account of their religious faith. Dr. King goes on to say :—

"It occasions a line of cleavage in society, the highest interests of which demands that it should, as far as possible, be one. It perpetuates distinctions, and almost necessarily gives rise to sentiments which are at once a reproach and a peril. I do not think the religious differences between the Roman Catholic and the Protestant churches, small or unimportant. As a Protestant, sincerely and firmly believing our faith to be more scriptural, I could not wish these differences to be thought of little account, but surely it is possible for the one party and the other to maintain steadfastly their respective beliefs without cherishing sentiments of distrust and hostility to the manifest injury of the public weal."

He adds at page 191 :

"The system itself of separate or sectarian schools appears to be incapable of justification on any ground of right principle or even of wise experience. I do not expect to see any permanent contentment in relation to the question while the system is maintained. The conviction will continue to be deeply and generally cherished, that the equities of the situation have been disregarded, and that the interests of the state have been sacrificed to meet the requirements of the Church of Rome."

Further down at page 192, he says :—

"The claims of our French speaking Roman Catholic brethren should be fairly and, if possible, even generously considered. They were early in this western land. They have done much and at great cost—cost not of money only, but of toil and suffering from the native races. But this claim the claim to teach the distinctive doctrines and rites of their church in schools sustained by public moneys—is one, I have no hesitation in saying, and as entertaining much regard for some among us by whom it is made, I say it with regret, which the state ought not to concede, should not feel itself at liberty to concede. It is a privilege which, under the system proposed, is not granted to any other church. No other desires to have the opportunity to teach the distinctive doctrines of Presbyterianism, or Methodism, or even of Protestantism, in the public schools, or if any cherish such a wish, it would be very properly denied them. There is no room therefore to speak of injustice to a class who happen to be in the minority, when exactly the same privileges are granted to them which are granted to other classes of the community. If it is a matter of conscience with the Roman Catholic Church (it is obviously not with all its members) that the whole body of the faith as held by it, should be taught even to the youth in attendance on school and in the day school. I see nothing else for it than that they should establish and support from voluntary contributions, the schools in which such teaching is to be given. But it were surely far better that our Roman Catholic fellow citizens should unite with us in securing a distinct recognition of our common Christianity within the public schools, leaving what is distinctive, and what many on the one side and on the other feel to be very important, to be taught to the children in the Sabbath school, or in the church, or better still, in the home."

Hon. Mr. OUIMET.—How do you explain the principle that it is unjust that public money should be used for the religious education of the people? I suppose because it is not fair that the Presbyterians, for instance, should be taxed to educate the Baptists or any other sects?

Mr. McCARTHY.—The clergymen of my church are anxious for separate schools.

Hon. Mr. OUIMET.—I do not know why they should not have them.

Mr. McCARTHY.—Then you break up the whole system.

Sir MACKENZIE BOWELL.—In Ontario, under certain circumstances, if there are a sufficient number of Church of England people living in a neighbourhood where the majority are Roman Catholics, they can form a separate school.

Mr. McCARTHY.—A Protestant school, but not a Church of England school. The Archbishop of Manitoba, who is an Aberdeen man, I believe, is very much imbued with the principles which prevail in England, where they are fighting strenuously for church schools. Where there is an established church, church schools would be logical, but in this country there is no established church, and you remember well the long struggle we had with regard to the clergy reserves, which was owing in fact to the jealous and hostile feeling that existed in the other Protestant denominations, as well as in the Catholic denomination, against the public lands of the province being used for the support of Church of England schools, although they had been set apart to the Church of England and the Church of Scotland, by King George III.

Sir MACKENZIE BOWELL.—I remember that when I was a boy writing for a newspaper, I used to write against the secularization of the Clergy Reserves.

Mr. McCARTHY. I can say that on that question I never changed my opinion, because from my boyhood I was in favour of the secularization of the clergy reserves.

Sir MACKENZIE BOWELL.—Your are a church man and I was not.

Mr. McCARTHY.—I am satisfied, speaking as a churchman, that my church has been better off and enjoyed a higher position in the ranks of her fellow churches, because she stands alone and has no unfair privileges over her sister churches, as she had when she used those lands which were set apart by King George for her benefit. Now, let us look at this question as regards the province of Manitoba. Remember you are asked now to set in motion machinery by which a local law can be made for Manitoba, and by which separate schools may be given to Manitoba. If that is to be given simply as a matter of right, and because at one period there were separate schools there, then there is no argument about it. If that is to be given on consideration of advantages or disadvantages, of expediency, or inexpediency, or of the wisdom of the measure as applied to that province,—and I humbly submit those are considerations which should prevail,—then you must take into account the circumstances of the province, and if you are in favour of separate schools, see whether it does not form an exception; and if you are against separate schools, conclude simply that there is no reason why they should be imposed on that province.

Hon. Mr. IVES.—Is it your opinion that the school Act of 1871, in so far as it created separate schools for the Roman Catholics, has become, by the interpretation that has been given it by the Privy Council, a part of the constitution of Manitoba?

Mr. McCARTHY—No, clearly not.

Hon. Mr. IVES.—You do not take that view.

Mr. McCARTHY.—Clearly not. They hold that the act of 1890 was not a good law; they hold that because the act of 1890 took away privileges which the Roman Catholic minority had by the School Act of 1871, that therefore they had a right to come here and complain, and call upon you to give them that school law back again. So, if you do not interfere, the Act of 1890 remains effective law.

Hon. Mr. HAGGART.—Is there any limitation to the remedy that we may order?

Mr. McCARTHY.—I suppose, judging by an expression that fell from one of their Lordships, it would be merely to restore rights that had been taken away.

Hon. Mr. HAGGART.—Suppose we made changes in excess of the old law, what would be the effect?

Mr. McCARTHY.—That might be investigated in the courts, every law is subject to that. That was not understood when this Act was passed in 1871, and probably that gave rise to this extraordinary question, because it was not recognized that laws could be declared *ultra vires* by the court. That was well understood on the American side where they have a paper constitution, but we had not a paper constitution, and no law was declared *ultra vires* until after Confederation, and after the passage of this Act. That would be a reason, probably, why this appeal was given to the Governor in Council. Now, let me remind you that this change in the law was not made hastily. I am glad to find in this history of Mr. Begg that within a short time after the law, in 1871, the question was raised, not by politicians, but by the people. On page 201 he says:—

"An agitation now commenced in the province on the school question and the following is the platform that was set down by a portion of the Protestant section of the community :

1st. The abolition of the board of education, and the creation of a department of education with a cabinet Minister for a head.
2nd. The establishment of a purely non-sectarian system of public schools.
3rd. The compulsory use of English text books in all public schoos.
4th. All public schools to be subject to the same rules and regulations.
5th. The appointment of one or more inspectors.
6th. The establishment, as soon as practicable, of a training school for teachers."

I need not trouble you with reading the rest. You will see what was afterwards embodied in the act of 1890. Now that was there in 1876, 5 years after the separate schools had been introduced. A section of the people commenced to agitate for a repeal of the separate school law, which they did not succeed in carrying out until 1890, 14 years after, so it cannot be said that the matter has been done hastily. Let me read you an extract from Mr. Hill's history also, to show that the question was up in the legislature long before it was treated as a government measure. At page 601, in Hill's History of Manitoba, he says:—

"Shortly afterwards John Norquay became Minister of Public Works, and Dr. Baird, Speaker of the House. The first session was naturally a long one, and all its members zealous. The government invited amendments to their measures, which were cheerfully furnished, and committees, after spending a month on a Queen's Bench and School Act, were ruthlessly wakened up at the close of the session, to find that the government had only done this as a blind, and passed their own bills over the heads of those who desired so much different. The Opposition were worsted, and their ideas of public schools buried—not however, for ever, as the session for 1890 has shown."

Now, Mr. Norquay was Minister of Public Works during the days when Mr. Archibald was Lieutenant-Governor of the province.

Hon. Mr. DICKEY.—He was appointed in 1874, and served two terms.

Mr. McCARTHY.—At all events, this shows that it was not a hasty act on their part.

Hon. Mr. DALY.—Have you anything to show that there was any agitation between the period that quotation refers to, and 1889?

Mr. McCARTHY.—No, I have not. The question was first raised in 1876. This history states that the agitation was kept up, but it was not adopted by any political party.

Hon. Mr. DALY.—I never heard of that.

Mr. McCARTHY.—Now Dr. Bryce, who was a member of the school board, and speaking therefore with knowledge, has written an article on the Manitoba School Question, which was published in the Canadian Magazine and also on page 283 of Mr. Ewart's book :—

"In conclusion the writer is of opinion that the people of Manitoba have followed a wiser and more patriotic course than that suggested by Mr. Ewart, with his lax and unphilosophic plans of so-called toleration. The problem facing Manitoba was unique. The province was made up of people of many nations, its speech is polyglot, with the majority English-speaking : it has eight or ten thousand Icelanders, it has fifteen thousand German speaking Mennonites: it has some ten or twelve thousand French speaking half breeds and Quebecers : it has considerable numbers of Polish Jews : it has many Hungarians and Finlanders : it has a Gaelic-speaking Crofter settlement. The Icelanders petitioned the education board, of which the writer is a member, for liberty to have the Lutherans prepare their candidates for confirmation in the school ; the Mennonites, with singular tenacity, have demanded separate religious schools."

I do not know what their religion is.

Hon. Mr. DALY.—It is the Lutheran religion.

Mr. McCARTHY.—Now, you will see it becomes a very important matter. Here were fifteen thousand people who were demanding separate religious schools, who had never come into the school system, and declined to come into it. Remember that at that time there was no power to tax, so that a man who was neither a Protestant or a Catholic, was exempt from taxation, and the Mennonites notwithstanding all the inducements, steadfastly refused to come into the school system, demanding that they should have separate religious schools. Mr. Bryce goes on :—

"The French had their Catholic schools, and their spirit may be seen when their late superintendent, Senator Bernier, refused to consent to a Protestant being a member of a French Canadian society. Many of the other foreigners are absolutely careless about education. What could patriotic Manitobans do?—They were faced with the prospect of whole masses of the population growing up illiterate. The Mennonites who came from Russia are more ignorant to-day as a people than when they came from Russia 18 years ago. Yes, British Manitoba has been a better foster-mother of ignorance than half-civilized Russia had been. The only hope for the province was to fall back on the essential rights of the province, and provide one public school for every locality and have a vigorous effort made to rear up a homogeneous Canadian people. It has required nerve on the part of the people to do this, but the first step has been taken, and in the mind of most there is the conviction that the battle has been won."

Now, just bear that in mind when you come to deal with the question as it otherwise presents itself. It was not merely a question between the English speaking majority and the French Canadians, or Roman Catholic minority. That was not the only difficulty that beset the Manitoba Legislature. They had all these various bodies of foreigners which had been induced to settle in the country, and who are, so far as I know, making good citizens, and therefore their settlement is to be encouraged. The legislature had the education of these people and those difficulties to look after, and in addition, the difficulties with which we in the older provinces are familiar, and to which I need not more particularly advert. Then, let me say something on the question of population, because it is impossible to disregard the question of majority. The minority does not rule, according to our system. The minority is not to be deprived of rights, but the ordinary way for the minority to obtain their rights is by agitation, and by appealing to what I think can always be appealed to where rights are invaded, and that is the good sense and fair-mindedness of the majority, no matter of whom that majority may be composed. That is our system, be it right or be it wrong. Now let us see how that stands here. In the first place, who does my learned friend appear for? Looking at the record I find none of the French names on the petition that is presented here, and for whom my learned friend appears. Looking at the petition, page 20 of the case that was referred to the Privy Council, the names are, His Grace the Archbishop of St. Boniface, the Bishop of d'Anemour, Joseph Messier, Priest of St. Boniface ; T. A. Bernier, J. Dubuc, L. A. Prudhomme, M. A. Girard, A. A. LaRivière, M.P., James E. Prendergast, M.P.P., Roger Marion, M.P.P., and four thousand other names. On page 21 the members of the Executive Committee of the National Congress are all French names. Then the third one, which is on page 31, contains also the same French names. The petitioners that appear on this document are not those whose names I find upon the face of the petition. These people—I say it with no disrespect, because they have rights, no matter where they live—the most of them live in the one district of Provencher in which the bulk of the French people are settled.

Hon. Mr. OUIMET.—It is one of your grounds for objecting because they are only Frenchmen.

Mr. McCARTHY.—That would be a good ground, but it is not the ground I am putting forward here. I mention these things because we had here a representative of the Irish Catholics, who came on behalf of himself and those who sympathize with him.

Hon. Mr. CURRAN.—Has he any credentials of any kind?

Mr. McCARTHY.—You have heard what he said yesterday. I do not represent him in any sense. He told you yesterday that he was a public school trustee, that he was a member of the Roman Catholic Church, and in full communion with the church, and as such he has a right to be heard, I suppose, just as much as even a Frenchman.

Hon. Mr. ANGERS.—And he told us his two daughters were teaching.

Mr. McCarthy.—Now, I say it is significant in this regard, that if the proportion of Catholics, small in itself, is yet to be cut down by any considerable number of them who are satisfied with the system, it reduces, in my opinion, the ground upon which the minority might claim indulgence, because it is an indulgence, at the hands of this Council. Now, let me deal with the question of population, but, first, I may dray the attention of the Council to this fact. At the time, Manitoba was set apart as a province, the population was said to be 12,000. Of these, 5,000 were French half-breeds, 5,000 were Scotch half-breeds, and 2,000 where what were called Canadians in those days, or whites in the older provinces. The population of the Red River settlement in 1870 was composed of about 2,000 whites, 5,000 English half-breeds and 5,000 French half-breeds, or Métis. There was another division into 3 parts, English, French and Canadians. There was a cross division into three parties, viz., the English, the French and the Canadians. Here is a citation from Begg's history, describing the population at that time :

"The French half-breed, called also Métis, and formerly Bois-Brulé, is an athletic, rather good-looking, lively, excitable, easy going being. Fond of a fast pony, fond of merry making, free-hearted, open-handed, yet indolent and improvident, he is a marked feature of border life. Being excitable, he can be roused to acts of revenge, of bravery and daring. The Métis, if a friend, is true, and cannot in too many ways oblige you. Louis Riel was undoubtedly the embodiment of the spirit of unrest and insubordination in his race."

Then he says of the English half-breeds :—

"As different as is the patient roadster from the wild mustang, is the English-speaking half-breed from the Métis."

So apparently the population included five thousand of the wild mustang and five thousand of the patient roadster. And the Canadians were two thousand pioneers who had gone into the country at that early day. Now these twelve thousand people passed a separate school law and if they had not done so the schools Act of 1890, which is now in question, would not have been passed, and this question could not have arisen until a separate school law had been passed. Gentlemen forget that the complaint is that because these ten thousand half-breeds chose to pass a separate school law the 150,000 or 200,000 people,—I believe that is about the estimate of the population of Manitoba now,—who are not the least intelligent of the sons of the older provinces, must never pass a law to alter that.

Sir Mackenzie Bowell.—Were these five thousand English half-breeds all Protestants?

Mr. McCarthy.—No ; some were Catholics.

Hon. Mr. Daly.—They were not all half-breeds, I fancy, but included other natives —the Selkirk colonists.

Mr. McCarthy.—I do not pretend to know. But Mr. Ewart quoted that and used it in the Privy Council as a correct statement. I believe you quoted from Begg?

Mr. Ewart.— Yes.

Mr. McCarthy.—I understood that some of the English half-breeds were Catholics, and so that majority was obtained. It is trifling almost with the free people of Manitoba to tell them that because 10,000 half-breeds passed a separate school law in 1871 the province was for ever bound down to that system. Now according to the last census there was a population in Manitoba of 152,506, of whom 20,571 were Roman Catholics.

Hon. Mr. Ives.—Before you leave that point, as the Roman Catholic population was very small and confined to Provencher the disturbance would be relatively very small if a separate school system were in force.

Mr. McCarthy.—If you were to pass a remedial law for Provencher?

Hon. Mr. Ives.—I mean so long as the Roman Catholic population is comparatively small and confined to one part of the province the disturbance caused by a separate school system would be much less than it would be in Ontario, where the Catholics are scattered all over the province.

Mr. McCarthy.—Of course, that necessarily follows.

Hon. Mr. OUIMET.— Remedial legislation would apply only to a small minority.

Mr. McCARTHY.— Of course, you can do that if you like, I suppose. Your remedial legislation might be only for a district. So long as you do not grant too much in excess you can grant anything less you see fit.

Hon. Mr. OUIMET —This legislation would not concern the majority in any way?

Mr. McCARTHY.—That depends upon what you call concerning them. If the majority are concerned in having the Catholics identified with themselves, if they are concerned in having these Catholics cease to be French and English.

Hon. Mr. OUIMET.—Would that be the object?

Mr. McCARTHY.—Undoubtedly, I think that would be a great object, and I think the object.

Hon. Mr. OUIMET.—That they may cease to remain French and Catholic.

Mr. McCARTHY.—Let them remain Catholic but not French. That is the object— as Mr. Bryce stated it—to make the people homogeneous. In the one district of Provencher you have 9,896 Catholics, or nearly half the Catholics in the whole province. Leaving Provencher out the question you have a population of 131,000 Protestants and 11,000 Catholics, or ninety-one to nine. And this great province with its 64,000 square miles—and let me call attention to the fact that this is larger by 14,000 square miles than New Brunswick, Nova Scotia and Prince Edward Island taken together, this province undoubtedly is destined to be one of the greatest provinces in the Dominion and already a great factor in the wealth of the Dominion, is the subject to be dealt with. And it seems to me that you assume a great responsibility if you interfere with laws that the local legislature have adopted. I have taken up the census and I find that it is only in the following census subdistricts that there are more than 200 Roman Catholics leaving Provencher for the moment out of the question :—

Lisgar.—Assiniboia, 390; Belcourt, 826; St. Francis Xavier, 699; St. Laurent, 989.

Marquette.—Elm River, 267; Portage la Prairie, 211; Riding Mountain, 243; Rosedale, 336.

Selkirk.—Brandon City, 201 ; Bremda, 209 ; Lorne, 1,180 ; Sifton, 500.

So that we have here but twelve out of seventy-three districts in which there are more Catholics than 200 outside this one constituency (for Dominion purposes) of Provencher.

Hon. Mr. DALY.—That must be the census of 1881. There was no municipality of Bremda in 1891.

Mr. McCARTHY.—It may be a mistake in the name. But I took the figures down and directed them to be copied ; but even if the name is wrong the numbers are right. Look at the population of the province as it has grown. I take it first as to the number of Catholics and next as to the number of French. We are told that in 1871 there were 12,000 people, of whom the minority were Catholics. In 1881 the total population was 65,954, of whom 12,246 were Catholics, or about eighteen per cent.

Hon. Mr. OUIMET.—But they had grown 10 per cent.

Mr. McCARTHY.—But the other had grown ten hundred per cent.

Hon. Mr. OUIMET.—From immigration.

Mr. McCARTHY.—In 1885 the population had grown to 108,640, of whom 14,431, or 13 per cent, were Roman Catholics. In 1891 the population was 152,500, Catholics 20,571 or 13 per cent. If you take the French separate from the Roman Catholics you will find this result :—In 1871 the French were 41 per cent, that is assuming that my learned friend's figures are correct. In 1891 there were 9,949, being 15 per cent of the population. In the census of 1885 for the first time there were separate columns for the enumeration for Half-breeds and French, showing 6,821—Quebeckers I suppose they would be called— and 4,869 Half-breeds, in all 11,190, or ten per cent. In 1891 the number was 11,102, or 7 per cent. So that the Roman Catholic population was 20,000, of whom 11,000 were French, most of them in one district, as to whom the system enforced—I fancy I am not mistaking it—was practically the Quebec system of schools, the French language being taught by teachers who did not understand the English language. There were 15,000 Mennonites, speaking their own tongue, demand-ing a separate system of schools, and as far as I can see, with just as much right to have the public money appropriated to their schools as the French. There was a large body of Icelanders, with whom there seems to have been difficulty according to the passage I have read from Mr. Bryce. Other elements were coming in to fill up the province. The desire of the Provincial Legislature was to do away with illiteracy among the people, to make the people Manitobans and Canadians, not French or Mennonites, not Poles or Polish Jews. And so this system of schools was adopted. Was that unwise so that it should be over-ruled, and replaced with a system inimical to the public interest?

Hon. Mr. DICKEY.—If you are through with the figures respecting the French, may I ask if, with regard to the Mennonites, Poles and so on, you agree with the intimation of the Privy Council that no rights for them are established under this judgment?

Mr. McCARTHY.—Of course; I am only dealing with the question of schools.

Hon. Mr. DICKEY.—Arguing it on the grounds of expediency?

Mr. McCARTHY.—Yes.

Hon. Mr. DICKEY.—Do you admit that these minorities are in a different position?

Mr. McCARTHY.—Yes; they have no right to come here and complain—there is no doubt about that. I wish to say, and it cannot be too often repeated, that in the distribution of legislative powers between the Dominion and the provinces the subject of education is assigned to the provinces, and that for wise and good reason. The fact that this body is invested with power to over-rule and to impose a law upon the province, does not preclude the Council from consideration what would be the wisest and best for the people of Manitoba. You are not, I hope, going to restrain or degrade the province of Manitoba to satisfy the province of Quebec? You are dealing with the rights of the people under legislative authority given you for the benefit of the people to be governed and not for the benefit of anybody else. Therefore, it becomes a very serious matter as it appears to me, when you are asked to repeal a law that has been solemnly adopted. I desire to recall to your recollection a case of dealing with the power of disallowance on the question of education. I wish to fortify my position with reference to the earlier records. The reports and the history will show that everything there was against any interference with the question of education. How was it that the parliamentary majority made up at one time of those on one side of the House and at another time of those on the other side of the House, expressed themselves as opposed to interfering with a law regulating education. Some, perhaps, will say that it was because of a dislike to interfere with provincial rights, but that will not answer, at all events, completely; because men in public life, who had no scruple at all upon the abstract question of provincial rights joined in these resolutions, and none more heartily than the president himself (Sir Mackenzie Bowell), against any interference with the subject of education. Was it that the subject was felt to be a delicate one to interfere in? Was it that the matter was so purely one of local concern? I will only give you the facts and allow you, gentlemen, who are as competent as I am and more so, to draw a proper deduction. The Minister of Marine and Fisheries brought this question up in 1872 and pressed it forward. His resolution you will find at page 35 of the Journals of 1872.

Sir MACKENZIE BOWELL.—That is the New Brunswick case.

Mr. McCARTHY.—Yes.

Sir CHARLES HIBBERT TUPPER.—It came up several sessions.

Mr. McCARTHY.—Yes; I am going to trace the resolutions to show the deliberation with which the matter was handled, and that, notwithstanding the strong regret expressed by the majority in Parliament that the law had been passed, yet a tremendous majority thought it best not to interfere.

Sir MACKENZIE BOWELL.—That refers to a province in which they had neither by law nor usage any rights in separate schools.

Mr. McCARTHY.—It dealt with a case in which the province had the right to pass the law.

Sir CHARLES HIBBERT TUPPER.—There had been no separate schools at any time.

Mr. McCARTHY.—At that time it was a disputed point whether the rights of Roman Catholics had been interfered with. It was settled by the Privy Council afterwards that the Act was not a violation of the terms of the British North America Act.

Sir MACKENZIE BOWELL.—But here you are dealing with a case in which the Privy Council says that rights have been interfered with.

Mr. McCARTHY.—I am going to try and apply the case I give.

Hon. Mr. COSTIGAN. If you quote the resolution to show the strong feeling of parliament and the delicacy felt in dealing with the rights of the provinces, you should also, before you leave it, refer to the vote of 1873.

Mr. McCARTHY.—I am going to. At this time Sir John Macdonald's government was in power, of which government you were a supporter. I am going to show it was received then and also to show that it was disposed of when Mr. Mackenzie was in power.

If there is no chance of my getting through perhaps this will be a convenient place to break off.

The Council adjourned until 11 a.m to-morrow.

OTTAWA, March 6, 1895.

The Privy Council met at 11 o'clock a.m.

Present :— Sir Mackenzie Bowell, Sir Adolphe Caron, Hon. Mr. Costigan, Sir Charles Hibbert Tupper, Hon. Mr. Foster, Hon. Mr. Haggart, Hon. Mr. Ouimet, Hon. Mr. Daly, Hon. Mr. Angers, Hon. Mr. Ives, and Hon. Mr. Dickey.

Mr. McCARTHY.—I find that the Minister of the Interior was in error in saying that there was not a census sub-district of Brenda in his constituency, Selkirk. I do not know whether it still exists under that name, but you will find in the census from which I took the figures which I quoted, that there is a census sub-district known as Brenda.

Hon. Mr. DALY.—There was a place of that name.

Mr. McCARTHY.—I mean that it was in the census as I gave it when I quoted the figures, showing the number of Roman Catholics in the several districts in which they numbered over 200.

Hon. Mr. DALY.—The reason I raised the question about it was that the municipality has been wiped out and I did not know but that you were quoting from the census before 1891, when the municipality existed.

Mr. McCARTHY.—I do not know whether these census sub-districts are intended to be municipalities or not.

Hon. Mr. DALY.—They are.

Mr. McCARTHY.—Then, of course, that adds to the force of my contention. If these are municipalities, you will see how impossible it would be for 200 people, scattered over a large township, to organize for the formation of schools of any efficiency. I gave you the different sub-districts, 12 out of 73, which have more than 200 Roman Catholic population.

Hon. Mr. DALY.—You must make a distinction between townships and municipalities. A township has only 36 sections.

Mr. McCARTHY.—What size is a municipality?

Hon. Mr. DALY.—Some have six townships and some nine.

Mr. McCARTHY.—That makes it still larger and still adds to the force of my argument.

Sir MACKENZIE BOWELL.—May not this be a village?

Mr. McCARTHY.—When there is a village it is quoted as such. For instance Morden is a village and is so marked ; Virden is a village and it is so marked.

Mr. McCARTHY.—Mr. President, if you will permit me to retrace my steps a little, I think, upon reflection, that I can take a course which will shorten my argument and avoid repetition to a certain extent. I had partly dealt with the system of education and had endeavoured to point out that the first question for the consideration of this board, —if I may be allowed to apply to this Council the name which is applied to the Judicial Committee—is the general question of separate as against national schools. I am not going to weary you with a repetition of what I said yesterday upon that point. I was asked by the Minister of Public Works (Hon. Mr. Ouimet) and promised to give to-day a definition of what I meant by national schools, and it is perhaps as fitting that I should give that now as at any other stage of the discussion. When I spoke of national schools I meant schools common to and enforcible upon the whole people. That would be a national system of education, and it might possibly be combined with a denominational system if the people were all agreed. Of course that can practically never be in this country: we can never have national schools, which are at the same time denominational schools. Applying my observations to the purpose before us I meant a system of national schools which can reasonably and fairly be accepted by the people as a whole, and I will submit that a non-sectarian or even a secular system if that was thought preferable, might be dealt with and treated as a system of national education. Contrasted with that is the system including what were known as separate schools, but what were in reality nothing more or less than church schools—Roman Catholic church schools. They are called separate schools, because that was the term used in connection with the agitation raised in the province of Ontario, but, as a matter of fact, they are church schools. We know that in England—or perhaps we do not know, but we might know, the fact being public—that there are church schools in existence belonging to the State Church, which had been in existence as parish or church schools long before Mr. Forster introduced his Educational Act, and which were connected more or less directly with the educational system of the country. But it is impossible for us to base our system upon that of England, because there there is a State Church which we know is attacked by a very large proportion of the population, and upon which the present government are now opening an attack in the principality of Wales, where the church is, perhaps less defensible upon any ground than amongst English people, because there the great majority belong to what are called dissenting bodies and not to the State Church. So that you have here the contrast practically between the system adopted in Manitoba—because I am quite willing to accept that as an example of national schools under the non-sectarian system of education on the one hand, with the church school system on the other hand. So that if you will understand me as speaking of a national system of schools as meaning a non-sectarian system of schools, such as we have in Ontario and Manitoba—because they are practically identical—and if you will understand the system that is contended for by my learned friend as a separate or church school system, I think there can be no difficulty in our following the different lines of thought which these systems suggest. Now, in addition to what I said with reference to the benefit flowing from the national system of schools, a school system that is accepted by the bulk of the people and which is fairly open to all the people, I think that if you will consult the educational statistics of the world you will find that illiteracy prevails in those countries where church schools are the rule and that there is a freedom from illiteracy where the schools are separate from and not under the control of the Church, but under the control of the State and carried on upon non-sectarian lines. I invite the attention of the board to that statement—I think it will be found throughout the continent of Europe that those countries where the Church have most control—take Italy for example—illiteracy is far more prevalent (the disproportion is in some cases enormous) than it is in Protestant states, not because one is Protestant and the other is Catholic, but because in the Protestant states, speaking generally, the system of education is national, non-sectarian or secular as it may be; the chief object of education in the other countries being not education but the teaching of the doctrines and tenets of their religion. So that any legislative body that has been charged with the responsibility of determining whether the schools should be national or church schools has been compelled to reach the conclusion that national schools are the better of the two. I invite your attention to the system of schools in Switzerland, and also to the system in Belgium, where, although the great majority of the people are Roman Catholics, the schools are non-sectarian or secular. In Italy you will find that the result of their school system was to leave the people in a hopeless state of ignorance until the late change. Relatively you will find the same thing in Ireland as compared with Scotland or England. I will lay before you a few statistics which I have not had time to verify myself, but which have been compiled with care and which I believe to be reliable. These figures, I think, will show that my observations are warranted by the facts.

Sir CHAS. HIBBERT TUPPER.—Is your view based at all upon the extent of religion taught in the schools or upon the fact of religion being taught at all?

Mr. McCARTHY.—It is not based upon the question of religion being taught at all, but upon the result of church teaching as distinguished from secular teaching.

Sir CHAS. HIBBERT TUPPER.—So your observations are not directed to any form of religion?

Mr. McCARTHY.—I do not desire to speak in disrespectful terms of any form of religion. That has not been my practice hitherto, and I certainly shall not adopt that rule in speaking here for the province of Manitoba.

Sir CHAS. HIBBERT TUPPER.—I hope that my question did not suggest that. But let me follow it with a further question : Do you approve of banishing all religion from the schools ?

Mr. McCARTHY.—Speaking for myself, of course I do not.

Sir CHAS. HIBBERT TUPPER.—But speaking as in this argument ?

Mr. McCARTHY.—I understand that the province of Manitoba does not approve of banishing religion from the schools, that the great majority of the people of Manitoba think that the schools ought not be secular.

Sir CHAS. HIBBERT TUPPER.—So it is a question of the extent to which religion is introduced ?

Mr. McCARTHY.—A question of extent as you say, but also a question whether that ought to be regulated and managed by the State or regulated and managed by the Church, There are the two antagonistic systems, and the question is which is the most beneficial in achieving the object which the State has in view, the education of the people. The State is not concerned in the teaching of any form of religion, but it is concerned in making capable and intelligent citizens, and in giving them sufficient education to attain that result.

Hon. Mr. DICKEY.—What do you think are the guarantees in the state school of the greater efficiency ?

Mr. McCARTHY.—I cannot tell you. I have not been able to devote time to that subject and during this argument I have regretted that the province had not time to send an educationist who could speak as an expert in these matters. I only speak of results. I cannot give the reasons for the results, but I find it universally the case that in schools that are under control of the Church, the people are not educated so well or so generally as in those countries in which the schools are wholly under State control.

Hon. Mr. DICKEY.—Do these statistics that you quote show in any way the degree or extent of control or inspection ?

Mr. McCARTHY.—No, you have to study the system itself for that. If you take the statistics I have here you will find the results they show to be very striking indeed.

Hon. Mr. OUIMET.—According to your own knowledge or any opinion that you may have, is the system which now prevails in Manitoba wholly secular ?

Mr. McCARTHY.—No.

Hon. Mr. OUIMET.—What kind of religious teaching is given ?

Mr. McCARTHY.—I am going to deal with that. My learned friend did deal with it and it will be my duty to attempt to remove the misapprehension which might follow what he said.

Hon. Mr. OUIMET.—I think you indicated a belief that no public money ought to be paid for the propagation of any religious dogma.

Mr. McCARTHY.—That is the distinction; if you will pardon me. What the people of Manitoba say is that they are not justified in paying for the propagation of the Methodist faith as it differs from the Presbyterian or Roman Catholic ; they are not justified in spreading the doctrines of the Presbyterian church, the Church of England or any other ; but, as God is believed in by the great majority of the people of thi country, as there are some principles common in great degree to all the churches—of course the agnostics would differ wholly, the Jews cannot accept our religion, and so on— but so far as religious truth is held in common by the great bulk of the people, we will permit a form of prayer which can be used by all or nearly all. But even this is done with the safeguard of a conscience clause which permits any parent who objects to any form of religious exercise to withdraw his child while that exercise is being engaged in. Your view, if I may be permitted to say so,—of course I have no means of knowing it otherwise than it has been publicly expressed—is that the teaching of your own religion, that is the Roman Catholic faith, in schools supported by public money, is quite justified. But, if so, the Presbyterians would have a right to demand a separate school in the same way for the teaching of his religion, the same with my own church, the same with the Methodist, and so on. But if all our exclusive rights are acknowledged in that way it is impossible that a separate school system can exist, and therefore, we must forego the observance of our extreme rights and agree upon something common to us all, and what I hope to establish before I am done is that the Roman Catholics have shown by experience and practice they can and do accept the system now prevailing in Manitoba, and that they can and do accept it in preference to their own system, the educational facilities being better than in the church schools. I will show that that is the practical result, and I may say that that is a result authorized by His Holiness of Rome himself. So that the attempt of this minority in Manitoba who oppose this system is to be more Catholic than the Pope. Now to give you the figures to which I refer. As I say, they were not compiled by myself, but I have taken them on the assurance of the Attorney General, whom I represent, that they have been compiled with care and are to be relied upon :—

"The census of the United States for 1880 showed that out of its total population over 10 years of age only 9·4 per cent were unable to write. In Victoria, in 1881, 92½ per cent of the population fifteen years of age and over could both read and write, and only 3½ per cent were entirely illiterate. In England during the year 1890 only 7·2 per cent of the males and 8·3 per cent of the femals signed by mark in the marriage register. In Scotland only 4·30 of the males and 7·38 of the females signed by mark in the marriage register in 1889. These are countries where Roman Catholicism and its methods of instruction are not in the ascendant. Turn but for a moment and glance at the illiteracy prevalent in countries where Roman Catholics are numerous and more or less supreme. While in Scotland, in 1886, out of a total vote polled of 447,588, only 7,708 were illiterate, in Ireland, in the same years, out of a total vote polled of 450,906, 98,404, or about 14 times as many of the voters in proportion were unable to read or write. In Italy, where the Roman Catholics had 51 Archbishops, 223 Bishops, 53,263 churches and chapels, 76,560 parish priests and 28,991 religious persons to help enlighten the people, no less than 53·89 per cent of the males and 72·93 per cent of the females were, in the year 1881, unable to read and write. In Spain, where Roman Catholicism is the established religion and Protestants dare not proclaim a church service——"

That is hardly true now, for you will remember that Lord Plunkett attempted to establish a branch of the Church of Ireland and created a great deal of trouble by it—

"—where there were in 1884, 32,435 priests, 14,592 nuns, 78,564 churches, and 1,684 monks, 30·64 per cent of the males and 41·37 per cent of the females were not even able to read when the census was taken in 1887. In Portugal and its islands, where the state religion is Roman Catholicism and the Protestants do not exceed 500 in number, the number of illiterate inhabitants in 1878 was 3,851,774, or 82 per cent of the total population including children. All the above figures and many more of like interest may be found in the Stateman's Year Book of 1892 and cannot be successfully challenged."

Let me add to that the statement that these separate schools in the province of Manitoba —I am speaking now of the year 1890 when the Act abolishing the separate school system was passed—were nothing more or less than French schools. They are so spoken of to this day. The teaching was wholly in the French language, and according to Mr. O'Donohue's statement which you heard yesterday, the French teachers—with perhaps such exceptions as would merely prove the rule—did not understand a word of

English. The same difficulty therefore presented itself to the people of Manitoba that four or five years ago aroused this province as it has not been aroused for many years, that of a system of French schools which, contrary to the School Act were being used in the county adjoining the province of Quebec. In order to meet that difficulty, as you are aware, Sir Oliver Mowat's government ordered an inspection and afterwards adopted a bilingual series by which it was hoped that English would be gradually introduced, because it is utterly impossible that a Frenchman, who does not understand a word of English, can teach children in the English tongue. That, whether successful or not, is the attempt made in the province of Ontario to deal with the problem presented by the overflow of the French speaking people of the province of Quebec into the neighbouring counties of Ontario. Now let us see, judging from our own statistics, what has been the result in the province of Quebec of their system of teaching. I quote from the last Statistical Year Book of 1893. I beg you to look at the table at page 168, where you will find proof that the province of Quebec, whose system of teaching was in partial operation in the province of Manitoba, appears to be in every respect the lowest among the provinces in the scale of education. This table is prepared by official authority. The first are the figures showing the relative standing of the provinces as to children under ten years of age able to read. In that respect the standard of the province of Quebec is the lowest. Prince Edward Island is first, Ontario second, Nova Scotia third, Manitoba fourth, New Brunswick fifth[1] the North-west Territories sixth, and Quebec seventh. In the table relating to children between ten and twenty years of age able to read, Ontario is first, Manitoba second, Prince Edward Island third, Nova Scotia fourth, New Brunswick fifth, the North-west Territories sixth, and Quebec seventh. I need not trouble you with all these, but generally I may say that Quebec stands seventh in the list in every one of these tabulated statements except two—the table showing the proportion of females between ten and twenty able to read, and that showing the proportion of females between ten and twenty able to write—and in these Quebec is number six, being above the Northwest Territories, but below all the other provinces. So we see that the system which partially prevailed in the province of Manitoba, but which has been changed by the legislature, which was properly charged with the management of educational affairs, is demonstrated to be the most inefficient that exists throughout all the provinces of Canada. Now, if this Council is of the opinion—for I do not know what the opinion of the Council may be, though I may have a shrewd suspicion, but not as appearing on behalf of the province of Manitoba—that a system of national schools is a proper one, I trust they will allow that system to continue in force in this case. I do not say that it might not be possible, notwithstanding that national schools are better as shown by the results we have than church schools, that the church system might be better for the province of Manitoba. Such a thing is possible, but if you are of that opinion, I would like to know upon what ground you are going to carry that opinion to the extent of directing—because your order will be an order from the Queen's representative—the province of Manitoba to change its school law. If you agree that, as a general thing, separate or church schools are not so efficient in promoting education as public schools, then, before you can order a change in Manitoba, you must be satisfied that there is something in the province of Manitoba which makes it an exception to the general rule. I venture to think, with all respect, that the facts which I gave you yesterday concerning the province, instead of pointing it out as an exception to the general rule, mark it out as a locality in which a national system of schools, once established, ought not to be interfered with by this Council. One point with reference to that. You may say :— This would be all very well if this matter came before us unfettered by any local condition and if we felt free to advise the Crown as to what would be best for the people of Manitoba. We might then say we would not interfere with the system of education established. But we feel ourselves hampered, cribbed—cabined and confined if you please—by the terms of the 22nd section of the Manitoba Act and must look at this not so much with a view to deciding what would be beneficial as with a view of saving the susceptibilities of the minority who, perhaps, have a right, after a fashion, to expect a different state of things. Now I do not know whether I made my meaning clear yesterday, but I endeavoured to say that the subject of education has been given over to provincial control in Manitoba as in the other provinces and that all that has been given to this Council or to His Excellency the Governor General in Council is, in case a system of separate schools duly established were afterwards abolished to hear the petition of those who felt themselves aggrieved and to act upon it if you thought it advisable. But in hearing that appeal you should put yourselves in the position of the legislature of Manitoba and look at the statement from their standpoint. There is nothing to show that this action on the part of the legislature of the province has been actuated by bigotry. There is not a word that has been cited, there is not a word that can be cited, to show that their action has not been *bonâ fide* and designed to establish the system which according to their best opinion would be most in the interest of the whole province. There has been no desire to wrong this minority, small as it may be, French as it may be ; the desire has been to promote the interest and welfare of the people of the province as a whole. And these considerations are just as pertinent to the advisers of His Excellency as they were to the representatives of the people of the province. The people of the province had this duty cast upon them in the first place, and, while there is a technical right in the minority to come here and have the opinions of the majority revised and their acts over-ruled, you can only over-rule them just as a higher court over-rules the judgment of a lower—upon consideration of the case itself. You must have before your mind consideration of the position of the province itself and decide the case on that ground, and not to gratify the feelings of the people in any other province, as I said yesterday. You must do what is best for the people of the province of Manitoba.

Hon. Mr. OUIMET.—As between parties in an ordinary court, would you say that the Court of Appeal was bound to do what was best for both parties or to stick to the law ?

Mr. McCARTHY.—They must stick to the law ; I don't think there is any doubt of that. But what I have pointed out to you, and I am glad that my learned friend here has agreed in that, is that your decision is to be given upon the merits of the case. The law as it has been interpreted by the Privy Council is that you have a right to consider the case ; but there is no law providing what you shall do. You are perfectly free, and before you over-rule the action of the province, you must come to the conclusion that on the merits of the case the province is wrong.

Hon. Mr. OUIMET.—Have we not to come to a conclusion as to the minority ? Have we not to consider their rights ?

Mr. McCARTHY.—No ; as I pointed out yesterday if that was the only question there would be no object in coming here to argue the case. The position that the Minister of Public Works (Hon. Mr. Ouimet) takes is that if the system of separate schools is established in Manitoba it must remain for all time. But that is not the law. The law is that the separate school system having been established, the abolition of it so affects the minority that, under the law, they have a right to appeal to the Governor General in Council and ask him to make an order to re-establish the system if he thinks fit, and then the Parliament of Canada will have jurisdiction to deal with his order.

Hon. Mr. CURRAN.—Then we are not bound by the constitutional rights at all ?

Mr. McCARTHY.—I am quite willing to answer my friend if I can make my meaning any plainer, but I do not know that I can do so. You are bound by the constitu.tion—I have endeavoured to say so. But I have also endeavoured to say that the constitution does not say that if separate schools are established they must remain. It provides that if separate schools are established and then abolished, those who feel that they are prejudiced by that abolition may come to this Council and ask for a consideration of their case.

Hon. Mr. CURRAN.—And for the maintenance of their constitutional rights.

Mr. McCARTHY.—There is no constitutional right about it.

Sir CHARLES HIBBERT TUPPER.—I understood your argument to cover the idea that that clause in the constitution ought not to be there and that, though it is there, it ought not to be acted upon—I mean the clause under which the appeal is made.

Mr. McCARTHY.—I do not mean it in that sense. You are acting in this matter and what I have contended is that you are bound to act according to good sense and judgment.

5½

Sir CHARLES HIBBERT TUPPER.—And that no remedial order ought to be given?
Mr. McCARTHY.—Just so.
Sir CHARLES HIBBERT TUPPER.—Under any circumstances—as I understand it.
Mr. McCARTHY.—That is a pretty big proposition. I do not think that it would be necessary for me to show that under no conceivable circumstances should such a thing be done. But I will say that no events in our history that I know of would justify interference in such a case as this.
Sir CHARLES HIBBERT TUPPER. Your position would be the same if the large majority were Roman Catholic and that majority were to bring in a system objectionable to the Protestants you would resist any remedial action?
Mr. McCARTHY.—So long, as in the case of Manitoba, there was a conscience clause.
Sir CHARLES HIBBERT TUPPER Then it would depend upon circumstances?
Mr. McCARTHY. - This law could not have been passed if, in the judgment of the Privy Council, the legislature had established Protestant schools. The Barrett case in that event would have been decided the other way. If the Act put those who did not attend the schools in any unfavourable position, if it provided that no child should be eligible for promotion in the public service or for appointment in the public service unless he could produce a certificate of attendance at the public schools, that decision would not have been given in the Winnipeg case. But the Privy Council held that this Act does not compel anybody to do anything; it only establishes public schools which all may use.
Sir MACKENZIE BOWELL.—Does your argument apply to the Confederation Act so far as it affects the old provinces of Quebec and Ontario? I refer to section 93, subsection 3, which says:—

" Where in any province a system of separate or dissentient schools exists by law at the union, or is thereafter established by the legislature of the province, an appeal shall lie to the Governor General in Council from any act or decision of any provincial authority affecting any rights or privileges of the Protestant or Roman Catholic minority of the Queen's subjects in relation to education."

Mr. McCARTHY.—That does not provide that if separate schools are established they are to be perpetual. If you will apply that it illustrates my meaning. Of the four provinces that formed the Dominion at first two had separate school systems. By the constitution separate schools were made perpetual in those provinces, the other provinces if they chose to establish separate schools had the right to do so. If they did so they would be in the same position as Manitoba occupies, and if the separate school system was abolished the minority had the right to come here and complain. But the separate schools were not made perpetual. In Quebec and Ontario the separate school system is part of the organic law. But provinces like Nova Scotia and New Brunswick which had no separate school system at the time of Confederation, might establish a system and, five years afterwards, repeal it ; but if they did so the minority could do as the minority in Manitoba is now doing—apply to the Dominion Executive and afterwards to the Dominion Parliament. In other words it is withdrawn—I do not know whether except to lawyers I can make myself plain. The control of legislation is vested in these provinces subject to this reservation—that if they establish separate schools and afterwards withdraw them, the minority can come and ask the Dominion Executive and afterwards the Dominion Parliament to restore them ; not because there is no right in the provinces to abolish separate schools, but that that circumstance will give the Dominion authorities the right to investigate the whole subject and, if necessary in their judgment, to over-rule the action of the province.
Sir MACKENZIE BOWELL.—Then, I understand you that in Ontario the legislature can repeal all the amendments made to the Separate Schools Act by which the separate school system has been extended in our province?
Mr. McCARTHY.—Yes. All the advantages that have been given under the Mowat administration—(putting the question in that way)—
Sir MACKENZIE BOWELL.—That is what I mean.
Mr. McCARTHY.—If those advantages were taken away the Roman Catholic minority would have the right to come here and ask to have them restored.

Hon. Mr. IVES.—Suppose the legislature of Quebec were to abolish the dissentient schools, as the Protestant schools in Quebec are called, is it your opinion that the remedy of the Protestants of Quebec would be by the use of this appeal?

Mr. McCARTHY.—No.

Hon. Mr. IVES.—What would be their remedy—disallowance?

Mr. McCARTHY.—No: the Act would be *ultra vires*, and the courts would so declare it.

Hon. Mr. IVES.—But if the law is being executed, the fact that it is bad does not help the people.

Mr. McCARTHY.—But the law could not be enforced; it would be *ultra vires*.

Hon. Mr. IVES.—I understand that in this judgment their Lordships say that this law cannot be enforced in Manitoba. I understand that the decision goes the length of saying that the law of 1890, in so far as it imposes taxes upon Roman Catholics, cannot be enforced.

Mr. McCARTHY.—No, no, you have not read it.

Hon. Mr. IVES.—Yes, I have.

Mr. McCARTHY.—I beg pardon; I withdraw that. But I think no one else would have come to that conclusion. The decision is that the law is a good law, but that this Council can set in motion proceedings by which the Dominion Parliament can, to a certain extent, modify it.

Hon. Mr. IVES.—I understand you to mean that in such a case as I speak of there should not be disallowance, that the minority in Quebec would not have this right of appeal, and the only satisfaction the people would have would be in the fact that the law would be bad law.

Mr. McCARTHY.—I do not know what better you would have. The law would be waste paper. It would be just the same as if in Ontario we attempted to deprive the minority of their separate schools. The Roman Catholics of Ontario cannot be deprived of their separate schools, and the same is true of the dissentient schools in Quebec.

Hon. Mr. IVES.—But they could pass the bill in the legislature.

Mr. McCARTHY.—But it would not be worth the paper it was written on.

Sir CHAS. HIBBERT TUPPER.—According to the public press the Manitoba Government intend to take that stand. It is said that if a remedial order is passed they will resist or ignore that law. Sometimes it does not much matter whether it is good law or bad law, if it is still enforced.

Hon. Mr. DICKEY.—Does not that appear in the Queen's speech in opening the legislature?

Mr. McCARTHY.—I have not seen the Queen's speech, but I should think the Lieutenant Governor would not be allowed to say that. But I understand that the position of the Manitoba Government is that they will resist by every constitutional means in their power the passage of any remedial order and that they will not obey the order, which is something that they have a perfect right to do.

Sir CHAS. HIBBERT TUPPER.—I had no reference to the Queen's speech.

Sir MACKENZIE BOWELL.—Mr. Sifton, the Attorney General, is reported to have said so.

Mr. McCARTHY.—I have here the Queen's speech. It says:

"By the judgment of the Judicial Committee of the Privy Council recently pronounced on an appeal from the Supreme Court of Canada, it has been held that an appeal lies to the Governor General in Council on behalf of the minority of this province, inasmuch as certain rights and privileges given by prior provincial legislation to the minority in educational matters had been affected by the Public Schools Act, and that, therefore, the Governor General in Council has power to make remedial order in respect thereto. Whether or not a demand will be made by the Federal Government that that act shall be modified is not yet known to my Government. But it is not the intention of my Government in any way to recede from its determination to uphold the present public school system, which, if left to its own operation, would in all probability soon become universal throughout the province."

No person could object to that statement. The Government of the province has a perfect right to take this position, and, if sustained by the Legislature, this Parliament will have jurisdiction to enforce the remedial order, if the Council think fit to make any such remedial order. I am not answerable for the statements made in the press, and I am not going to make any statement on a point such as that suggested by the Minister of Justice (Sir Charles Hibbert Tupper).

Sir CHARLES HIBBERT TUPPER. I referred to the report of an interview with the Attorney General of Manitoba and then only to illustrate the hypothetical position of affairs suggested by Mr. Ives, and to show that sometimes it was poor satisfaction to the people to know that the law is bad; even bad law is sometimes enforced.

Mr. McCARTHY.—I do not want to occupy any better position than to be sure that a law is *ultra vires* if I do not want to obey it.

Sir CHARLES HIBBERT TUPPER.—I am not differing from you at all, but was merely illustrating the position.

Mr. McCARTHY.—I have pointed out some of the considerations, though I am afraid very few of the considerations which actuated the people of Manitoba, and I have shown that it is the will of the people of Manitoba you are asked to overrule in this matter. I would now give you a history of the legislation, because, no doubt, you would desire to know before you would over-rule or coerce a free legislative body exactly how its will was carried out. You will remember that I stated yesterday that the agitation for the abolition of the separate school system commenced, apparently, in the fall of 1876. As to that agitation, I am not able to give you the facts, but in glancing over the history of Manitoba I gathered that it was in 1876,—that is five years after the separate school system was introduced—that the people began to agitate for a change. A section of the people took hold of the question and laid down a platform, on the lines of which they claimed that the change should be effected. But it was not until 1889, so far as I know—and I speak subject to correction—that any political party took the question up, and became convinced that there was a majority of the people prepared to endorse the change and carry it into effect. In August, 1889, at a place called Clearwater, Mr. Smart, who was then a member of the Greenway Government, the present Government of Manitoba, announced that the Government had determined upon the policy of abolishing the separate school system and establishing a public school system, with a Department of Education and a Minister of Education, following in the wake of the Ontario Administration, and adopting the policy they had pursued. It was in the following year, 1890, that the matter became a subject of legislation, and I want to point out to you the various votes that took place upon it, and you will see with what unanimity the question was carried. The question first arose on the 10th March, and by reference to the Journals of the Legislative Assembly of that date, you will see that the following motion was moved by Mr. Gillies, who was then the leader of the Opposition, seconded by Mr. Roblin. This was on the second reading of the bill, and Mr. Gillies moved in amendment:—

"That, whereas by section 93 of the British North America Act it is declared that where in any province a system of separate or denominational schools exists by law at Union, or is thereafter established by the legislature of the province, an appeal shall lie to the Governor General in Council from any act or decision of any provincial authority affecting any right or privilege of a Protestant or Roman Catholic minority of the Queen's subjects, in relation to education, with power to the Parliament of Canada to make laws for the execution of the decisions of the Governor General in Council in connection with such an appeal—"

You will excuse me if I do not read the intervening clauses. The resolution goes on:

"Whereas it is desirable that a uniform system of public schools should be established—"

Remember this is the resolution of the leader of the Opposition—

"—wherein all the youth of the province may receive elementary education, without the possibility of legislation providing for the same, being subject to repeal or revision to the Parliament of Canada, or any other than the legislature of this province, which alone should deal with this vital subject; and,

"Whereas in view of such special provision, applicable to the province of Manitoba, grave doubts exist as to the validity of the legislation embodied in this bill, the effect of which is practically to abolish the system of denominational schools existing in the province, at and since its formation, and it is inexpedient that such an important matter should be passed by this House before its legality has been authoritatively determined or the Manitoba Act so amended as to clearly provide for such abolition;

"Therefore, be it resolved that the bill be not read a second time, but that such steps be taken as will secure an amendment, by the Imperial Parliament, of the British North America Act or the Manitoba Act, whereby the right of the legislature of Manitoba to deal with educational matters in the province shall be firmly and clearly established without appeal to the Governor General in Council or to the Parliament of Canada."

This was the view of the Opposition, adopting the proposed system in its broadest terms but proposing delay, so that the questions of law should be settled by the repeal of those clauses which appear to interfere with the free power of the legislative body. That resolution came to a vote and it was voted down by 30 to 5. The five who voted "yea" were Messrs. Gillies, Norquay, O'Malley, Roblin and Wood, not by any means all the Opposition, which consisted at that time of ten or twelve members; it certainly was more than five. Another amendment was moved to give the bill the six months' hoist, and this was voted down by 7 for to 19 against, the seven who voted "yea" being Messrs. Gelley, Jerome, Lagimodière, Marion, Martin (Morris), Prendergast and Wood. I do not even see Mr. Fisher's name here ?

Hon. Mr. ANGERS.—Does his name appear on the other side of the vote ?

Mr. McCARTHY.—No.

Mr. EWART.—He was away sick, I believe.

Mr. McCARTHY.—At page 91 of the Journals will be found another amendment declaring that:

"Whereas the Bill before this House involves most important educational principles, and most radical changes in the existing school laws; and

"Whereas it is an essential privilege of the people to pronounce upon so important a question, before it is introduced in the House through their representatives; and

"Whereas this House is of opinion that the electorate is against the principles of the Bill—

"Resolved, that it is due to the electorate that this House do not endorse the principles of the said bill before the same is submitted to the said electorate."

This was voted down by 6 for to 22 against and the second reading was carried on the same division reversed: Then, on the third reading of the bill at page 107 of the Journals, another long resolution was moved by the French member, Mr. Gelley—I think he is French——

Mr. EWART.—Yes.

Mr. McCARTHY.—This resolution declares that whereas grave doubts exist as to the constitutionality of the bill, and so on, therefore that the bill " be referred back to a committee of the whole House " to make certain amendments. That was voted down by 11 for to 25 against, and the bill was finally passed by 25 for to 11 against. Now, I need not trouble you with the changes made in 1891-92, because there seemed to have been no division on them. The changes were slight, and there was no division of the House upon them. In 1892 an election took place. You will remember the objection— and there was some force in it—that when this bill was brought up it was in the third session of that legislature, that the subject had not been before the people at the time of the previous election and that an opportunity ought to have been afforded to the people to pronounce upon it before it was dealt with by the legislature. But the election came on in 1892, and I say without fear of contradiction by my learned friend or anybody else that the great question before the people in that election was the question of the schools. Pamphlets were issued on either side and the people were instructed and educated on the question. In 1893 the new House met and the matter came up for decision before it. The repeal of the bill was moved in the House consisting of forty members, as you will find that in the Journals of 1893, page 97. On the vote being taken 34 voted to sustain the Act and only 4 against, Messrs. Fisher, Jerome, Paré and Prendergast. Of the 34 at least one was a French representative, Mr. Martin, the same gentleman I believe, whose affidavits were read by my learned friend Mr. Ewart the other day. So that in a House of 40, with 39 to vote (one being in the chair), 38 did vote, and only 4 for the repeal of the bill. And it must be remembered that this was after the measure had undergone the most thorough and exhaustive discussion in the constituencies and after the people had pronounced upon it. All those who voted for repeal were French representatives, except Mr. Fisher, who is my learned friend's partner, and that is the only way I can account for his having given poisoned and falling away from his Liberal views and the principles he formerly held.

Hon. Mr. ANGERS.—Is any one who changes his views "poisoned"?

Mr. McCARTHY.—That depends upon what the change is. Mr. Jérôme is from Carillon, which, I believe, is in Provencher. Then, Mr. Paré is from La Verandrye, and he and Mr. Prendergast also, I believe, are from Provencher. And so, in the whole province, except my friend—or rather my learned friend's friend, for I am not acquainted with him—Mr. Fisher, all the representatives, except the three representatives from the one Dominion constituency of Provencher, are in favour of the law and against its repeal. And even Provencher is not unanimous, for I believe that Mr. Martin was one of the representatives of Provencher. Then you know about the bill of 1894, the disallowance of which has been urgently pressed upon you. That bill was carrying out the principles of the School Act of 1890. The six months' hoist of that bill was moved by Mr. Jerome and the vote stood 4 for to 31 against. So that if the deliberate opinion of the province upon the question, a question which had been agitated in the province from 1876 has any weight, you have here evidence of what that opinion is. I have told you the position of one political party, but I have here also the Conservative platform in the election of 1892. I was astonished to hear my learned friend say that he represented in this matter the Conservatives in the province of Manitoba. I do not mean to say that he appeared for them, but he said he spoke the opinions of the Conservatives of Manitoba and was astonished that the Conservatives here should differ from those in Manitoba. He mistakes very much the views of the Conservatives of Manitoba. I have here the Conservative platform of 1892:—

The Opposition hereby declare:

1. That they are in favour of one uniform system of public schools for the province.

2. That they are ready and willing to loyally carry out the present school act—should it be held by the Judicial Committee of the Privy Council of Great Britain to be within the legislative power of the province.

3. That in the event of such school act being held by the Judicial Committee of the Privy Council of Great Britain to be beyond the legislative power of the province; then they will endeavour to secure such amendments to the "British North America Act" and the "Manitoba Act" as will place educational matters wholly within the legislative power of the province of Manitoba without appeal to Governor the General in Council or the Parliament of Canada.

So I have given you the views of the Liberal party, of the Conservative party, showing practical unanimity in the province on this question of education. Another point I have brought before you and which cannot certainly have been without effect, was the inefficiency of the French school system. The two kinds of schools were started practically upon an equality and there was no apparent reason why one should grow to be better than the other. Let me give you an example, which has been published, and never contradicted, of the kind of questions put in the examination of a first class teacher in the separate schools. If this is the standard required of a first class teacher, we cannot be very much astonished if the scholars do not show very great advance in in the path of learning. Here is part of the examination:

"*Catechism.*

"(1.) What is the church? Where is the true church? Ought we to believe what the Catholic Church teaches us, and why?

"(2.) What is the Eucharist? What is necessary to do to receive with benefit this great sacrement?
"(3.) What is sanctifying grace? How is it lost?
"(4.) Name and define the theological virtues.

"*Comportment.*

"(1.) How is a letter addressed, when written to a prelate, to a priest, to a professional man? How are such letters concluded?
"(2.) In conversation, what titles do you employ in speaking to these same persons?

"*History.*

"(1.) Describe the defeat of the American armies near Chateauguay.
"(2.) Who was St. Thomas Becket? What difficulty had he with Henry II.? How did he die? What was the fate of Marie Stuart? Write a short note on the Treaty of Paris. Who was then Governor of Canada?

"*Geography.*

"What is the capital of England?" "What is the capital of Canada?" and so on. This is a fair example of the examination for first class teachers in the separate schools under the old system, as I am informed, and the legislature thought that the system was not working satisfactorily. These and other papers were sent as examples of the efficacy of their schools by the Catholic section of the board of education to the Colonial Exhibition at London in 1886. Now another point I submit to you is that this system has been in force for five years, but it has not had quite a fair trial. I will ask Dr. Blakely to set me right with regard to the figures if I am wrong. The former system was to divide the legislative grant between public and separate school boards according to the number of school children, a census of the school population being required by the law to be taken. Having ascertained the sum payable to the Protestant and the Catholic boards these sums were subdivided according to the number of schools. And this is a point to be noted. I was surprised to learn that there were no less than 11 separate schools in Winnipeg, but I found equal cause for surprise in the fact that there were 88 others. If one did not understand the sense in which the word "schools" is understood, the figures would be misleading. There is nothing unjust about it, but one must understand this point in judging of it.

Sir MACKENZIE BOWELL.—Is the division not made per capita?

Mr. McCARTHY.—Yes, between the two kinds of schools, but the subdivision is according to the number of schools or classes.

Hon. Mr. FOSTER.—Is that true of both boards?

Mr. McCARTHY. Yes; I am not suggesting that there is anything unfair about it, but it is misleading if you do not understand it. This was one grant of public money. But there was another grant, according to a method different from the system in Ontario. The law provided that the township councils should vote $20 per month for each school. Our system in Ontario is that the trustees make up an account of what they want and demand the sum. They can collect it themselves or call upon the municipal council to collect what they want. In Manitoba it was township money, but the township had no discretion in the matter as to the amount to be given. Until the Act of 1894 was passed, in townships that were favourable to the separate school system they had been paying this grant to the separate schools. The Act of 1894 was intended to do away with that granting of public money to separate schools which had been continued, and to bring the school system into harmony. I use this to show that this system has enabled separate schools to be carried on with public money, so that the public school system, established under the law of 1890 has not had a fair trial, though it has been in existence for five years. I have put in a list of the schools in Manitoba showing the number at the time of the passing of the Act.

Hon. Mr. FOSTER.—Was there any general principle upon which they made a division of classes, and was that general principle observed in the two sets of schools?

Mr. MCCARTHY.—There is no principle common to both. It is almost impossible to find out what principle was followed in the French schools, because the reports are not always printed, and when printed they are in French.

Mr. EWART.—And you cannot read them.

Mr. MCCARTHY.—And, as my learned friend observes, I cannot read them.

Hon. Mr. FOSTER.—Was the division into classes merely arbitrary?

Mr. MCCARTHY.—Dr. Blakely tells me that they were made up into classes according to grade.

Hon. Mr. FOSTER.— Would that be like a department—primary, secondary and so on?

Mr. MCCARTHY.—Yes ; the children in one grade would be one class.

Hon. Mr. FOSTER.—That would be what we would call a form?

Mr. MCCARTHY.—Yes.

Hon. Mr. FOSTER.—Then there would be some general principle.

Mr. MCCARTHY.—I am not bringing this forward to show that there was any unfairness in the division of the provincial grant, but what I have stated shows that up to 1891, they were able to get public money for separate schools in those townships that were favourable to separate schools—$20 for each class.

Hon. Senator BERNIER.—Twenty dollars for each school.

Mr. MCCARTHY.—I am informed that it was to each class in towns and to each school in the country. The list of schools that I have put in shows that there were 91 French schools in receipt of public money under this system, at the time the bill was passed.

Hon. Senator BERNIER,—They should be called public schools.

Mr. MCCARTHY.—It does not make any difference what they are called. I have taken the facts from the public documents and I give the names given in those official papers. I am able to show also that of these schools 36 have come in under the public school system. You know from what Mr. O'Donohue said what pressure the people have been kept under ; but, notwithstanding the pressure exerted by their priests and religious teachers, they are coming under the public school system and many have come in since this new amendment to the school law was passed. I bring this forward to show that you are not dealing with the matter simply as it stood in 1890. but as it stands in 1895, or it may be as it will stand in 1896. The withdrawal of this $20 a month of public money has forced many of the schools to come in and adopt the public system. I have here the report of Mr. Young, Inspector of Public Schools. This report was made at the end of 1894 and covers the whole of that year.

Sir MACKENZIE BOWELL.—Is he the inspector of French schools? (Report filed Exhibit " Q. ")

Dr. BLAKELY.—He is the inspector of the south-eastern division, in which the schools are nearly all French schools.

Now, as to whether these are Protestant schools and in that sense offensive to the Catholic people, so that their children cannot fairly attend them. I point out to you that the law distinctly declares that they shall be non-sectarian schools, and I add to that the self-evident fact that if they are not conducted upon a non-sectarian basis the right of any objecting parties is to appeal to the law. The Legislature, whose acts you are called upon to amend, declared the schools to be non-sectarian. If through the action of the advisory board or for any other reason they are not carried on as non-sectarian schools, those who are not carried on according to the law of the province, and anybody aggrieved can appeal to the courts at much less expense than that involved in sending learned counsel down here to Ottawa. The schools as established are not amenable to the allegation of my learned friend. His argument was substantially that the religious exercises under this Public Schools Act of 1890 are identical with those of the Protestant schools under the Act of 1871, and that, if they were Protestant in 1871 they are Protestant still, although their prayers are adopted by the advisory board under the School Act. I dispute both my learned friend's facts and his conclusions. I have before me the religious exercises as they were required under the Protestant system and also those under the Public Schools Act of 1890. If you will permit me I will draw your attention to the difference. In 1887 the regulations of the Protestant section of the Board of Education regarding religious exercises provide:—

"1. Every school established and in operation under the authority of the Protestant section of the Board of Education for Manitoba shall be opened and closed daily with prayer and the reading of a portion of Scripture ; and it shall be the duty of the teacher of each school to allot a suitable portion of each school session to this exercise and to conduct the same as herein directed."

Now we come to what these exercises are to be :—

"Bible reading. The Bible shall be used as a text book in the Protestant schools of Manitoba. A supply for use in each school may be obtained by the trustees, otherwise each pupil from standard 3 upwards shall be required to provide himself with a Bible in addition to his other text books."

This is not to be found in the present regulations. It is not required and not permitted.

The regulations of 1887 further provide :—

"The selections for reading shall always include one or more of the lessons in the authorized list given herewith, but any other selection from Scripture may, in the discretion of the teacher, be read in connection with them."

This list is practically the same, with a modification to which I will draw your attention in a moment, but the discretion in the second part of the section is not permitted.

Sir ADOLPHE CARON.—You mean under the new regulations ?

Mr. McCARTHY—Yes. The third clause with regard to Bible readings in the old regulations is as follows :—

"The Scripture lesson in each school shall follow the opening prayer and shall not occupy more than 15 minutes daily. Until notes and questions are provided under the authority of the board, the reading shall not be accompanied by commentary or explanations.'

The Scriptures permitted under the old system were as follows :—Part 1, Historical ; Part 2, Devotional, didactic, prophectic : Part 3, the Gospels : Part 4, the Acts of the Apostles : Part 5, selections from the Epistles, and Part 6, Miscellaneous. Under the present regulations the only Scripture readings permitted are Part 1, Historical, and Part 2, the Gospels. Then it is provided that these Scriptures may be either from the English version of the Bible or from the Douay version. Now I may ask my learned friend to point out what he objects to in these Scripture readings. They are less than are allowed in Ontario, although we Ontario people know that the late Archbishop Lynch approved of the Scripture readings and allowed the new edition popularly known as the Ross Bible to be issued. I believe that this was copied from the Ross Bible, but to prevent there being any possibility of complaint on the part of minority it is confined to the historical part to the Gospels and the Scripture may be read from either version, and I suppose they are practically identical.

Sir MACKENZIE BOWELL.—Is what is known as the Ross Bible used in the separate schools of Ontario ?

Mr. McCARTHY—No, but the reason why the Archbishop claimed the right to interfere with the reading of the Scriptures in the public schools is that a large portion of the children under his charge were attending those schools. Now let me draw your attention to the prayer, which is identical under the two regulations, only the closing prayer being now provided for. Under the old regulations it is preceded by the Lord's prayer, after which it proceeds :

"Most merciful God, we yield Thee our humble and hearty thanks for Thy fatherly care and preservation of us this day and for the progress which Thou hast enabled us to make in useful learning; we pray Thee to imprint upon our minds whatever good instruction we have received and to bless them to the advancement of our temporal and eternal welfare, and pardon, we implore Thee all that Thou hast seen amiss in our thoughts, words and actions. May Thy good providence still guide and keep us during the approaching interval of rest and relaxation so that we may be prepared to enter on the duties of the morrow with new vigour both of body and mind; and preserve us, we beseech Thee, now and for ever, both outwardly in our bodies and inwardly in our souls for the sake of Jesus Christ, Thy Son, Our Lord. Amen."

That is the prayer together with the Lord's prayer. Now on the evidence I have given you, I submit that my learned friend's statement of the facts is not correct. I believe that nobody could object to this form of prayer. Objection is taken to the instruction given in commandments, etc. The regulation is as follows:

"To establish the habit of right-doing, instruction in moral principles must be accompanied by training in moral practices. The teacher's influence and example, current incidents, stories, memory gems, sentiments in the school lessons, examination of motives that prompt to action, didactic talks, teaching the Ten Commandments, etc., are means to be employed."

All I can say, is, without entering upon the theological question as to whether the commandments can be taught from the Protestant and Roman Catholic standpoints at the same time, that the remedy for this is simply that of having this withdrawn if it is offensive. Within the programme of studies, which also I have here, there are no less that nine grades or forms. My learned friend does not object to all these, and I think he could not find ground for objection except in the one he has called attention to. What he said on that subject might lead you to believe that the case was merely an example of the others, but I think he has given the only one to which objection can be taken that is the history curriculum in the seventh grade—English, religious movements, Henry VIII and Mary. Now he says that the history of England cannot be taught, so far as that period is concerned, from the Roman Catholic standpoint and the Protestant standpoint in the same school. And I will admit, with the little knowledge that I have of the subject, that it is a difficult point. But the remedy is a simple one and it ought to be a simple one. What we ought to be concerned with is the truth. We know the difficulty of ascertaining the truth with regard to a historical incident of thirty or forty years ago; how much more difficult to ascertain what really happened in the reign of Henry VIII? We know that it has been the habit of historians to write the history of that period from their own standpoint—not history but a partisan statement. We also know—at least I do not pretend that I knew until I was told—that the tendency has been among more recent writers to correct that fault, and to have histories as near the truth as can be given. The history in use is Miss Buckley's History, which up to quite a recent time has been the fairest history that has been written upon this subject; so fair th t I am informed,—and I speak subject to contradiction if I am wrong—that it has been in use in the convent schools, which are not subject to Government inspection. So we find that in the religious exercises there is nothing that can be complained of. We find that in a curriculum there is only one subject that is objected to and with regard to that I have given an explanation. Miss Buckley's history was in use in this province up to a recent time, when the department had a history prepared in which certain phrases which had been pointed out as objectionable from a Roman Catholic standpoint were omitted. But all these are mere matters of detail. If these points are not arranged on a non-sectarian basis the administration of the syst m is to that extent in defiance of the law and that can be corrected. And I can speak for the Education Department that they are happy to correct anything of that kind and they have no desire to force upon the people of Manitoba history or religion in any way offensive to their religious convictions. What they desire is that the whole people should be united in one system of schools and brought together in harmony. Now it is said Catholics cannot attend these schools and that if this system is continued the effect will be that while the Catholics continue to pay their taxes for the public schools, they will have to pay for the support of other schools which they can conscientiously attend. This is set forth in clause 11 of the petition. Now I can speak from my own knowledge and experience. He e in the province of Ontario the Catholics have the right to separate schools and yet the result is that more than half the Roman Cathol c children are attending public schools voluntarily.

Hon. Mr. OUIMET.—May I ask under what authority you state that?

Mr. McCarthy.—I suppose anything that Mr. Fisher says will be good evidence. He spoke the other day in the legislature, and I think he rather over-stated the facts when he said that far more than half attended the public schools.

Hon. Mr. Ouimet.—Mr. Fisher is not before us.

Mr. McCarthy.—He is represented I mean he is the champion of minority in Manitoba.

Sir Mackenzie Bowell.—Do the school reports show that with regard to Ontario?

Mr. McCarthy.—They do not show it in terms, but I base the statement upon a calculation which I will give you and which you can accept or not as you think right. I find that the school population in the province of Ontario—this is taken from the last school report—is 595,238. This includes Catholics, Protestants and all. The Roman Catholic portion of that population is 100,324. The total number not attending schools is 86,000, the relative portion of which for the Roman Catholic schools would be 19,000, leaving 81,000 to be provided with school accommodation. The number attending separate schools is 37,166, leaving 43,797 attending the public schools.

Hon. Mr. Curran.—Have you anything to show how many Catholic children are attending public schools in those places where separate schools are established?

Mr. McCarthy.—No, except as I am going to point out, I have not had time to go into this matter minutely. The petition asserts that Roman Catholics cannot attend the public schools ; I am proving that they do.

Hon. Mr. Curran.—Where there are no separate schools.

Hon. Mr. Dickey.—Will you tell me in what sense you use the word "attending." Do you mean registered?

Mr. McCarthy.—I understand this to be actual attendance.

Hon. Mr. Foster.—It must be the registered attendance.

Mr. McCarthy.—I am not sure that I understand the Secretary of State's (Mr. Dickey) question. I take the figures as they appear in the reports and I use the word "attendance" as applying in the same way throughout.

Hon. Mr. Daly.—This represents the public schools, not the high schools or collegiate institutes?

Mr. McCarthy.—Exactly. This is what Mr. Fisher said, speaking of the Ontario school system : " Every child in the land is taught in a State school. The immense majority of the Roman Catholic children go to public schools, rather preferring them to separate schools. In Ontario there are 700 municipalities and in 500 of these at least there are no separate schools. Separate schools have not been increasing in number, except for a short time when Mr. Meredith was weak and foolish enough to join Mr. Dalton McCarthy in an attack on separate schools, which led to a boom in such schools."

Sir Mackenzie Bowell.—So you see the effect of what you are doing.

Mr. McCarthy.—I give you the benefit of what Mr. Fisher said. I am not ashamed of what I have done. I may give you an example of what I know myself in my own county—not my own riding, but the whole county of Simcoe The whole Roman Catholic school population is 2,317. There are only three separate schools with a total attendance of 221. So there is a total of more than 2,000 Roman Catholic children not attending separate schools in that county. I know several townships in which the Roman Catholics are in sufficient numbers to support separate schools in efficiency in which no such schools have been established. Now, on this question, I give an authority that will be accepted by everybody among the minority in Manitoba, though I do not know that the Premier will accept it. I give you the words of the Most Rev. Francis Satolli, delegate of the Apostolic See to the United States of America. You may remember that this question of separate schools was brought up by Archbishop Ireland, one of the ablest prelates of the church, he taking a position on which his brethren differed from him. He thought that the Roman Catholic children were falling behind in the race of life by reason of the inefficiency of the educational system under which they are trained, and he said that he could see no reason why the Catholic children should not attend the public schools. That discussion resulted in Mgr. Satolli coming to this continent. And here is the letter in which he wrote his decrees, representing, as I understand, the Congregation of the Propaganda. I got this document from the library. It bears the imprint of John

Murphy & Co., printers to the Holy See, Baltimore, U.S.A. The first paragraph is a general instruction:

"All care must be taken to erect Catholic schools to enlarge and improve those already established, and to make them equal to the public schools in teaching and in discipline."

The next section is:

"When there is no Catholic school at all — "

That meets the Solicitor General's (Hon. Mr. Curran's) case.

" — or when the one that is available is little fitted for giving the children an education in keeping with their condition, then the public schools may be attended with a safe conscience, the danger of perversion being rendered remote by opportune, remedial and precautionary measures, a matter that is to be left to the conscience and judgment of the Ordinaries."

I pass from there to No. 5 :—

"We strictly forbid any one, whether Bishop or Priest, and this is the express prohibition of the Sovereign Pontiff through the Sacred Congregation, either by act or by threat to exclude from the Sacraments as unworthy, parents [who choose to send their children to the public schools.] As regards the children themselves this enactment applies with still greater force.

"6. To the Catholic Church belongs the duty and the divine right of teaching all nations to believe the truth of the Gospel, and to observe whatsoever Christ commanded; in her likewise is vested the divine right of instructing the young in so far as theirs is the Kingdom of Heaven ; that is to say, she holds for herself the right of teaching the truths of faith and the law of morals in order to bring up youth in the habits of a Christian life. Hence, absolutely and universally speaking, there is no repugnance in their learning the first elements and the higher branches of the arts and the natural sciences in public schools controlled by the State, whose office it is to provide, maintain and protect everything by which its citizens are formed to moral goodness, while they live peaceably together, with a sufficiency of temporal goods, under laws promulgated by civil authority.

"For the rest, the provisions of the Council of Baltimore are yet in force, and, in a general way, will remain so ; to wit. : 'Not only out of our paternal love do we exhort Catholic parents, but we command them, by all the authority we possess, to procure a truly Christian and Catholic education for the beloved offspring given them of God, born again in baptism unto Christ and destined for heaven, to shield and secure them throughout childhood and youth from the dangers of a merely worldly education, and therefore to send them to parochial or other truly Catholic schools.' United with this duty are the rights of parents which no civil law or authority can violate or weaken.

"12. As for those Catholic children that in great numbers are educated in the public schools, where now, not without danger, they receive no religious instruction at all, strenuous efforts should be made not to leave them without sufficient and seasonable instruction in Catholic faith and practice. We know by experience that not all our Catholic children are found in our Catholic schools. Statistics show that hundreds of thousands of Catholic children in the united States of America attend schools which are under the control of State Boards, and in which, for that reason, teachers of every denomination are engaged. Beyond all doubt, the one thing necessary, i.e., religious and moral education according to Catholic principles, is not to be treated either lightly or with delay, but on the contrary with all earnestness and energy.

"The adoption of one of three plans is recommended, the choice to be made according to local circumstances in the different States and various personal relations.

"The first consists in an agreement between the Bishop and the members of the School Board, whereby they, in a spirit of fairness and good-will, allow the Catholic children to be assembled during free time and taught the Catechism ; it would also be of the greatest advantage if this plan were not confined to the primary schools, but were extended likewise to high schools, colleges, in the form of a free lecture.

"The second : to have a catechism class outside the public school building, and also classes of higher Christian doctrine, where, at fixed times, the Catholic children would assemble with diligence and pleasure induced thereto by the authority of their parents, the persuasion of their pastors, and the hope of praise and rewards.

"The third plan does not seem at first sight so suitable, but is bound up more intimately with the duty of both parents and pastors. Pastors should unceasingly urge upon parents that most important duty, imposed both by natural and by divine law, of bringing up their children in sound morality and Catholic faith. Besides, the instruction of children appertains to the very essence of the pastoral charge : let the pastor of souls say to them with the Apostle : ' My little children of whom I am in labour again until Christ be formed in you.' Let him have classes of children in the parish, such as have been established in Rome and many other places and even in churches in this country with very happy results.

"These words I hope the pastors will take to heart. If they would do this duty in their own sphere, there would not be this trouble about the state educating the children in secular matters.

" Nor let him, with little prudence, show less love for the children that attend the public schools, than for those that attend the parochial ; on the contrary, stronger marks of loving solicitude are to be shown them ; the Sunday school and the hour for catechism should be devoted to them in a special manner, and to cultivate this field let the pastor call to his aid other priests, religious, and even suitable members of the laity in order that what is supremely necessary may be wanting to no child."

I do not want to have it supposed that I read only those portions that are suitable for my own argument, so I lay this document before the Board in its entirety. I think it will establish the fact that Catholic children can attend the public schools and the allegation of a grievance in that regard in the petition is not well founded and ought not to lead you to any such result as the petitioners seek by their prayer.

The Council adjourned until 2.30 p.m.

AFTER RECESS.

The Council resumed at 2.30 p.m.

Mr. McCarthy.—I have the honour to say, in finishing the history of the question, whatever may be said as to its merits, that the matter of the threatened interference has been dealt with by the local legislature during the present session, and I have read to you an extract which my learned friend kindly furnished me from the Lieutenant Governor's speech at the opening of the session, and I will just supplement that by the resolutions and the vote upon those resolutions with reference to this threatened interference. Mr. Fisher, on the House going into Committee of Ways and Means, proposed :

" 1. That while this House is determined at all times to maintain to the fullest extent that the constitution warrants its exclusive power to make laws with respect to education, yet it recognizes that the highest judicial tribunal in the realm has recently decided that 'such exclusive power is not absolute, but limited,' and that the limitation was embodied in the constitution as a 'parliamentary compact,' between the Dominion and the protection, amongst other things, of the rights and privileges of the Roman Catholic minority in relation to education, including rights and privileges that were acquired by them since the union.

" 2. It has been also adjudged by the same tribunal that 'the rights and privileges' of the Roman Catholic minority in relation to education, which existed prior to 1890, have been affected by the Public Schools Act of that year.

" 3. The same tribunal has further decided that in the event, which is now foreshadowed, of this legislature being called upon to remove the grievance in the judgment referred to, and in the further event of the legislature declining to do so, a case will have arisen where "the parliament of Canada is authorized to legislate on the same subject.

"4. That this House is always prepared to abide by the constitution, which is the safeguard of our provincial rights, and will not be a party to its violation, nor will it seek to impair the efficiency of its provisions for protecting the rights and privileges of any class of Her Majesty's subjects. At the same time the House would deplore the occurrence of anything calling for the exercise by the Parliament of Canada of its authority to legislate on the subject of education, the ultimate effect of which it is impossible to foresee.

"And having regard to the suggestions of the tribunal referred to that 'all legitimate ground of complaint would be removed if the present system were supplemented by provisions which would remove the grievance upon which the appeal is founded, and were modified so far as might be necessary to give effect to those provisions,' without a repeal of the present law, this House is ready to consider the grievance referred to with a view to providing reasonable relief, while maintaining, as far as possible consistent with that object, the principles of the present act in their general application."

Upon that coming up a debate took place and the Attorney General moved the following as an amendment:—That all words after the word "while" in the original motion be struck out and the following substituted therefore : " This House loyally submits itself to the provisions of the constitution as interpreted by the Judicial Committee of Her Majesty's Privy Council. It is hereby resolved that the exercise of appellate jurisdiction by the Governor General in Council in such a way as to lead hereafter to the alteration of the principles upon which the public school system of Manitoba is founded will be viewed with grave apprehension. That an interference by the Federal authority with the educational policy of the province is contrary to the recognized principles of provincial autonomy. That this House will by all constitutional means and to the utmost extent of its power resist any steps which may be taken to attack the school system established by the Public Schools Act of 1890, which is believed to be conceived and administered in the highest and best interests of the whole population of Manitoba."

The amendment was carried, as appears from the report of the Manitoba *Free Press*, 28th February, by a vote of twenty-two to ten. Three gentlemen who voted, Messrs. McFadden, Frame and Lyons, all stated that they considered both resolutions uncalled for and voted against them. The debate, consisting of a speech by Mr. Fisher, and a speech by the Attorney General, and also some shorter addresses to the House, may be put in as being worthy of preservation for the history of this interesting occasion.

Hon. Mr. FOSTER.—That is simply a newspaper report?

Mr MCCARTHY.—That is all. I think they have no other report than that. I now recur to the place that I left off yesterday afternoon for the purpose, and make the statement so that you will see I am not wasting time in my citations, of demonstrating what is perhaps sufficiently well known, but which I cannot too strongly enforce, that the deliberate will, deliberate conviction, of both of the great parties in Canada, sanctioned by public opinion of all shades and classes, is that in school matters there should be no interference by the central body, and I will follow that up by pointing out to this Council that the proposal that is now made to interfere is a far harsher remedy, a far more drastic means of interference, far more humiliating to the province than would have been the disallowance of the Act of 1890. I say it advisedly that it would have been far better for the province that the Act of 1890 should be disallowed, than that there should be the interference which is threatened by those proceedings. I will endeavour to show you why, before I close. I was commencing to refer, yesterday, to the question on the schools which first arose, namely, with regard to the New Brunswick law, and I had got as far as to read certain documents, though not yet reported. Mr. Costigan's resolution, which, perhaps, you will be good enough to consider as read, is as follows :—

"That it is essential to the peace and prosperity of the Dominion of Canada tha the several religions should be followed in perfect harmony with those professing them in accord with each other, and that every law passed either by this Parliament or the local legislature disregarding the rights and usages tolerated by one of such religions is of a nature to destroy that harmony ; that the local legislature of New Brunswick in its last session in 1871 adopted a law respecting common schools prohibiting the imparting of any religious education to pupils, and that prohibition is opposed to the sentiments of the population of the Dominion in general and to the religious convictions of the Roman Catholic population in particular :—That the Roman Catholics of New Brunswick, without acting unconsciously, send their children to schools established under the law in question and are yet compelled like the remainder of the population to pay taxes to be devoted to the maintenance of those schools :—That the said law is unjust and causes much uneasiness among the Roman Catholic population in general disseminated throughout the whole Dominion of Canada and that such a state of affairs may prove the cause of disastrous results to all the confederate provinces, and praying His Excellency in consequence at the earliest possible period to disallow the said New Brunswick school law."

Hon. Mr. OUIMET.—What date was that resolution ?
Mr. MCCARTHY.--1872.
Sir CHARLES HIBBERT TUPPER.—You had passed that subject, had you not ?
Mr. MCCARTHY.—I was going to recur to it ; I would retrace my steps, as I said this morning. This resolution was moved on the 20th of May and the debate was not concluded. The next time the question came up was on the 22nd May, as will be found at page 148 of the Votes and Proceedings, when the Hon. Mr. Gray moved in amendment to leave out all the words after " Canada" in line two, and to substitute the following :—

"That the constitutional rights of the several provinces should be in no way impaired by the order of this Parliament ; that the law passed by the local legislature of New Brunswick respecting common schools was strictly with the limits of its constitutional powers and is amenable to be repealed or altered by the local legislature, should it prove injurious or unsatisfactory in its operation ; that not having yet been in force six months, and no injurious consequences to the Dominion having been shown to result therefrom, this House does not deem it proper to interfere with the advice that may be tendered to His Excellency the Governor General by the responsible ministers of the Crown respecting the New Brunswick school law."

Hon. Mr. Chauveau moved in amendment to the said proposed amendment that all the words after " that " in the original motion be expunged and the following inserted in lieu thereof : "an humble address be presented to Her Majesty, praying that she will be pleased to cause an Act to be passed amending ' the British North America Act, 1867,' in the sense which this House believes to have been intended at the time of the passage of the said Act, by providing that every religious denomination in the provinces of New Brunswick and Nova Scotia shall continue to possess all such rights, advantages and privileges with regard to their schools as such denominations enjoyed in such province at the time of the passage of the last mentioned Act ; to the same extent as if such rights, advantages and privileges had been then duly established by law."

Then I pass on to page 167, where the vote is taken on Mr. Chauveau's amendment which I have just read. The vote is 34 for and 126 against, including in that vote Sir John Macdonald, Alexander Mackenzie, Mr. Blake, the leaders of all parties, and of course it was lost by a large majority.

The question being then put on Hon. Mr. Gray's proposed amendment. Mr. Colby moved in amendment thereto that all after the word " that " be expunged and the following substituted in lieu thereof :—" this House regrets that the School Act recently passed in New Brunswick is unsatisfactory to a portion of the inhabitants of that province and hopes it may be so modified during the next session of the legislature as to remove any just grounds of discontent that now exist."

That being advice to the province it was carried by a majority, 117 to 42. Then Mr. Dorion moved that the following words be added to Mr. Colby's motion, Mr. Colby's amendment having been carried :—

" And this House further regrets that to allay such well grounded discontent His Excellency the Governor General has not been advised to disallow the School Act of 1871 passed by the legislature of New Brunswick."

Bringing up the disallowance quite clearly. That was voted down by a majority of 117 to 38, and then the question being put on the main motion as amended, the Hon. Mr. Mackenzie moved that the following words be added thereto :—

" And that this House deems it expedient that the opinion of the Law Officers of the Crown in England, and if possible the opinion of the Judicial Committee of the Privy Council should be obtained as to the rights of the New Brunswick Legislature to make such changes in the school law as deprived the Roman Catholics of the privileges they enjoyed at the time of the Union in respect of religious education in the common schools, with the view of ascertaining whether the case comes within the terms of the 4th subsection of the 93rd clause of the North America Act, 1867, which authorizes the Parliament of Canada to enact remedial laws for the due execution of the provisions respecting education in the said Act ;" which was agreed to.

And here is the result of the whole :

" The question being then put on the main motion as amended, it was agreed to on a division and is as follows :—

" That this House regrets that the School Act recently passed in New Brunswick is unsatisfactory to a portion of the inhabitants of that province and hopes that it may be so modified during the next session of the Legislature of New Brunswick, as to remove any just grounds of discontent that now exist and that this House deems it expedient that the opinion of the law officers of the Crown in England, and if possible the opinion of the Judicial Committee of the Privy Council should be obtained as to the right of the New Brunswick legislature to make such changes in the school law as deprived the Roman Catholics of the privileges they enjoyed at the time of the Union in respect to religious education in its common schools, with the view of ascertaining whether the case comes within the terms of the 4th subsection of the 93rd clause of the British North America Act, 1867, which authorizes the Parliament of Canada to enact remedial laws for the due execution of the provisions respecting education in the said Act."

So the matter ended there for that session.

The Hon. Minister of Marine asked me what had been done in 1873. On the 14th of May, the House resumed the debate on the amendment which was carried by 98 to 63, and amongst those who voted in the negative, was the President whom I have now the honour of addressing.

Sir MACKENZIE BOWELL.—The government of that day did not act upon that resolution.

Mr. McCARTHY.—I do not know that Sir John Macdonald refused to act.

Sir MACKENZIE BOWELL.—It is the amendment we are talking about. You will find it laid down in Todd more clearly.

Mr. McCARTHY.—Yes ; that amendment was carried by 98 to 63.

Hon. Mr. COSTIGAN.—You seem to lay great stress upon the fact that the House did not express anything beyond sympathy in regard to that question.

Mr. McCARTHY.—No, no, not sympathy.

Hon. Mr. COSTIGAN.—You had some yourself.

Mr. McCARTHY.—Yes, but sympathy and legislative Acts are two different things. Then in 1874 the Minister of Marine and Fisheries renewed his motion in the same terms, I think, as in 1872, but it was withdrawn. In 1875 he again brought up the resolution, at page 188 of the Votes and Proceedings, and this time the Privy Council had determined the question. Then it was brought before them *ex parte*, and at the time when the Minister of Marine and Fisheries brought this question up that I am now referring to, it was in the position that it is at present, that is to say, the law was understood, for the question came up in this way : The Minister of Marine moved the resolution in 1872, at page 166, and then it is followed by the amendment of Hon. Mr. Gray, and then by Hon. Mr. Chauveau's amendment in amendment, that all the words after " that " in the original motion be expunged and that an humble address be presented to Her Majesty praying that she may be pleased to cause an Act to be passed to amend the British North America Act. That seems to be exactly what Mr. Chauveau moved in 1872. Then upon that, the vote for alteration in the British North America Act was 31 to 126 against, and that appeal to an alteration seems to have been opposed by the leaders of both parties—I do not think the present Prime Minister voted, — but Mr. Blake, Mr. Costigan, Mr. Alexander Mackenzie, Sir John Macdonald, Mr. Joly and Sir Charles Tupper voted against it. Mr. Costigan's motion was brought up on the 18th of March, 1875. Mr. Costigan's motion was in the same words as originally. Then, Mr. Mackenzie moved in amendment that:

"In the opinion of this House, legislation by the Parliament of the United Kingdom encroaching on any powers reserved to any one of the provinces by the British North America Act, 1867, would be an infraction of the provincial constitutions, and that it would be inexpedient and fraught with danger to the autonomy of each of the provinces for this House to invite such legislation."

Mr. Cauchon moved in amendment :—

"This House regrets that the School Act recently passed in New Brunswick is unsatisfactory to a portion of the inhabitants of that province, and hopes that it may be so modified during the next session of the Legislature of New Brunswick as to remove any just grounds of discontent that now exist.

"That this House regrets that the hope expressed in the said resolution has not been realized.

"That an humble Address be presented to Her Most Gracious Majesty the Queen embodying this resolution, and praying that Her Majesty would be graciously pleased to use her influence with the Legislature of New Brunswick to procure such a modification of the said Act as shall remove such grounds of discontent."

That motion being put was lost on a division of 60 to 124.

A further debate arising, the House continued to sit until midnight. The House divided on the question, resulting in, 114 yeas and 73 nays. Mr. Baby then moved in amendment to the main motion as amended, that all the words after "that" be left out and the following inserted in lieu thereof:

"This House regrets that the position of the Roman Catholic minority in the province of New Brunswick with regard to their educational rights is such as to cause great dissatisfaction to a large portion of Her Majesty's subjects in the Dominion :

"That this House is of opinion that any legislation which will restore harmony among persons professing different religions, and remove any feeling of uneasiness now existing among any portion of Her Majesty's subjects, is greatly to be desired :

"That by resolution passed by the House of Commons on the 30th May, 1872, it was regretted that the school Act recently passed in New Brunswick was unsatisfactory to a portion of the inhabitants of that province."

He terminated by moving that an humble Address be presented, and so on. The Speaker ruled this out of order. The question then being put on the amendment as amended, it was agreed to, 121 yeas to 61 nays. The question being put on the main motion as amended, it was agreed to, 119 yeas and 60 nays. Then Mr. Costigan moved in amendment, that the said committee be instructed to add the following to the proposed address :

"But this House reserves to itself the right to seek by Address to Her Majesty, an amendment to the British North America Act, 1867 ; should the present motion prove insufficient to bring about an amendment of the New Brunswick School law satisfactory to the minority of that province."

The Speaker ruled that amendment out of order. Then the address was as follows :—

"That in the opinion of this House, legislation by the Parliament of the United Kingdom encroaching on any powers reserved to any one of the provinces by the British North America Act, 1867, would be an infraction of the Provincial constitution, and that it would be inexpedient and fraught with danger to the autonomy of each of the provinces, for this House to invite such legislation."

That on the 29th day of May, 1872, the House of Commons adopted the following resolution :—

"This House regrets that the School Act recently passed in New Brunswick is unsatisfactory to a portion of the inhabitants of that province, and hopes that it may be so modified during the next session of the Legislature of New Brunswick, as to remove any just ground of discontent that now exists ;

"That this House regrets that the hope expressed in the said resolution has not been realized. That we most humbly pray that Your Majesty will be graciously pleased to use the influence of Your Majesty with the Legislature of New Brunswick to procure such a modification of the said act as shall remove such grounds of discontent."

It was ordered that the said address be engrossed.

Now, the debate that took place on that address, to be found in the *Hansard* for 1875, and more especially the speech of the then Premier and the present Premier, are well worthy of consideration, I mean on this motion of Mr. Costigan. The substance of Mr. Mackenzie's remarks is that he regretted very much the legislation of the province of New Brunswick, depriving the Catholics of any portion of their privileges. But he said this, as will be found on page 610 of the *Hansard* of 1875 :—

" But, Sir, there is a higher principle still which we have to adhere to, and that is to preserve in their integrity the principles of the constitution under which we live. If any personal act of mine, if anything I could do, would assist to relieve those who believe they are living under a grievance in the province of New Brunswick, that act would be gladly undertaken and zealously performed ; but I have no right—this House has no right—to interfere with the legislation of a province when that legislation is secured by an Imperial compact, to which all the parties submitted in the Act of Confederation. So soon as the majority of the people of New Brunswick, so soon as the Legislature of New Brunswick, shall see fit to make such arrangements as will remove the cause of discontent, I am quite satisfied that province will find it to its advantage to do so. It is unfortunate that in any province of the confederated Dominion there should be any cause for complaint when precisely the same privileges are enjoyed in the large and most prosperous provinces, and while I feel bound to move an amendment to the hon. gentleman's motion which will place on record my views of the Federal compact and the obligations that rest upon us in connection with it, I shall, at the same time, gladly accord my support to any course which, in the opinion of Parliament—if it corresponds with my own opinion—will tend in any way to further the object that the minority in New Brunswick have in view, that is, to obtain the same privileges and rights that they enjoyed at the time of entering the Union, and which they supposed they were entitled to under the compact. Sir, I have no intention to discuss this matter further, because I conceive that it is quite sufficient to make the remarks I have offered, to indicate my own personal feelings, and to indicate the course that I propose to take. I have merely to say this, whatever may be our religious proclivities or feelings, whatever may be the feelings which actuate us in relation to local grievances, it is not well that we should endanger the safety of any of the provinces in relation to matters provided for in the British North America Act, which is our written constitution. Sir, it must be apparent to every one that if we were to attempt violently to lay hands upon that compact for the purpose of aiding a minority in New Brunswick who have a grievance, no matter however just that grievance may be—and from my point of view I think it is one they have a right to complain of—however much we might entertain that feeling, we have no right to do anything that will violate our obligation to defend the constitution under which we live. I may point this out to honourable gentlemen in this House and to the country, that if it were competent for this House, directly or indirectly, to set aside the constitution as regards one of the smaller provinces, it would be equally competent for this House to set it aside as regards the privileges which the Catholics enjoy at this moment in Ontario."

Now, I point out the significance of these words, because that is just as much a part of the constitutional power of disallowance which is invoked, as was the power of the province of New Brunswick over the subject of education ; therefore, the language must be understood with reference to the well understood principles of the constitution under which we live. There could have been no violation in annulling that law, the violation was in interfering with the matter of education which, while it may have been disallowed, was one in regard to which it would have been a grievous wrong to the province, and fraught with serious consequences to the Dominion, if there had been any interference. Now, I think you, Mr. Premier, took a much stronger, and safer, and better ground. At page 616 I find you reported as follows:—

" Mr. Bowell desired to offer a few remarks in explanation of the vote he was about to give. He intended to vote against the amendment of the hon. member for Quebec Centre, and for this reason : because he (Mr. Bowell) was opposed to the passage of any resolution by the House that would interfere in any way——"

That was the Address to the Queen. You agreed with the resolution of Mr. Mackenzie saying there should be no interference, but you declined to follow the addition, that which proposed to express regret that New Brunswick had not modified the law, and to ask Her Majesty to use her influence with the Legislature of New Brunswick to make a change.

" He was opposed to any resolution by the House which would interfere in any way, directly or indirectly, with the legislation of the province of New Brunswick, or any other province upon any question, and if he understood the motion aright, it was similar in character to that which was proposed by the hon. member for Stanstead two or three years ago, which asked the interference of the Imperial Government. If the motion proposed by the Hon. First Minister, which raised a fair and square issue, had been put to the House without any milk-and-water amendment, he would have had great pleasure in voting for it."

That is what you said, and you voted for the principle that the House should not interfere with the legislation of New Brunswick in the school matters of that province, but you would not adopt the words proposed to be added as a soothing syrup in connection with it, by asking the Queen to use her influence to interfere with the will of the province. Now, it will be in the recollection of the hon. gentlemen of the Privy Council that shortly afterwards the question of education in Prince Edward Island came up. They passed a school law in that island, and the strongest efforts were made to have it disallowed, when Mr. Mackenzie's Government was still in office. In a blue-book containing the school laws and other educational matters in Assiniboia, Prince Edward Island, the North-west Territories and Manitoba, including the judgment of the Supreme Court respecting the appeal from the minority in Manitoba, and printed by order of Parliament, you will find an account of the Prince Edward Island case, when petitions were presented, in substance the same as the petitions now before you. In the Minute of the Executive Council, in answer to these petitions, and to which I referred the other day, I find this language :—

"The great principle that the public moneys shall not be appropriated for the purpose of teaching sectarian dogmas or creeds, is one which a large majority of the people of this province value very highly, and which they will not surrender without a struggle, commensurate with the importance they attach to the principle itself. It has been the underlying principle of our educational laws for years, and though attacked in many ways and from many quarters, has so far been preserved intact."

Then Mr. Laflamme, who was then Minister of Justice, went into all the complaints which formed the subject-matter of the petition. His conclusions are all that I will trouble you with. He considered all the objections, and finally came to this conclusion :—

" Great stress has been laid on section 15 as imposing an unjust tax upon the parents neglecting or refusing to send their children to the district school, thereby causing a deficiency in the average attendance, and leaving absolutely to the discretion of the trustees to determine the amount and to levy an assessment on the parties.

" This provision I consider to be severe and giving somewhat arbitrary power to trustees in fixing the penalty and in the selection of offenders. It confers the power of levying an additional tax at the discretion of the trustees. The previous laws give the right to trustees to levy the amount of the deficiency on the district, which necessarily comprised those who complied with, and those who refused to submit to the law. If we are bound to consider the right of regulating education as absolutely appertaining to each province, except where the privilege of establishing separate schools existed by law, it must be admitted that they have equally the right to attach to the provisions of such laws the conditions and penalties required to secure its object : however arbitrary or unjust the mode of enforcing it may appear, it would not seem proper for the Federal authorities to attempt to interfere with the details or the accessories of a measure of the Local Legislature, the principles and objects of which are entirely within their province."

This agitation began in 1872 and went on till 1877, and here again we find that both the great parties in the country seem to have adopted as their rule that there should be no interference in matters of this kind. I do not know how it can be better put, or more strongly, than it was by Sir John Thompson in the debate on this question in 1893. I read from *Hansard*, page 1793 : —

"The principle had been well settled in this legislature time and again that no statute regarding education passed by a province ought to be destroyed by disallowance. On the contrary, if it were *ultra vires* of the legislature, that fact ought to be ascertained and established by judicial decision. I shall refer in a few moments to the precedents by which that was well laid down and well established. But it was obviously, from start to finish, a principle which would commend itself to the common sense of any government and any legislature."

Then, speaking of the case of Prince Edward Island, he said :—

"That case was obviously parallel to the New Brunswick case, as to the want of sanction of law for the privileges which Roman Catholics enjoyed at the time of the Union, and therefore the repealing Act was declared to be *intra vires* of the provincial legislature, and not to be interfered with. The complaint of the Roman Catholic minority of Prince Edward Island was as strong as the complaint from the province of Manitoba."

Then he quotes from Mr. Blake's speech, which I find in this same volume, page 1810. Mr. Blake's speech was quoted by Sir John Thompson with approval. Mr. Blake says :—

"Those members who have long been here will well remember the New Brunswick school case, which was agitated for many years, and in the course of which agitation, I hoped that some political aspects of that and of analogous questions were finally settled—settled, at all events, for the party with which I had acted, and for the humble individual who is now addressing you. I regard it as settled, for myself, at any rate, first of all, that as a question of policy—there shall be no disallowance of educational legislation, for the reason that in the opinion of this parliament, some other or different policy than that which the province has thought fit to adopt would be better."

Now, the reason I trespass on your time by making these quotations is this : that when you reflect for a moment on what is asked here, I think you will agree with me that the interference by the Council in this matter, an interference which is to give jurisdiction to Parliament, would be a greater violation, would be more humiliating, as I have stated already, to the province, than disallowance itself. Disallowance would mean merely that that particular statute is wiped out from the Statute-book, and the province would still be free to go on and re-enact that law, as we know that to have been done in the province of Ontario in the case of the Streams Bill, which was disallowed certainly twice, and was again re-enacted, but finally remained law. That gives time for consideration and reflection. It shows that the view taken by the central body and the view taken by the legislative body, are antagonistic. It enables the people of both the central and local bodies to have an opportunity for reflection and consideration, and ultimately, under our system, it is to be hoped that the right course will be adopted. But what are you asked to do here ? You are asked to take the first step in the passage of a law, a law which, when passed, so far as the province is concerned, is absolute and irrevocable, and I venture to say so far as this Parliament is concerned, is absolute and irrevocable. The power of this Parliament is limited to pass such remedial law as may be necessary to carry out an order made by this government. Now, Parliament makes that remedial law, which cannot be interfered with by the local legislature, or even by

Parliament itself. Under these circumstances the jurisdiction for exercising the power of control passes away, except that it resides with the Imperial Parliament.

Sir MACKENZIE BOWELL.—That is, that the Parliament of Canada cannot repeal or amend its own Acts?

Mr. MCCARTHY.—Its own Act passed under this section.

Sir CHARLES HIBBERT TUPPER.—Of course, the local legislature could get into the same position in the event of disallowance if, in the event of a remedial order being considered likely to occur, they agreed to legislate.

Mr. MCCARTHY.—Of course, if they legislated they could prevent all these happenings. What I mean is that if the local legislature refuses to carry out any order that is made here, then there is a power in the central body to pass it. But just as there is a power to pass that law, it is a power ad hoc, that power being exercised, it comes to an end.

Hon. Mr. OUIMET.—Do you propose to cite authorities in support of that proposition?

Mr. MCCARTHY.—I can give you the authorities if that would be of any service to the Council, on the equiva'ent question of powers.

Hon. Mr. DALY.—The Globe has given us authorities on exactly the same lines.

Mr. MCCARTHY.—I can hand in authorities showing that when a power is given to a trustee to be exercised, and is exercised by the trustee, it is then gone and he cannot revoke it. I think the lawyers in the Council will agree to that. The question is whether this is not just an ad hoc power. Legislation with regard to education is given to the province, with that exception. Parliament had the power in 1871 to create a province; Parliament therefore had power to assign a certain portion of its authority over that territory which was then called Manitoba, reserving to itself this particular figment of authority respecting education, and that being exercised, it appears to me that power is gone.

Sir CHARLES HIBBERT TUPPER.—I suppose it is hard to find a parallel case in a legislature?

Mr. MCCARTHY.—You cannot find any.

Hon. Mr. IVES.—Do I understand you to say that in case a less measure of justice were given, it might be supplemented?

Mr. MCCARTHY.—Yes, and I say so still. But you cannot withdraw. If you pass a remedial order in the terms of my learned friend's bill, and Parliament at the first session, did not go the whole length of that, there would then be authority in another session to implement so far as necessary, the measure, and only to that extent, in order to carry out the intention of the Governor's order. Now, can you imagine, with the feeling that exists throughout the Dominion with regard to provincial rights and the non-interference by the federal authority, anything more irritating, anything more calculated to disturb, and to create ill-feeling, and to destroy the harmony which should prevail, than the passage of a law in Ottawa, by this Parliament, for the purpose of settling educational matters in the province of Manitoba? Remember, it is not because you have the power to do it that it is always wise to exercise that power. Let us not forget that Manitoba was almost driven to the verge of rebellion a short time ago by the disallowance of her railway laws; let us not forget that Sir John A. Macdonald found it necessary to abandon that policy of disallowance which had been pursued for some years in regard to vetoing its railway bills which interfered with the general policy of the central government regarding the Pacific Railway. Don't let us forget that the act of the Imperial Parliament which imposed the Tea Tax was a valid and legal act, but it brought about the Revolution. The Imperial Parliament has power to pass laws for Canada, the Imperial Parliament is omnipotent wherever the British flag flies. Its power is not questioned, but what is questioned is the wisdom, and the propriety, and the statesmanlike policy of exercising that power. I speak with the greatest possible deference to this body, but I speak with all the strength of language that I can command, to warn you that you are now asked to take the first step in creating a line of difficulties which, I venture to say, the youngest man sitting on that council board will not live to see the end of. And all for what purpose? Why, Sir, in a population of probably 190,000 in Manitoba, there appears to be 10,000, or 15,000, or 20,000, if you like, who desire to continue the system of French and Catholic schools which was established by an enactment passed when the legislature cannot be said to have been controlled by very great wisdom, as I do not think the intelligence of those few half-breeds can compare at all with the intelligence of the later settlers who have gone in ; I say because these people passed that law is it pretended that the province is never to be at liberty to repeal it ? When the province repeals it deliberately, shall a body come here and, *ex debito*, ask successfully that the Governor in Council shall annul the School Act and restore that which they, in their wisdom and justice, thought ought to be repealed ? Now, I appear here representing not merely an individual but a province, who are seeking to do what they think in their judgment is best for themselves, seeking to work out their system under difficulties that we are not capable here, perhaps, of appreciating to the full. We cannot realize the enormous task which has been cast upon them of providing for the education of the people, not merely those from the older provinces of Canada, but the immigrants from foreign countries, whom they are endeavouring to weld together into a homogeneous population. Under these circumstances I venture to think that this Council will hesitate before they take a step which will limit or deprive the local legislature of this right. Let me remind you that this question is to be viewed, not in the light of the interests or feelings of the province of Quebec, or of any other part of the Dominion, but in the light of the interests, and welfare, and prosperity, and peace of the province whose law you are asked to change and to amend. Viewed in that light, and regard being had to the circumstances which I have had the honour to submit to the Council, I fully realize that I have not been able to grasp, in the time at my disposal, or to master the intricacies of this question, so fully as I would have liked, in order to present it properly. I ask the board to remember, that the last word has not by any means been said on this question of the education of the people of the province of Manitoba. Now, while my learned friend, Mr. Ewart, quarrelled with what he called a neutral system of schools, I want you to remember that there are just two systems, or three if you like. There is the denominational system—and, if you want a definition of that, you will find it in the case of New Brunswick, which appears in the official document I quoted from, showing what a denominational school is. I say that while my learned friend complained of this form of religious exercises which was prescribed by the advisory board, you will recollect that the Hon. Mr. Pelletier speaks in strong language of the preference on the part of his people for a system permitting religious instruction in schools, instead of the secular or godless system to which reference was made. Mr. Pelletier, in the speech from which I quoted yesterday, says

"Mr. Laurier declares that he would only settle the school question in case the schools were Protestant. If, therefore, he considers that the schools are neutral or without any religion he will do nothing. I have no hesitation in saying, gentlemen, that between the system of Protestant schools and neutral schools, both being had, the Protestant school is yet to be preferred to the neutral schools, from many points of view. In a Protestant school principles are taught to the children which Catholics do not admit. In the neutral school the child is made an atheist, and he is brought up in ignorance of God and of all those religious principles which should be inculcated into the minds of the young in order to prepare them for the battle of life. In the Protestant schools the children are taught what we Catholics believe to be errors, but they teach at least that there exists a God whom all should adore and to whom all should pray. The child is led into error in the manner of practising this belief in God, that he or she is directed towards altars before which, in our opinion, they should not kneel, but they are taught at least that their heart and their intelligence should regulate their existence in view of a future and immortal life. At each day they should bow the head under the beneficient influence of prayer, because faith and prayer are the two grand qualities of man. In the neutral school, where all religion is banished, doubt, scepticism and incredulity are prepared, and a population grows up without religion, which is the greatest of all evils. In the Protestant school children are taught that the truths of our religion are not applicable as we understand them, but the parents can, perhaps, counterbalance these theories received at school and correct the errors which may have taken root. In the neutral school it is taught to the child who has prayed at home that prayer is not necessary. Religious education for the child is the accessory and necessary complement of instruction. Therefore in the neutral school this principle is reversed, or it is rendered inapplicable. It has been asked why not speak of religion to children in their family, and speak to them of other things in their schools? and to it is has been added that common schools could be established for all creeds. This is impossible."

I read that as the best answer to the argument of Mr. Ewart in regard to the exercises of prayer that are in force in these non-sectarian schools. Therefore I conclude by saying that the schools, being non-sectarian by law—so that if they transgress that law they can be corrected by the courts, as the administration of any other law can be corrected—the schools being such as even Mr. Pelletier says are to be preferred to a secular system, being such as that a majority of the Roman Catholic children of Ontario are frequenting them, being of a character such as that, according to the highest mandate, the authority which all Catholics revere and respect, they are bound to send their children to them, is this school system of Manitoba to be disallowed and upset by an order from this Council? Now, I ask pardon of the Council if I make a personal reference, which I am very sorry indeed to be obliged to do. I have endeavoured to conduct my argument without any personalities, or without any reference to parties, or to the reasons of my speaking here in a representative capacity on behalf of the Government and the Legislature of Manitoba, but perhaps, without contradiction, this allusion that has been made by Mr. Ewart would be taken as an admission on my part that it was correct. He made a quotation—I do not know why he did not do it in a manly way, I do not know why he made it all. I do not know what my view has to do with this question, but on page 15 of his argument he quotes from a Dr. Morrisson, a gentleman whom I have not the honour of knowing, and who does not seem to know very much of what he is talking about. He says:—

"Anticipating the appearance of this question in the arena of federal politics, Mr. McCarthy and his Protestant Protective Association have entered upon a campaign of open hostility to the Roman Catholic church, her religion and members."

Now, I say there is not one word of truth in that from beginning to end. I am not connected, and never have been connected, with the Protestant Protective Association. This is not the first time I have disclaimed it. I never was even a member of the order of which you, Mr. Premier, was at one time, and perhaps still may be, a distinguished ornament. I have never had anything to do with any such body of men.

Sir MACKENZIE BOWELL—If you had, perhaps you would not have made the reference you did up west.

Mr. MCCARTHY.—I never said one word against the order.

Sir MACKENZIE BOWELL.—No, but your information about it was wrong.

Mr. MCCARTHY.—That may be so, but my father was a member of the order, and I would not like to say anything that would reflect upon him, or the order to which he belonged.

Sir MACKENZIE BOWELL.—I would like to have been there to meet you.

Mr. MCCARTHY.—I am willing at any time to meet you on the stump or elsewhere. Now, I want to deny that I have entered on any campaign of open hostility to our Roman Catholic fellow subjects. I never yet, and I hope I never shall, make any charge or accusation against my Roman Catholic fellow subjects. I respect their right and acknowledge their right to their religion, just as I claim the right to exercise my own judgment as to what religion I shall follow. Therefore, it is a slander, and I am sorry my learned friend has seen fit to put it into a document which will be widely circulated; I regret still more that if he was determined to do it, he did not have the manliness to do it in a direct manner, instead of quoting the language of another. In conclusion I beg to thank the Council for your patient and attentive hearing. I certainly cannot complain of any want of attention and of respect for the gentlemen whom I represent— and I shall take care so to report to them; and whatever effect may be given to my arguments, they have had at the hands of this Council a most attentive hearing, and I thank you for your kindness in that regard.

Mr. EWART.—I do not think that I said, although so reported, "Mr. McCarthy and his Protestant Protective Association." I think what I did say was "Mr. McCarthy and the Protestant Protective Association." However that may be whatever I said I certainly did not intend to connect Mr. McCarthy with the Protestant Association. As to the other part, I think that I could fully justify myself were this the proper place. However, I am very glad to take my learned friend's disclaimer that he has never shown any hostility to the Roman Catholic Church upon general principles, and I am sorry to say in partial justification of the language I used that certainly the Roman Catholics have taken his strenuous attacks upon the Jesuit Order, which is a very widespread branch of their church, as an attack upon their church. I do not think that if my learned friend were to take his little hatchet and cut off an important branch of a tree and afterwards deny that he hit the tree that he would go down to posterity as a shining example of heroic truthfulness, it seems to me that he would rather be taken as making some subtle distinction between the branch and the tree itself. However, I am very glad to hear my learned friend say that he does not intend to attack the Roman Catholic Church, and I would like his disclaimer to go further and say that he does not now intend to attack a very important branch of that church or again to charge some of the members of it with having poisoned one of the popes.

And now I come to Mr. O'Donohue's statement. He was asked for his credentials. He left hurriedly, I may tell the Council, and he was unable to get the credentials before he came away. His co-religionists feeling that possibly he might be asked for them, determined to rectify the matter, and called a mass meeting the second night after he left. They have sent them after him, and as he will not have an opportunity of addressing the Council again, I shall read those credentials for him :—

"On Thursday night at St. Mary's school a mass meeting of Catholics was held. Matters of importance were discussed, especially Mr. John O'Donohue's departure for Ottawa on the mission of testifying as a representative Catholic before the Governor in Council on the school case. Severe discussion ensued, and all present strongly denounced Mr. O'Donohue's posing as a representative Catholic. The meeting was unanimous in denouncing him. The secretary was instructed to draft a resolution.

"A resolution was then put, unanimously carried, and directed by the meeting to be wired at once to Mr. J. S. Ewart, Ottawa. The resolution as carried and sent to Mr. Ewart is as follows :—

"'We Catholics of Winnipeg, in mass meeting assembled, resolveth herewith :

"'Having heard of the departure of one John O'Donohue, a trustee of the Protestant school board of Winnipeg, for Ottawa, for the alleged purpose of testifying before the Governor in Council on the Manitoba school case, on behalf of the Government of Manitoba, and posing as a representative Catholic of this province ;

"'And inasmuch as the said Government of Manitoba failed to contradict the aforesaid allegation, when questioned thereon, on the floor of the House by a member of the same ;

"'That said John O'Donohue is not, nor never has been, a representative of the Catholics of Manitoba, on the school question, or upon any other question ;

"'And that we strongly and emphatically repudiate any and all such enforced representation by him.. Carried unanimously.

"'(Signed)   "'D. SMITH,
                    "'Chairman.
             "'O'CONNELL POWELL,
                    "'Secretary.'

"Following the above considerable discussion ensued. It was then moved by J. J. Golden, seconded by Mr. Carroll :

"'That we, the Catholics of Manitoba, again reiterate the fact that we are a unit on the question of having our own schools, and that there is no better proof of the same than that while paying our taxes to and supporting the so-called public schools, we have at the same time maintained our own schools for the education of our children. Carried unanimously.'

"Moved by Mr. Carroll, seconded by J. A. Richard :

"'Inasmuch as the Honourable Attorney General stated on the floor of the House,

" ' He had always maintained that a large number of Roman Catholics did not agree with the proceedings taken in their name, and that a large number of them preferred the public school system to any other system.

 * * * * * *

(After having read certain statistics purporting to show the illiteracy prevailing in Catholic countries.)

" It would be a shame and a disgrace to perpetuate such a state of affairs in this country. Taxes had been paid by Catholics for the support of schools under the old system, but those controlling the school had failed in their duty."

 * * * * *

" He did not wish to say anything derogatory of any religious creed, but if the Roman Catholic clergy were allowed to override the people of this country the same undesirable condition would prevail here as in other countries where they predominate.

 * * * * *

" If the present school law compelled Catholic children to attend school and swallow Protestant religion (it would then take away a natural right of the Catholics). But the law did not do this, and having this fact in view the legislation was neither unfair nor ungenerous.

" We the Catholics of Winnipeg assembled here in mass meeting repudiate all such assertions, and at one and the same time characterize them as maliciously false or wilfully ignorant. Carried unanimously."

These, gentlemen, are the credentials of Mr. O'Donohue. Now for his evidence. He tells us that the teaching in the French schools is bad. He does not understand French and he bases his opinion on what he heard or saw in those schools. It does not require words to displace testimony of that kind. He was however sent to curse and remained to bless; for he tells us that the convents are remarkably distinguished for the good education they impart to their scholars. Now, Mr. O'Donohue knows, (and I should not at all be surprised if it was the fact, with reference to two members of his own family) that almost all the female teachers in the Roman Catholic schools in Manitoba receive their education at those convents. These are the female teachers in Manitoba whom Mr. O'Donohue condemns, who receive their education in the convents where it is such that Mr. O'Donohue can recommend it, and he tells us that it is really better than the education given in the Protestant schools. Another part of his evidence is that there is a large number of the French half-breeds who are unable to sign their names. I do not know at all if the figures are accurate—for my part I am quite content to have it known that there are a great many who are unable to read and write. But what does Mr. O'Donohue draw from that—that these Metis who are unable to read and write have been to the French schools? I return to the charge upon the public schools. I say to my learned friend, that there are a large number of persons in Manitoba who cannot read or write—what do you think of your public schools ? My learned friend would reply : They never went to our public schools. I say that they never came to our schools, and why do you charge up the illiteacy to us rather than to the public schools ? Now what is the fact with reference to these French half-breeds? We have taken responsibility in connection with them and to the best of our ability we have discharged that responsibility. Who are these French half-breeds? They are more Indian than they are English or French, and a great many of them up to within the last few years could not speak either English or French. They were not those who have settled upon farms nor who had the benefit of parents who were educated such as the Scotch half-breeds who were educated before they came to us and settled on farms. They were not such people at all, but belong to the *coureur des bois*, the *voyageurs*, those restless individuals who until within the last few years hardly owned more than a wigwam or tent. They have now to some extent settled down. Prior to that the good fathers of the Catholic Church followed those roving bands and gave them such education as they could, and I say it redounds to the credit of those Catholic fathers if they have been able now to show such a result that twenty-five per cent of such roving bands are able to sign their names and carry on agriculture to such an extent as to deal with Mr. O'Donohue for implements.

My learned friend Mr. McCarthy commenced very good humouredly by warning the Council against my book because he said that I have had a long connection with this case and was probably very much prejudiced. Prior to his argument, I would have been quite prepared to admit that being only human I probably was very much prejudiced in this case, but after having heard my learned friend's address I am quite prepared in comparison to claim not only perfect sanity but the most perfect impartiality. My learned friend and I have been practising before the bar for a great many years now, before judges whose fundamental principle was that there never was a wrong without a remedy. It has been the boast of the Court of Equity that it implemented the common law system just because there were wrongs for which there were no remedies, but since the Court of Equity has been in operation, and that has been a great many years, the principle has been that there is no wrong without a remedy. But my learned friend seems to have got into a new region altogether, almost into another world, some place where two and two cease to make four. For the last twenty-five years my learned friend and I have been going before courts where we prove that we have a grievance and that the court has jurisdiction, and what do we get? We always get relief—for twenty-five years we never thought it necessary to prove anything further. Although I have listened to his able argument I have not found out what more we have to prove. We have a grievance and there is not a remedy. I say we have got into a region that I am not at all familiar with, and therefore I do not know that I shall be able to meet my learned friend's contentions. Adding two and two together do not now make four. What is the result?—nothing, in the region in which my learned friend has been arguing. He has gone further than that—not only may there be a grievance and the power to remedy, but no remedy, but he has taken the broader ground that where there is a power there may be no corresponding duty. For instance with reference to the very subject of disallowance we are speaking about, it would seem that there is the power to remedy, but there may be no corresponding duty to consider whether you are going to exercise that power or not; there may be some other principles which would actuate you in the matter. Now I desire to read the language of an authority equal to my learned friend, in which it is said:—

"I venture, sir, to ask the House seriously to consider the position in which we stand. The worship of what was called local autonomy which some gentlemen have become addicted to is fraught, I venture to say, with great evils to this Dominion. Our allegiance is due to the Dominion of Canada. The separation into provinces, the right of local self-government which we possess is not to make us less citizens of the Dominion, is not to make us less anxious for the promotion of the welfare of the Dominion; and it is no argument to say that because a certain piece of legislation is within the power of a local parliament, therefore that legislation is not to be disturbed." (That is as I have understood the purport of my learned friend's argument.)—" By the same Act of Parliament, by which power is conferred upon the local legislature the duty and power —because where there is a power there is a corresponding duty,"—(My learned friend will, I think, agree with that at all events)—"are cast upon the Governor in Council to revise and review the acts of the legislative bodies. If you are to say that because a law has been passed within the legislative authority of the province therefore it must remain, we can easily see, sir, that before long these provinces, instead of coming nearer together, will go further and further apart." (My learned friend has argued the other way.) " We can see that the only way of making a united Canada and building up a national life and sentiment in the Dominion is by seeing that the laws of one province are not offensive to the laws and institutions, and it may be to the feelings of another.— I will go so far as to say that they must be to some extent taken into consideration."

I am sure that everyone will be astonished to the last degree to know that that language is the language of Mr. Dalton McCarthy in the Hansard of March, 1889. It is a sound and just view, but two and two do not make four in the atmosphere in which we are to-day. What was the question under consideration. It was the Jesuit Estates Act, where it was thought there ought to be Dominion interference although no harm was done. Now having squared myself with my learned friend to some extent, although I hope in a manner not at all offensive to him, I wish to take up a few of the arguments which he has adduced here, and I shall trouble the Council with another reference to historical matters.

With reference to this historical argument the only point in dispute between my learned friend and myself is as to the fourth bill of rights. He did not point out anything wrong in my book, in fact he even referred to it, and I think that I proved in that book that the fourth bill of rights was the one referred to and I think I shall clear up any doubt about it. My learned friend proposed to prove by the "clearest possible testimony" that it was the third bill of rights that the delegates took down, and not the fourth. He commenced his argument under a complete misapprehension and I am sure it will be noticed by every one that he had to change his argument before he finished. His idea was this, that the third bill of rights was adopted by the council of 24 or the legislative assembly, then, having established that, as he thought he could, he was going to say that this fourth bill of rights was not before the council at all or the legislative assembly, that it was altered by the executive. That was the line he was pursuing; but I corrected him and pointed out that neither bill had been before the assembly and he forthwith changed front, and he asked you to assume that it was the third bill of rights that the Council had prepared and that someone had afterwards altered it. No bill of rights was before the legislative assembly, and the only question is, then, whether it was the third or fourth bill of rights that was prepared by the executive of that legislative assembly. He asserts that the third bill of rights was prepared and was afterwards altered, but for that assertion he has nothing but the witness of two individuals, and I wished to point out the extent of their evidence. The first one is Mr. Begg, and it may be sufficient to displace all his authority to say, that although writing in 1894, he never heard that there was any discussion as to whether it was a third or fourth bill of rights. He never pretended to investigate that question and in fact in an interview that I had with him he so admitted. The only other testimony he offers is that of Mr. Taylor, who says that he saw a copy of this bill, but whether it was the same bill, we do not know: so that statement may go for what it is worth. Now, that is the whole evidence of my learned friend. His great mistake was in adopting, from the language of a pamphlet that was written before my book, the statement that the fourth bill of rights was never heard of until 1890, and he says significantly, that is just the time when it was wanted; that it was produced in 1890 when it was wanted in the interest of these separate schools. He says it was never heard of before then. My learned friend did not listen to what I had stated and proved in my opening plea, that the original of this fourth bill of rights——

Mr. McCARTHY.—The affidavits were withdrawn, and you cannot refer to them now.

Mr. EWART.—I did not withdraw, however, the certified copy of that bill of rights produced from the Department of Justice, and that copy of the bill of rights has been in the Department of Justice no less than 16 years prior to "the first time when it was even heard of." This fourth bill of rights was first heard of in 1870, and it is now of record in the Justice Department, as having been put in at the Lepine trial, which was the most celebrated trial that ever took place in Manitoba, as early as 1874, and put in with evidence proving that it was the original bill of rights.

Sir CHARLES TUPPER.—Who put it in at the trial?

Mr. EWART.—I think it was the defence.

Mr. McCARTHY.—You must produce a certified copy.

Hon. Mr. DICKEY.—It is not printed.

Mr. EWART.—It ought to be printed, all the affidavits ought to be printed. Now there was another point in my learned friend's argument where, as it seemed to me, that the Mr. McCarthy whom I have known for a great many years, and have always admired, not only for his great legal and political attainments, but for his unimpeachable integrity—where it seemed to me that Mr. McCarthy had got away from himself to-day; because I cannot imagine that Mr. McCarthy, under the influence of anything but some overwhelming passion or dominating prejudice, would have referred to these pledges and promises which I produced and proved here—I do not mean by affidavits, but in other ways—in the slighting way that he has referred to them. For instance, with reference to the compact made at the time of the union of Manitoba with Canada, when a great treaty was made by which half the territory that Canada now possesses, was added to its domains, although that treaty was made under Imperial sanction and under the view and direction of Imperial officers, although he admits that "the minority perhaps, had a right, under the circumstances, to expect a different state of things" from that to which they are subjected to-day, my learned friend, instead of meeting my argument, and saying directly, no, there was no such compact, has said in this technical fashion, It is not in the bond, and we must be governed by the exact language.

Mr. McCarthy.—What agreement?

Mr. Ewart. —The compact in the Manitoba Act.

Mr. McCarthy.—I do not quite understand you.

Mr. Ewart.—The Manitoba Act is the agreement. My learned friend does not deny that we have on record the view of Sir John A. Macdonald (who was the negotiator of that treaty) that separate schools had been obtained for the new territory. He can see for himself that it was the opinion of their Lordships of the Privy Council, indicated clearly enough, that such was the intention. What they say is that the draughting is defective,—that they cannot say that the intention was put in clear language. My learned friend knows that in the course of his practice, dozens of agreements have been reformed on account of defective draughting, but he has never raised against an application to reform them such an argument as he has raised with reference to this compact, that because the draughting was badly done, therefore the agreement, when its intention is known and ascertained by direct testimony, should not have its agreed force. That is all my learned friend has to say. He advises you to take the advice of their Lordships of the Privy Council, who say it is better to be governed by the exact words. No doubt a court of law has to do that, but when my learned friend advises you to do what a court of law does, when he advises Parliament to do what a court of law does, to be bound by its own language when it knows that that was not its own intention, then I say he is giving you bad advice.

Then, with reference to one of the other contracts, to one to which Mr. Greenway was a party, he interposes a denial by telegram, and says that Mr. Greenway has denied it. Referring to the interviews Mr. Greenway had with the Reverend Vicar General, first at the Archbishop's palace and in the following morning at Mr. Alloway's office, my learned friend interposes, I say a denial. Mr. Greenway has denied that before. He has given a general denial to the whole statement, but he has never denied, and dare not deny, that he did pay a visit to the Archbishop's palace, and made an appointment with the Vicar-General for the next morning in Mr. Alloway's office to get his answer, and that in pursuance of what was done there, Mr. Prendergast joined his administration. Mr. Greenway never attempted to deny that, and if he does, I will prove it by a sheaf of affidavits. My learned friend has interposed again a technical objection to the other promises that were made. He cannot deny them, for they never have been denied. As to the first, when the French Catholic members assented to the abolition of their great safeguard they had in the Senate, my learned friend's criticism now is that what they were particularly thinking of at the time, was not the schools but the French language. But there is no doubt that the language of the promise covers the schools as well as the French language, and that the promises given were wide and general in their terms. My learned friend says, as a technical objection to that, Why, what business had these people to make those promises? They were the representatives of the people in the legislative assembly asking the French members to give up a safeguard which they had. My learned friend says, Yes, they made those promises, but those whom they represented on that occasion are not to be bound by them, there was no mandate to make those promises. I do not pretend that, as a matter of law, if we had the signature of every individual in Manitoba at that time to these promises, they would be legally binding upon the parties. I cannot say that ; I cannot even say that if the province had declared by an act of the legislature so and so, that would be binding. His objection goes no further than this, that technically they were not legally bound. I admit that, but still I dare say that the Mr. McCarthy, whom I have known to this date, has never interposed objections of that kind, to his own promises, or to those of his friends. Then with reference to Mr. Martin's promises, promises he was authorized to make by the Liberal party, my learned friend interposes the same objection, he says that Mr. Martin was not authorized to make that statement. Now, I do not pretend to say that the Liberal party was absolutely bound by what Mr. Martin said on that occasion; but I would put it to the Liberal party, and ask if they are going to act upon principles of that kind? I do not think my learned friend would have a very high opinion of them; I do not think he would predict for a party that acted upon principles of that kind, a long lease of life. It would be impossible, I am glad to say, for any political party to live two years in Canada and have anything of a respectable following, which laid down as a principle that they could make promises in profusion at the polls, but the moment they were returned to power they could break them. Now, I ask the Liberal party, if they are prepared to accept such principles, if they are prepared to adopt the view that their lieutenants and their leaders may go before the people at a critical election, and obtain power by virtue of those promises, and then turn round and say they were not authorized. It seems to me all these promises have a direct bearing upon the petition we are arguing here to-day. It seems to me that if we can prove, not only that we have had rights, and have lost them, but that we have been tricked out of them, that is a very strong argument for their restoration, and for giving a lesson to the tricksters.

I do not intend to follow my learned friend very far in his long discussion as to whether this Council is sitting now as a judicial body or not. If I were to say anything, it would be nothing more than this, that I should think that one could not either affirm positively that they are acting as a judicial body or a non-judicial body. I should think that in some senses they are judicial, in other senses they are not. But, I would say that they have to proceed in this matter in a judicial manner, and they have to bring to bear upon it a judicial spirit. There is a grievance here, there are complaints and there are defendants. We come before you as an appellate jurisdiction, with our grievance in the shape of a complaint,—by a complainant complaining against a respondent. I think therefore you should proceed in this matter in a judicial spirit, to investigate the complaint upon the lines justice, and fairness, and reasonableness demand, and to decide upon the line of duty, not upon the line of mere political expediency as to what you should do under the circumstances. I may be permitted to read here a quotation from a speech of Mr. Blake, where he says:

"But, Sir, besides the great positive gain of obtaining the best guidance, there are other, and, in my opinion not unimportant gains besides. Ours is a popular government and when burning questions arise inflaming the public mind, when agitation is rife as to the political action of the Executive or the Legislature—which action is to be based on legal questions, obviously beyond the grasp of the people at large;—when the people are on such questions provoked by cries of creed and race, then I maintain that a great public good is attainable by the submission of such legal questions to legal tribunals, with all the customary securities for a sound judgment; and whose decisions passionless and dignified, accepted by each of us as binding in our own affairs involving fortune, freedom, honour, life itself are most likely to be accepted by us all in questions of public concern."

This language seems to me to afford a strong reason for adopting the suggestion, I might almost say, the ruling, of their Lordships of the Privy Council. My learned friend has, perhaps, properly characterized what they have said in some portion of their judgment as *obiter*, that is, that what they said was not absolutely necessary in order to give answers to the questions that were put to them. Nevertheless it seems to me that Mr. Blake's language affords a good reason for being influenced by what their Lordships have said, and for adopting the suggestions which they have made.

Mr. Ewart here suspended his argument until to-morrow.

Mr. McCarthy.—I beg to refer the hon. gentlemen of the Council to chapter 25 of 54 and 55 Victoria, which is the Exchequer Court Act. I draw you attention to the fact that an act of Parliament is merely advisory.

At 4.30 p.m. the Privy Council adjourned.

OTTAWA, March 7, 1895.

The Privy Council met at 11 o'clock a.m.

Present:—Sir Mackenzie Bowell, Sir Adolphe Caron, Hon. Mr. Costigan, Hon. Mr. Foster, Hon. Mr. Haggart, Hon. Mr. Ives, Hon. Mr. Ouimet, Sir Charles Hibbert Tupper, Hon. Mr. Daly, Hon. Mr. Angers, and Hon. Mr. Dickey.

Mr. EWART.—Before commencing my reply to Mr. McCarthy's arguments, I think it would be well that I should summarize what, in my opinion, those arguments were. It seems to me that he had nine of them, and I would like to state them, because I intend to take them up and answer each in detail, and I hope satisfactorily to all. His first argument was that there should be no coercion of a great province, more particularly when, by so doing, its jurisdiction would be taken away, and still more particularly in a local matter. His second argument was that separate schools were bad in themselves, and there were various sub-headings under that one heading. The third was that the present schools in Manitoba were non-sectarian, and therefore unobjectionable. His fourth was that Catholics can and do send their children to the public schools, instancing such cases both in Ontario and Manitoba. As a fifth argument, he gave us a history of the school case for the purpose of showing that Manitoba is not only a unit upon this question, but that it had proceeded with the greatest deliberation possible. He then said that before the Council could interfere, it would have to come to the conclusion that a separate school system was the best possible system, or at all events, preferable. As a seventh argument, he defined national schools and gave some reasons for approving of them. His eighth argument was that the New Brunswick case showed that the determined and settled policy of the Parliament of Canada, was non-interference in matters relating to education ; and his ninth argument was that, at all events, there are very few Catholics in Manitoba, and the injustice therefore cannot be very great. Commencing with the first, namely, that there should be no coercion of a great province, at all events, in purely local matters, and by the offensive method of appeal, I say that is not the true way to present the case before the Council. What we are complaining of is coercion, and what we ask the Council and Parliament to do is to stop that coercion. My learned friend pleads for liberty for the people ; that is what we plead for. My learned friend has mistaken the position. It is we who are pleading for liberty for the people, liberty to have their own schools conducted in the way their consciences dictate. My learned friend says, No, let Manitoba coerce all these people and dragoon them by force, by applying one screw after another, to come into line and send their children to schools which their consciences disapprove. He argued that in no possible case ought the Dominion interfere. I ventured to quote, against that position, his own language. I would remind him, further, that that has not been the practice, and that that has not been the policy with reference to the important subject of disallowance. For instance, in the Ontario Streams case, a case with which my learned friend, I think, was professionally identified, he succeeded in getting the Dominion Government to intervene three times, upon this principle—as can easily be found by reference to the record—that vested rights should not be interfered with ; that individual property was there taken away without compensation ; and the principle was then laid down distinctly, and it seems to me in accordance with justice, that where vested rights are taken away, that where flagrant injustice is found to have been done, that where it is made clear that the province is coercing and improperly interfering with the rights, even of one single individual, that is a case for interference by the supreme authority vested in His Excellency in Council. Then the Jesuit Estates Act, although there was no interference in that case, proceeded upon precisely the same principle. It was not doubted that if there was a case made out for interference, as in the case of the Streams Bill, a case where vested rights were taken away and an injustice done, there should be interference. But we all remember that it was said, Why, nobody is complaining of this. Nobody knew anything about it until some gentlemen in Toronto pointed out to them that there was some hidden injustice in the Act. So far as the Protestants in Quebec were concerned, the Act was passed without complaint ;

and afterwards, when certain points with reference to the Act were brought to their attention, they asked the Government to amend them, and they were amended. Now, I say that these two cases proceeded upon the same principle, namely, that when a grave injustice is done, a case for interference is made out.

But my learned friend says, in answer to all that, and in answer to what I have read from his own speech, that that will apply to every case except education. I think it would be interesting to take his language, and while reading it, to make the exception that he suggests. I am sure when I have finished, that, while he will still say that the principle he laid down would be a very useful one for this occasion, it is one that I think, he would be heartily ashamed of :—

"The worship of what is called local autonomy, which some gentlemen have become addicted to, is fraught, I venture to say, with great evil to this Dominion— except in connection with education. Our allegiance is due to the Dominion of Canada —except in relation to education ; the separation into provinces, the right of local self-government which we possess—except in relation to education, - is not to make us less citizens of the Dominion, is not to make us less anxious for the promotion of the welfare of the Dominion—except in connection with education, and it is no argument to say that because a certain piece of legislation is within the power of the local parliament, therefore that legislation is not to be disturbed—except in connection with education. By the same Act of Parliament by which power is conferred upon the local legislature, the duty and power—because where there is a power there is a corresponding duty— except in cases relating to education—are cast upon the Governor in Council to revise and review the Acts of the legislative bodies—except in cases relating to education. * * * If you are to say that because a law has been passed within the legislative authority of the province, therefore it must remain—except in relation to education— we can easily see that before long these provinces, instead of coming nearer together, will go further and further apart—unless it be in cases relating to education. We can see that the only way of making a united Canada and building up a national life and national sentiment in the Dominion, is by seeing that the laws of one province are not offensive to the laws and institutions, and it may be, the feelings of another—except in matters relating to education."

Now, he was wrong in saying that his language had no reference to education. It was laid down as a general principle, a principle with which I think all reasonable men will agree ; but he says now that it had no reference to education. Why did he speak of it then with reference to the Jesuits Estates Act ? That, it seems to me, had something to do with education : the lands were set apart for educational purposes ; and one of the questions debated with reference to the Jesuits Estates Act, was the assertion that the money was not properly applied to education, but was left to the disposition of His Holiness of Rome. And why should we make an exception with reference to education—of all things in the world ? Why single out education ? Because the constitution, the very clause of which we are debating here to-day, provides specially for education ? My learned friend says there should be no disallowance, there should be no interference in any case, except with reference to education. And why no', when the constitution makes particular reference to that very subject, and a particular provision for interference upon that subject ? I would suggest to him that there is another subject that he may much better except from the generality of subjects, than education, and that is finance. Is the Dominion to interfere with provincial finances ? I should think a much stronger case could be made out for finance than for education, if any exception is to be made, and the Jesuits Estates Act was a matter relating to finance.

Mr. MCCARTHY.—Your bill proposes to interfere with local finances.

Mr. EWART.—No.

Mr. MCCARTHY.—Yes, you say that the grant for educational purposes should be divided.

Mr. EWART.—What we say is that we want to be restored to the enjoyment of the rights we had before they were taken away.

Then my learned friend says this is a drastic way of interfering, one that would be objectionable to the local legislature I cannot see that disallowance seems to me more objectionable than interfering in any other way, when there is a jurisdiction over the subject. In the case of disallowance, there is simply destruction. My learned friend says that it may lead to reconciliation. Well, that is not our experience so far. So far from disallowance leading to reconciliation, it leads to heartburnings and to re-enactment of the statute. I cannot see why there should be any objection on the part of the province to the exercise of jurisdiction here. If the province were supreme in this matter, if the province had exclusive jurisdiction in this matter, then I could very well understand that the province would say, This matter is within our jurisdiction only, keep your hands off. But when it is not such a case, when the jurisdiction is here according to the constitution, what grounds have they for argument ? Apart from the constitution, of course, you can argue anything you like ; but what ground for complaint have they, under the constitution, that the Dominion Government or Parliament should interfere ? The Supreme Court at Ottawa undertakes, under Dominion legislation, to interfere with the decisions of our own courts. What business have they to do it ? The reply is, That is the constitution, and if you don't like it, of course, agitate and get it changed.

My learned friend says that if the Parliament of Canada passes an act, such act remains for ever, it can never be undone. I do not agree with him on that point. But if he is right, it seems to me that it is an argument that ought to apply more to the Provincial Government, to the Provincial Legislature, than to the Dominion authorities. It seems to me that his argument means this, Don't remedy this wrong that has been done because, if you do, you cannot take away that remedy afterwards : that is, let this grievance remain unremedied, because if you apply the remedy the remedy is going to remain. Now that seems to me an extraordinary argument. It may be an argument to apply to the local legislature :—You are losing your jurisdiction. But I do not agree with him that Parliament would not have power to repeal. If you will allow me, I will make a suggestion how to obviate all difficulties. The Dominion could pass a statute for a limited time and then it would run out. That is one way of relieving the difficulty. That, however, would not suit us at all, because we might have just as bad a government at the end of 10 years as we have now. Then, there is another suggestion. The Dominion Parliament could pass an Act which would be in force until repealed, and as soon as it was repealed, it would cease to have force, not because of the repeal, but because of the provision in the original statute.

Hon. Mr. HAGGART.—Do you mean to say we could assume jurisdiction for ever by putting in a clause of that kind, that we preserve the power always of repealing it afterwards.

Mr. EWART.—Yes, of repealing the statute afterwards.

When he says that this is purely a local matter, I cannot agree with him at all. It does not seem to me at all to be a matter of indifference to the whole Dominion, that the principle of coercion should actuate legislation in Manitoba, and whether vested rights are to be interfered with there or not. It seems to me Canada is interested in the progress of Manitoba, as of every other province, and an injustice there cannot be tolerated without injury to the whole. Suppose, however, that it is merely a local matter, then, the only complaint is that under the constitution the local legislature is not supreme. I would like to point out that the local legislature is more supreme over its local affairs than is any state in the Union. No state in the Union has power to take away vested rights, but the province of Manitoba to-day has more power with reference to vested rights—and that is what we are dealing with here—than has any of the States ; and yet Manitoba objects and says she has not got power enough. I say that the only objection is with the constitution, if it has not given her greater power than any state in the Union. In the States such legislation is *ultra vires;* here, however, the province has power to pass legislation, subject, not to be declared *ultra vires*, but to be overridden by the better judgment of Parliament. There are a variety of local matters, however, other than these which are provided for in the constitution, that are beyond the powers of the local legislature. For instance, there is one that, if it were in force in Ontario, I think my learned friend would have pointed it out long before now : there is one with reference to Quebec, namely, that Quebec is utterly unable to alter twelve of her own constituencies ; she is prohibited from doing that by the British North America Act. What is more absolutely a local matter than arranging constituencies for the

Legislative Assembly? yet the province of Quebec cannot do it. And why not? Because it was so provided for the protection of the Protestants in the province of Quebec. That was not to be done, and they have never attempted to do it, and of course they are not going to do it. I say that there is a local matter, and yet the province has not supreme power to deal with it; because such is the constitution. No province is supreme in reference to matters relating to agriculture. Any province may pass a law with reference to agriculture, but the British North America Act gives power to the Dominion to override any such law. What is more local in its nature than a matter relating to agriculture? Yet, that is the constitution, we are bound by the constitution, and we cannot get away from it. Now, I wish to point out that at the time of Confederation this subject was brought up for discussion, and this power of disallowance was discussed at great length. It was suggested that the provinces should not have power to take away vested rights within those provinces. It was foreseen that in the provinces, some of them very immature, there might be an interference with vested rights, and a great injustice done; but it was thought better to reserve the disallowance power for the central authorities. I do not wish to trouble you with long quotations from the debates, but I will give you merely a citation from Mr. Clement's book on the Canadian constitution, page 173:—

"Throughout the debates it was clearly recognized that the exercise by the Dominion Government of the power of disallowance was to be exercised in support of federal unity, *e.g.* to preserve the minorities in different parts of the confederated provinces from the hands of the majorities."

Now, my learned friend used an argument—I think it was suggested by the Secretary of State—that if the Roman Catholics were in the majority in Manitoba, and they provided for public schools according to their way of thinking, ought the Dominion to interfere? He says, No, if there was a conscience clause for the benefit of Protestants. There would be a case, he thinks, if the Roman Catholics did what the Protestants have done here, unless the Catholics provided for the conscience of Protestants.

Mr. McCarthy.—No, you did not understand me. If they established denominational schools, which I do not admit, and deny that they have been established here.

Mr. Ewart.—If they established schools according to their way of thinking, of course they would be denominational schools, and if they did not provide for the conscience of Protestants, then there ought to be interference; and yet we have here a system of schools with no provision for the conscience of Catholics, and there ought to be no interference! It shows the different ways one can look at the same thing.

His next argument is that separate schools are bad, and he gives quotations. I do not pretend to dwell long upon them in reply. He argued that the dogmas taught in the denominational schools violated the principle of the separation of church and state; yet he himself advocates the teaching of religion in schools where the population consists, as he read, of Icelanders, Mennonites, Polish Jews, French, Hungarians, Finlanders, and Gaelic-speaking Crofters, besides Protestants and Catholics. I hope he may never be asked to formulate a religion which is going to be suitable to all these. He says that separate schools are injurious to unity, and he quotes from Dr. King to that effect, a gentleman who, while advocating unity for the Catholics, has been for many years engaged in conducting a separate school, although of a voluntary character, which has for its object the withdrawal of Presbyterians and others from the common schools.

Then his contention with reference to separate schools is that they produce illiteracy. I have never been able to understand at all how it is that illiteracy is connected with church government or any other government of schools. I can very well understand that it has some bearing upon the character of peoples; it may have some bearing upon their character in this way, that some nations may not be so anxious for education as others. But I cannot see how it has any bearing one way or another upon the question, Which is the best system of schools?—because none of those schools produce illiteracy. It is not charged by my learned friend, or any one else, that if people go to those schools, or schools of any kind, they come out illiterate. He has given a good many statistics for the purpose of showing that in Catholic countries illiteracy does prevail. Now, he does not pretend that that is because of the Catholic religion; because he admits that in Belgium, which is almost entirely Catholic, illiteracy is almost unknown. He does not pretend, either, that it is because the schools are under church government.

Mr. McCARTHY.—Yes, that is what I do pretend.

Mr. EWART.—Well, if he does, all I can do is to refer him to England where, until 1870, all the schools were under church government, and more than one-half of them are under church government to-day. I do not think he will undertake to say that England is an illiterate country. However, I do not at all admit those statistics, which he says have been so carefully compiled. There have been handed to me some other statistics, which I will take the liberty of reading, and which, perhaps, are more accurate than those given by my learned friend. I have here a statement of the attendance at schools in different countries. In Norway, Sweden and Denmark, where the population is almost entirely Protestant, the attendance is 14 per cent. In the United States, where there are 51,000,000 Protestants and 9,000,000 Catholics, the attendance is 13 per cent. In Great Britain and Ireland, where the proportion of Protestants to Catholics is 29½ to 5½, the attendance is 12.3. In France, where the population is almost entirely Catholic, except the 4,000,000 that are put down as having no religion, and they are omitted from calculation, the attendance at school is 17 per cent, more than 3 per cent higher than any other country in the world. In Austria, which is almost entirely Catholic, having 20,000,000 Catholics to 400,000 Protestants, the attendance is 13 per cent, or about that in the United States. In Spain, which is almost entirely Catholic, the attendance is 10.6: in Italy, which is almost entirely Catholic, it is 9 per cent. So that these figures prove how foolish it is to rely upon statistics of this kind to support an argument for the purpose of founding legislation upon it.

Mr. McCARTHY.—If both sets of statistics are correct, what is the explanation of the fact that the larger the number attending schools, the larger the number who come out illiterate?

Mr. EWART.—The answer to that is that your statistics are all wrong.

Mr. McCARTHY.—That is not an answer.

Mr. EWART.—I think that is the best answer, and needs no other.

Mr. McCARTHY.—My statistics are taken from the Statesman's Year Book.

Mr. EWART.—Your statistics, even if they be true, do not prove anything with reference to education. My learned friend might as well argue, but perhaps the argument would come better from me, that the Protestant religion is unfavourable to art, to painting, to music and things of that kind. As a proof of that I would contrast England with Italy. I would say, too, as another proposition, that Protestantism was altogether unfavourable to culture of manners, politeness and so on, and I would refer him to England and Germany as against all the Catholic countries in the world. He would have to admit those facts, but he would not be willing to admit the deduction I draw from them. In the same way, when he says that in Catholic countries, his statistics show a certain amount of illiteracy, I tell him that all they prove is that the southern nations are not so eager for education as are northern nations. When he goes amongst northern nations he will find a Catholic nation like Belgium, eager for education, and well educated. The line he has drawn is not between Protestantism and Catholicism in their bearing upon education, but the line is between northern nations and southern nations. Anyone who knows anything at all about ethnology knows that these peoples differ in many respects, even upon the question of education.

Mr. McCARTHY.— Quebec is further north then Ontario.

Mr. EWART.—I think the only fair way to test a matter of that kind is to take the two systems under the same circumstances. Take them with the same environment and at the same period. For instance, let us take the separate schools and the public schools in Ontario. There we have the same kind of people, at least largely the same kind, living in the same country, subjected to much the same influences; and yet the Year-Book for 1893, to which my learned friend goes for his statistics, also tells us that the attendance upon the separate schools is about 5 per cent larger than in the public schools, and the cost is less. I think that is the only fair way to make the comparison.

Then he has another argument against separate schools. He quoted statistics to show that amongst the provinces, Quebec always stood at the foot. I observed, how_ ever, while he was reading, that he told us also that Ontario generally stood at the top of the list. If there are two provinces in which both the separate and the public school systems prevail and that of those two provinces one is at the top and the other at the bottom of the list, what he can make out of that, in the way of proving either in favour or against separate schools, passes my comprehension.

Sir CHARLES HIBBERT TUPPER.—I think Nova Scotia came third in his list; and though they have not a separate school system on the Statute-book, they have it in practice.

Mr. McCARTHY.—At the same time, in one province the Catholics are in a large majority and in the other the Protestants are in a large majority.

Mr. EWART.—Does my learned friend say that teaching a little religion in the schools is a bad thing for education? No, he does not say that; he says it is well to keep religion in the schools. But does he say that teaching the Catholic religion in the schools is a bad thing? I do not think he would say that after the disclaimer of yesterday. Then where is there anything that militates against the success of separate schools? In Ontario, for instance, they are working under the same rules and regulations as are the public schools, with the same kind of inspectors, the same books, and the same government regulations? They have a little Catholic religion taught there, and does he say that makes a difference? If so, I am afraid I shall not be able to give him credit for his disclaimer of yesterday.

Then he attacks the separate schools, particularly in Manitoba. I think we have been quite prepared to hear that in Manitoba the teachers are not up to the full standard that they are in Ontario. Where there are a great many schools with a very small attendance, and where the salaries are necessarily low because of the poverty of the people, one would be quite prepared to hear that the schools were not up to the Ontario standard. But the defect is not altogether upon the side of separate schools. For instance, if we take up the report for last year of the public schools in Manitoba and look at the statistics on page 8 with reference to teachers, we find that out of 997 teachers, 222 were put down as untrained, not quite a fourth of them, but still about one-fourth of them are altogether untrained.

Mr. McCARTHY.—Untrained at Normal schools.

Mr. EWART.—They have had no training as teachers, and I think that is not to be wondered at under the circumstances.

My learned friend read some examination questions for the purpose of showing how absurd some of the questions are which teachers are required to answer. Many of them, however, I, for one, quite approve, that is, if the catechism is going to be taught in the schools, and he says he has no objection to religion being taught in the schools. If the catechism is to be taught in the schools, I can see no objection to asking the questions upon it that my learned friend has read. Then as to those questions which were written, if not read, with a sneer, questions as to the way to address dignitaries — all I can say is that I wish that they had been taught in the schools when I was young. If we are going to have dignitaries, one thing we ought to know is how to address them. But the absurd questions are not altogether in the Catholic schools. I can give, if necessary, a number of very absurd questions that have been put at Protestant examinations, and I am sorry to say, even in the Civil Service examinations to the ladies employed in the post office department. I remember one that was put to those young ladies who are busy sorting letters all day, was this : "What is the deepest lake in the world?" No particular book was prescribed for studying that subject.

Hon. Mr. FOSTER.—They wanted a place to sink dead letters.

Mr. EWART.—I suppose that must have been the explanation of it. In an examination of Protestant teachers not very long ago, there was this question, "How many legs has a spider?" I think, however, the best way to answer such statements is to read from a pamphlet that was issued by His Grace the late Archbishop Taché, telling of the success of the Catholic exhibits sent over to the Colonial Exhibition in 1885:

"In the fall of 1885, Sir Charles Tupper visited the province with the view of having it take part in the International Exhibition which was to take place in England during the following year. The Catholic section of the Board of Education was invited to help in the exhibit. The proposition at first was met with little favour, it was after vacation ; the schools had hardly organized for the new year ; there was no time to prepare anything new ; nevertheless, the Canadian Commissioner was so pressing that objections were overruled, and a collection was made in some of the nearest schools out of the work of the pupils of the previous year. The most advanced had left their classes, some of the best work had been lost or carried away, and none had been prepared in view of the exhibition. Eight schools furnished samples of their work in different branches, the whole was forwarded to England, it was exhibited there, it attracted so much attention that every article exhibited was examined, re-examined, in such a way that when they were returned, their condition proved that they had passed through a great many hands. A diploma of merit and a medal of honour were sent to each of the schools, as well as to their superintendent, who had contributed to the exhibit, and we had a proof that such complimentary recognition was not merely a matter of form. Capt. W. Clarke, as every one knows, was the Manitoba representative at the Colonial and Indian Exhibition, and here is the way the gallant and intelligent representative wrote to the Superintendent of Catholic schools in Manitoba :—

"'LONDON, 27th July, 1886.

"'DEAR SIR,—I can speak with experience with reference to the excellence of your section, two of my daughters having been for a long time with the good sisters of St. Boniface, where their progress was as satisfactory to me as it was pleasant to them.
"'I am, sir,
"'Your obedient servant,
(Signed) "'WILLIAM CLARKE.
"'T. A. BERNIER, Esq.,
"'Supt. of Education.'

Mr. Clarke is not a Catholic, nor has he shown any tendencies towards Rome, but through his daughters he has acquired some knowledge of a Catholic school in Manitoba, and so was prepared to acknowledge without surprise the merit of their exhibit.

Sir Charles Tupper is not a Catholic either, and is known all over for his superiority and patriotism ; here is the way that the Canadian High Commissioner speaks of the Catholic schools of Manitoba :

"COLONIAL AND INDIAN EXHIBITION, 1886.
"CANADIAN SECTION,
"LONDON, 29th July, 1886.
"To T. H. BERNIER, Esq.

"MY DEAR SIR,—I duly received your letter of the 3rd inst., and thank you for the memorandum which you have prepared on behalf of your section of the Manitoba Educational exhibit. I shall be pleased to receive a thousand copies of the memorandum and to see that they are carefully distributed. The exhibit which you have taken such pains to collect has already attracted considerable attention, and I do not doubt it will add to the success of the Dominion at the exhibition.

"I remain, yours faithfully,
(Signed) "CHARLES TUPPER."

Is it possible? can anything good come from that (sort of) Nazareth? Yes, friends, come and see that Sir Charles Tupper does not hesitate to say that the exhibition of the ordinary work of the pupils of Catholic schools of Manitoba will add to the success of the Dominion at the exhibition. If you are not satisfied with such testimonies, listen to the following remarks published in the Canadian Gazette of London, on the 4th November, 1886 :—

"'It is generally believed, that of all the sister provinces, that of Manitoba is the least advanced towards civilization. We already know, that in many respects, such is not the case, but if we consider the excellent scholastic exhibition of that province, we see in what degree that impression is erroneous, especially in the matter of education.

"'The collection contains samples of books, exercises, scholastic material, etc., etc., coming from the Catholic schools as well as from the Protestant schools of the province.

"'The excellence of the work, and especially of the geographical charts, is incontestible. This is the more pleasing, if we consider the fact that many exhibits are dated from the year 1884, and the beginning of the year 1885. It is evident the exhibit is composed of the ordinary duties of the schools in all parts of the province, and not of work specially prepared for the occasion.

"'No pretention has been made to eclipse the school exhibits of the other provinces, but the collection that is under our eyes denotes that in one of the most recently 'organized' provinces of the Confederation, there exists a school system, which although respecting the faith and religious convictions of the population, offers to every one an education capable of fitting for the highest rank in the society, the child who is placed under its care.''

My learned friend's next argument was that Catholic children go to the public schools, both in Ontario and in Manitoba. He quite admitted, too, that that had been brought about, so far as Ontario was concerned, by a policy of friendship and concession; that because the Catholics were satisfied, and there was no struggle going on, they naturally drifted into the public schools. He quite admitted, too, that the effect of Mr. Meredith's agitation against Catholic schools, was not to drive them further into the public schools, but to drive them in the other direction, and that there had been a large increase of separate schools owing to that agitation.

Mr. McCarthy.—An increase, not a large increase.

Mr. Ewart.—It seems to me that there is here a great lesson for the province of Manitoba. Would it be justifiable for this Council and for the Dominion parliament to interfere, in order to carry out Manitoba's own object? If Manitoba's own object is to get all these children into one school, what is the proper way to go about it? Looking at Ontario, for example, is it by coercion? Is it by contesting the matter with the Catholics, or is it by conciliation, by letting them have their own way? If we are to believe his statistics for Ontario, clearly the latter course is the best one to follow. So I say that parliament would be helping the object that Manitoba says she has in view, by adopting the proper course to attain that object, and not the one that Manitoba, in its foolishness, has seen fit to adopt. But I deny the correctness of his statistics upon that point. There are a number of considerations which go to annihilate them completely. It must be remembered that a large number of schools in Ontario, although called public schools, are in reality separate schools, that is, the Catholic religion is taught there; that by a process of severe winking, such as my learned friend says Manitoba is quite willing to engage in, the schools, although public schools, are really of a character satisfactory to Catholics.

Mr. McCarthy—You are assuming I said that; I do not know that to be the case.

Mr. Ewart—I think you do know that that is being done in Manitoba. But I do not know that you know it is being done in Ontario.

Mr. McCarthy—I do not know that it is being done in Manitoba.

Mr. Ewart—My statement with reference to Ontario is based upon the opinions of a great many individuals. The County of Essex I would mention particularly as a county very much in point. Then, it must be remembered that a large number of Catholics in Ontario are scattered, and it is therefore impossible to get them together.

So far as Manitoba is concerned, he makes what would be a strong point without explanation, when he says that in the course of four or five years since the school acts have been in force, no less than 36 separate schools have come in under the public school system and have complied with the requirements of the statute. Now that is not so, and what has been done has been accomplished in the most objectionable manner. The Acts of 1890 were no sooner passed than a gentleman who spoke the French language, was employed to go into the Catholic school districts and visit the trustees and the parents, going from house to house, with the view of getting them to adopt the public school system. Then commenced what may be termed the temptation on the prairie. That gentleman, whether he was so instructed or not, used this argument: Come away from the Catholic schools, come into the public schools, and you will save money by it. You will get the Parliamentary grant, you will get your share of the municipal taxes, and you won't have to pay for the Protestant schools or the public schools, and at the same time support your own schools. However, he met with little success, as these statistics sufficiently show. For the first three years, he met with little success, although various expedients were resorted to. For instance, they were asked not to abandon the books which they had before, but merely postpone their religious training until after 4 o'clock. After he had got in a certain number that way, he found he could get no more. He had got, I think, about a dozen out of the whole province, with inducements of that kind, appealing to their poverty and appealing to their ideas of getting education for their children. The Act of 1894 was then brought into force, and, as he says himself, the effect of that was the withdrawal of $20 a month from the schools. My learned friend says, to quote his own language, "the withdrawal of $20 a month has forced them to come in." That is what it was passed for. They had not got more than a dozen schools out of all the separate schools in Manitoba. Prior to the Act of 1894, the Catholics could tax themselves, or rather procure from the municipalities where they were all Catholics, a sum of $20 a month. The Manitoba government put on another screw, and the result was that a large number of the schools came in. But to what extent did they come in? The Manitoba government or legislature had succeeded in turning the Catholic religion out the front door in order to gratify Protestants, or some of them, and then, in order to satisfy the Catholics, they said, " let it come in at the back door as long as you do not say anything about it." The fact is to-day—the superintendent may contradict me if it is not true—the Catholic religion is taught there exactly the same as before, in every one of the schools.

Mr. BLAKELY.—No.

Mr. EWART.—If he means it is not taught in the same way he probably means that it is not taught at the same time. Before 1890 it was taught during the school hours between 9 and 4 o'clock; since 1890 it has been taught from 4 o'clock to 4.30. That is the difference between the schools. Thus, what were Catholic schools before 1890, and what were called Catholic schools, are given credit for being public schools now. The difference between them is this, that then religion was taught between 9 and 4 and now the children are kept in for another half hour in order that it may be taught them.

Mr. McCARTHY.—I think that is permissible under the law.

Mr. EWART.— No, it is not permissible under the law.

Mr. McCARTHY. —Why not?

Mr. EWART.—I will read my friend the law.

" Religious exercises in the public schools shall be conducted according to the regulations of the advisory board. The time for such religious exercises shall be just before the closing hour in the afternoon."

So, according to the law it is just before the closing hour, and according to the practice just after the closing hour in the afternoon.

Mr. McCARTHY.— You hold political meetings in the public schools.

Mr. EWART.—Section 8 of the Act says:—

" The public school shall be entirely non-sectarian and no religious exercises shall be allowed therein, accept as above provided."

The Catholic religion is still taught, as it was before.

Mr. McCARTHY.—Not during school hours.

Mr. EWART.—But I am showing that the only difference is, that while formerly the Catholic religion was taught during school hours, now it is taught during the next hour thereafter. The advisory board have the power to fix the school hours as they like. They have fixed the hours from 9 o'clock to 4. Suppose they fixed the hours from 9 to 3.30, then if the teachers occupied the half hour after school hours in teaching religion, the state of affairs would be just what it is now. The only difference would be that the school hours would be changed a little. So, that what my learned friend objects to is not to the teaching of religion in the schools, but to teaching during school hours, insisting that the children should be kept in after school hours to teach it to them. Now, there might be something said in favor of that if there were Protestants in the districts affected as well as Roman Catholics, but where, as is the great majority of these cases, none but Catholics go to the schools in question, I cannot see the soundness of this objection. All this fight and turmoil is about the question whether the children should be taught religion just before or just after 4 o'clock.

Mr. McCarthy.—And all you are arguing for is for a change in the law which will enable the teaching of religion to be carried on half an hour before, rather than half an hour after four o'clock.

Mr. Ewart.—We want our rights secured by law and not left to the whim of the government.

My learned friend says that not only according to the practice in Manitoba and Ontario can the children attend the public schools, but he says that the Catholic doctrine permits it. My learned friend reminds me of what Lord Morris said in his rich brogue, when the case was being argued before the Privy Council. My learned friend may remember——

Mr. McCarthy.—I remember the brogue.

Mr. Ewart.—Speaking with reference to Dr. Bryce's affidavit, Lord Morris remarked : "This gentleman gives it as his individual opinion that the Catholic religion ought to be something entirely different from what it is." So my learned friend is trying to make the Catholic religion something entirely different from what it is. I have here a statement of the Catholic doctrine, and I can show it him in the original, but it is in a language I fear he would object to as much as he does to the French. It is in Latin, but I can give him a free translation :—

"The teachings of the Roman Catholic Church in relation to education were communicated to the American bishops by the late Pope Pius IX. and confirmed by Pope Leo XIII. that the members of the church should be warned against frequenting the public schools wherein the religion of the Roman Catholic Church is not taught.

"While this is the general principle, yet the Roman Catholic Church, not being inimical, as is so often alleged, either to elementary education or to instruction in the higher studies, permits its children to avail themselves of the advantages of the public schools in cases where there is no fear of perversion and where it is impossible to provide church schools."

So that it will be seen that public schools can be attended by Catholic children only under two limitations : first, that Catholic schools cannot be established and, second, that the public schools are free, at all events, from positive objection.

Mr. McCarthy.—But that has been changed by what I read from the ablegate.

Mr. Ewart.—I do not think so.

My learned friend goes into the history of the school Acts with a view of showing that the law has been adopted of set purpose and deliberate intention by the people of Manitoba. But he has been altogether too modest in the history of these school Acts. He forgets the part which he took himself—and he will forgive me for referring to him in this connection, because it is impossible to tell the history of these school Acts without referring to him. He says that the history commenced in 1876. Well, at that time Professor Bryce, who has taken an active interest in this question, wrote a pamphlet on the subject. But that is all that was done ; the pamphlet fell flat and dead. Thirteen years intervened without a single word of complaint. There was not a man in Manitoba who knew that there was a grievance with reference to separate schools. We did not hear a word about it. No political party, no politician, no clergyman, no private individual, so far as I know, said a word about it. The first word, so far as I know, was spoken by my learned friend.

Mr. McCarthy.—That is not correct.

Mr. Ewart.—It is absolutely correct.

Mr. McCarthy.--It is absolutely incorrect.

Mr. Ewart.—I think I can prove what I say. My learned friend is reported to have said on one occasion that he was forestalled in this matter by Mr. Smart, who was then a member of the Government of Manitoba, in his speech at Clearwater. But my learned friend is in error about that. Mr. Smart did speak at Clearwater, but he did not advocate the abolition of separate schools ; what he did advocate was the combination of the government of the two sets of schools under one power, and that is all he advocated. The first word said in favour of the abolition, or suppression rather, of separate schools in Manitoba, so far as I know (apart from Prof. Bryce's pamphlet in 1876), was spoken by my learned friend in Portage la Prairie in 1889. I think my learned friend's suggestion that he was not the first relates to what I have mentioned—he thinks he was anticipated by Mr. Smart at Clearwater. I want to read what my learned friend said at Portage la Prairie and what was said on the same platform immediately afterwards by Mr. Joseph Martin. I think Mr. Martin got his cue from my learned friend, but however that may be, he was the one who introduced the Schools Act, forced it upon his own government, and carried it. Then I want to read what Mr. Smart said at a subsequent period, this Mr. Smart who was supposed to have forestalled my learned friend by his announcement of a policy of the Government. I will read what my learned friend said at Portage la Prairie.

Sir CHAS. HIBBERT TUPPER.—This was in 1889 ?

Mr. EWART. - Yes.

Mr. McCARTHY.—In August, 1889, after Mr. Smart's speech.

Mr. EWART.—This was three days after Mr. Smart's speech at Clearwater and several days before his speech at Wawanesa. My learned friend said :—

" There was something for the politician to live for ; we have the power to save this country from fratricidal strife, the power to make this a British country in fact as it is in name. In order to acomplish this other issues must for the moment give way. We have got to bend our energies and let it be understood in every constituency that, whether a man call himself Grit or Tory, Conservative or Reformer, his record is clear, his principles are sound and no influence at Ottawa will induce him to betray his great trust. The speaker was glad to inform the meeting that the poor, sleepy Protestant minority of Quebec were at last awake."

My learned friend, as you will remember, had been arousing them with his Equal Rights Association and had had some success in opening their eyes.

" He trusted before many weeks to address a meeting in Montreal and to realize that that minority is sound to the core on this question. There is the separate school question here and in the North-west, and there is the French school question in Ontario ; we have all the work to do in our various localities ; let us do that first before we seek to traverse fields before more difficulty is to become encountered because vested rights have become solidified."

That is the first word said, apart from Dr. Bryce's pamphlet, so far as I am aware, for as to Mr. Smart's speech at Clearwater, I hope to show you that it does not relate to the suppression of separate schools. Mr. Joseph Martin was on the platform when my learned friend delivered his speech. He was a member of the Greenway Government, of which Mr. Smart also was a member. If Mr. Smart, a few days before had announced the policy of the Government, Mr. Martin would have known it and would have told the people what the policy of the Government then was—for it could have been no secret if it had been announced by Mr. Smart sometime before. But this is what Mr. Martin said :—

" He could not say that it had been announced by the Government at least not very definitely, what action they proposed to take in connection with the dual language and separate school system in this province, which were subject of an entirely similar nature with the discussion now going on with regard to the disallowance of the Act in Quebec. But he thought it had been very well known in this province for some years back what his own individual feelings were in regard to the use of two languages in the legislature."

I will read what Mr. Smart said at Wawanesa.

Mr. McCARTHY.—That is not all Mr. Martin said. If I remember rightly, he went on to say that he would abolish the dual language sytem.

Mr. EWART.—I have read what he said about separate schools.

Mr. McCARTHY.—I do not think he says he will do anything about separate schools, but that he will abolish the dual language system.

Mr. EWART.—That is what I am speaking about. He did not pledge himself as to separate schools, but if the Government policy had been announced he would have pledged himself on that question.

Mr. McCarthy.—It had already been announced.
Mr. Ewart.—His abstention from doing so is proof that it had not been announced. I will read you what Mr. Smart said a few days afterwards :—

"It was not his intention, neither by speech nor inference, to be understood as speaking disparagingly of Roman Catholics. They were as much entitled to their rights as any other people, and he would defend them as energetically as he would those of the Protestants. In referring to the schools, he did not set himself up as an educationalist, but as the matter had come before the Government, he spoke of it in a practical way. There was, he said, very much of an anomaly in it all. *While the state recognized both systems*, he did not undertake to discuss or take any side in the matter as to whether this was right or wrong."

Later on Mr. Smart spoke as follows :—

"The Liberal party is known to be the party of reforms, and the present Government is prepared to undertake the task of giving in the matter of the conduct of the educational system equal rights to all citizens of the province, and thereby making a reform, which should be received by every fair-minded man in Manitoba, with favour. *I do not wish to be understood in any of my remarks on this question to advocate the abolition of the separate school system. I am not prepared to express any opinion, at present, on this question, nor do I purpose discussing the question as to whether the principle of state aid to any class of denominational schools is or is not a correct one.* Sufficient it is for me now to point out under the existing laws the unfairness that exists, with a view to giving to the people the reasons for the changes which will shortly take place in the law pertaining to the carrying out of the educational institutions of the country. The whole department will be placed directly under a responsible Minister of the Crown and similar regulations as to qualifications of teachers, as to inspectors, normal schools, &c., will be made both in the case of separate schools as well as Protestant. This course will effect the saving of some thousands of dollars, which will go further to assist in reducing the taxation raised by the people of Manitoba."

I think I have now proved my point that my learned friend was the first to say anything about the suppression of public schools.

Hon. Mr. Daly.—You have not read what Mr. Smart said at Clearwater.

Mr. Ewart.—I will read what Mr. Smart said at Clearwater prior to my 'earned friend's address at Portage la Prairie :—

"The anomaly existing as to the separate school system was pointed out, and it was the Government's intention to overhaul the whole educational machine. The double-barrelled system must be abolished. The two superintendents, the two boards and two sets of inspectors must go, and a minister of education will be appointed (a present minister taking the portfolio who would administer the education department and be responsible to the people. The change would enable ministers to greatly increase the grants towards the support of schools, and would benefit the taxpayers."

So that it was a mere change in the regulation and control of schools that he spoke of. The first word as to the suppression of separate schools was spoken by my learned friend at Portage la Prairie

My learned friend says the School Acts were carried by large majorities in the Legislature elected in 1888. He is quite correct, but he forgets how these Government majorities were obtained. They were obtained by the promises—if I may refer to what is generally known, and is shown by the affidavits which were withdrawn—that were made to the Roman Catholics in that election. My learned friend says that after the acts were passed another election took place, in which he says, and expects me to admit, that the great question before the electors was the school question. He says that the result of an appeal to the country upon the question and after a full threshing out of the issue was a majority in favour of the Public Schools Act?

Mr. McCarthy.—In favour of the Public Schools Act?

Mr. Ewart.—Well, that is in favour of the government. He read almost immediately afterwards the declaration issued at that same election by the Conservatives as their platform, showing, as he says, that the Conservatives were in favour of abolishing separate schools. I do not think that any politician ever heard of such a thing before —both parties were on one side, both in favour of abolishing separate schools and yet that this was the great question before the people to be decided. Of course my learned friend used these two facts for a different purpose, but they are mutually destructive. In fact my learned friend is quite wrong when he says that that was the great question in that election, for it was not. The question of the schools was hardly debated at all, so far as I know, except in the French parishes, and there, of course, all were on the same side. It was not an issue in the election, because the matter was in the courts and it was not thought advisable by the Catholics to make an appeal to the electors at that time. My learned friend read this platform of the Conservatives for the purpose of contradicting what I have said in claiming that I represented really the matured opinion of the Conservatives upon this point. I did not intend to say, and I did not say, that at that time the Conservatives looked upon this matter in the light that we desire. What I did claim was that they looked at it in that light now, and that since the decision of the Privy Council they had seen what was best to be done and were quite ready to obey its behests and fall in with the suggestions of their Lordships of the Privy Council. And my learned friend gave me the evidence of that a little later, though using it for another purpose. He referred to Mr. Fisher's resolution for which the whole Opposition voted. Mr. Fisher's resolution, after recitals, says :—

"And having regard to the suggestions of the tribunal referred to, that 'all legitimate ground of complaint would be removed if the present system were supplemented by provisions which would remove the grievance upon which the appeal is founded, and were modified so far as might be necessary to give effect to those provisions' without a repeal of the present law ; this House is ready to consider the grievance referred to with a view to providing reasonable relief, while maintaining, as far as possible consistent with that object, the principles of the present acts in their general application."

What I said is that every Conservative in the House voted for that, and it is no contradiction of what I said as to my representing the matured opinion of Conservatives to show what was the Conservative platform in 1892 under totally different circumstances. And not only did Conservatives vote for that resolution, but Mr. Fisher, who is a very good Liberal, voted for it and I believe that a good many other Liberals outside of the House take that view of the subject also.

Then my learned friend raised the point that before the Council could interfere it must say that separate schools were better than public schools. Now I submit that there is a great variety of things that this Council might say without saying that. I can suggest seven, and no doubt I have not thought of all. One thing that the Council might say is that it would be best to leave matters of religion to the people themselves. A second is that the old law worked well for twenty years without a word against it and without the people knowing that there was any grievance, while since then everything has been turmoil and confusion. A third suggestion is that the Council might say that separate schools were agreed to at the Union and it might surprise Mr. Greenway very much by showing some regard for honourable engagement. A fourth thing the Council might say is, that Parliament has declared that it desired separate schools established, that in the case of New Brunswick, Parliament's decision has been in favour of separate schools, and, to put Parliament in possession of the matter, this Council ought to pass an order for that purpose. It might be said in the fifth place, that the policy of Parliament was indicated by its dealing with the North-west Territories, whose circumstances are very much the same as those of Manitoba. Parliament established separate schools in the North-west Territories, and, by large majorities refused to disturb them. Sixth, in all other parts of Canada except perhaps British Columbia there are separate schools by law or common consent. Seventh, the Council might say that the Manitoba government has itself re-established separate schools after four years' experience, and the only objection to their being sanctioned by the law is that they have some sentimental objections to being bound to do right. With reference to this last, I would like to read from my learned friend's address of the day before yesterday, what I consider the most important, or, at least, the second most important statement made during this whole debate, perhaps during this whole controversy, the only one to compare with it in importance being his declaration that we had a grievance, and that there was power here to remedy it, but that two and two did not make four. At page 30 of the second day's proceedings Mr. McCarthy is reported to have said :

" In the provinces that are free, we are told, and it is the best possible argument that can be urged, that so tolerant are the majority, so willing are they to yield rights which could not be legally claimed, that, to adopt the language of my learned friend, we wink at infractions of the public school law so that it becomes almost a separate school system. And they do it willingly. But it is one thing to compel people to do a thing, and it is another thing to leave it to their free choice. It is a strong argument in favour of allowing the people of Manitoba to work out their own salvation without interference."

Now what does my learned friend suggest here,—that the separate school system is wrong ? Not at all, but that it is right. And so tolerant are the majority that the Catholics may have a separate school system if they will only be kind enough to take it as a gift and not as a right guaranteed by the law. There is the whole point. " They are willing to wink at infractions of the public school law." These gentlemen say : Let us have the law one way and let us have illegal transactions going on in schools, and that is all right. Let us have the Catholic religion taught there and education carried on under religious auspices, and that is quite correct ; but the law must be one way even though the practice is the other. I do not think we are unreasonable in saying that we are not satisfied to have the law one way and the practice the other way. If we could be sure that the practice would remain the way we want it, it would make no difference of course. But with such a Government as we have to-day or with such a Government as we may have from time to time we are not sure that the winking will be carried on as steadily as heretofore, particularly when it is done for one purpose only, and that to induce us to come in under the public schools. But by winking they have allowed the separate schools to continue, only they must be carried on under the name of public schools.

Sir CHAS. HIBBERT TUPPER.—And I suppose that what you are afraid of is that it may be a long time between winks.

Mr. EWART.—That is very well put in. That is what we fear.

My learned friend undertook to give a definition of national schools. I think he was not successful. He said that national schools are those common to and enforcible upon all inhabitants. He thought they might be even denominational schools so long as there was only one system, but there must be only one system or they would not be national schools. I would oppose to that this definition :—National schools are those that are governed by the nation ; and I would add that in order to be truly national they must provide for the nation and not for a party. Now I say that my learned friend's definition is wrong in so far as it implies that it is a necessary feature of national schools that they should be enforcible upon all. Surely there can be national schools even though you have no compulsory clause. I say also he is wrong in saying that there must be one system for all. In England we have separate denominational schools as well as the public schools and one of the provisions is that these must be open to all. Yet my learned friend would not agree that these were national schools. In defence of my definition I would say that national schools are those governed by the nation, just as church schools are those governed by the church, just as denominational schools are those governed by the denominations. National schools are those governed by the nation, just as we say national railways are those owned and regulated by the government. It does not follow that all schools must be upon one system ; it is not necessary they should be exactly alike. I do not think it is a necessary part of a national railway system that all the railways should be of one gauge. We could have a national costume and yet have a great variety of tartans. Suppose there was a system of national schools in which, in Protestant districts, the Protestant religion was taught, and the Catholic districts the Catholic religion was taught, but all governed, regulated and inspected by the nation. Would the fact that one form of religious exercise was carried on in one and another form of religious exercise in another make these non-national schools. In order to be national they must provide for the education of the nation. What are the schools we have in Manitoba? They are national in the sense that they are governed by law, by Parliament, but they are not national in the sense of providing for the nation. In fact they leave a large part of the nation unprovided for, because they are schools that a large part of the nation will not attend. I claim that the schools that exist in Ontario to-day known as separate schools, are national schools. They are called separate schools as a name to distinguish them. Just as in a railway station you will find different waiting rooms, one for ladies, one for gentlemen. Nevertheless these are all public rooms. So in Ontario, some schools are intended for non-Catholics and some for Catholics, but all are national schools, each providing for a large part of the public and controlled by the government.

Now a few words with reference to the New Brunswick case. My learned friend gave you the whole history of the divisions upon that. What are the results as declared by the Dominion of Canada? One result is that the New Brunswick Acts were unjust, and the people had a grievance. That is fairly enough to be inferred from the different resolutions. Another result is that these Acts ought to have been disallowed, for Mr. Costigan's resolution of 1873 was passed so declaring. In the third place we see why the Dominion did not interfere in that case, viz.: because they had no jurisdiction to intervene, or they would have done so. Mr. Mackenzie, the leader of the Government after 1873 so stated in one of the paragraphs my learned friend read. In the fourth place we see that Her Majesty the Queen was asked to use Her influence to secure a remedy for the injustice that was done to the Roman Catholics of New Brunswick. The fifth point determined is that though there was an injustice, Parliament would go no further than asking Her Majesty to use her influence, but would not ask for such radical relief as an amendment of the whole constitution of the Dominion of Canada. Now, these results seem to me to be very important and to point in an entirely different direction from that indicated by my learned friend. He drew this inference from the history of the New Brunswick case, that Parliament would never interfere, that it was the declared policy of Parliament never to interfere, with any matters relating to education. I have shown you that the contrary conclusions are the ones to be drawn from an attentive perusal of the history of the case.

Then my learned friend says there are very few Roman Catholics in Manitoba, only from ten to fifteen thousand, and that therefore no very great damage will be done after all. That is just the trouble. If there were a few more we would not have to face this difficulty. When Mr. Martin first introduced these School Acts in the local legislature they provided for purely secular schools. The Protestants got together at once, headed by their ministers—which is a very proper thing for Protestants to do, but very wrong for Catholics—and they brought such influence to bear that Mr. Martin was forced to change his Act and to make it conform to their ideas regarding schools. But the Catholics were not strong enough to do that, and so they had to suffer. I do not think it makes it any the more creditable—my learned friend would say manly I suppose—that the people upon whom the injustice is perpetrated are few in number. We have it clearly enough established that the Government did not do what they wanted to do because they were opposed by those who were strong, but with regard to those who were weak the Government did what they pleased. My learned friend says—or rather if we may infer from his words at page 30 which I have quoted, he thinks—that no great harm will be done, because after all the people are so tolerant that they will "wink at infractions of the law" and so there will be in effect a separate school system !

My learned friend has been endowed by nature with faculties of unusually high order; let me beseech him to reflect upon the disrupting purposes to which he has for the last few years been applying his great talents. Let him remember that had it not been for him the "sleepy" Protestants of the province of Quebec would never have believed that they had suffered wrong or insult by the passage of the Jesuits Estates Act; and the unfortunate animosities stirred up by his agitation would never have been aroused.

Let him remember that had it not been for him, the Protestants of Manitoba would never have known that they had a grievance in the matter of Catholic schools; that but for him, the fellowship and respect, which prior to 1890 existed between Protestant and Catholic, between Presbyterian and Jesuit, would never have been interrupted, and that that harmony and co-operation between religious bodies which are so beneficial, not only for education but for religion itself, would never have been, as I am afraid they have been destroyed.

I beg of him to remember, that while it may be proper that respect should be paid in provincial legislation to the feelings of a small body of men in another province— namely to those of the members of an association which sprang up in a night and died in a night, it is all the more proper that respect should be paid to the feelings of a large body of men in the same province, and to the feelings of two millions of people in the other provinces.

Let him above all remember that the golden rule was not made for the use of Catholics and for the advantage of Protestants ; but for Protestants and Catholics alike, for him and for me, and for all the world beside.

Let him turn from his efforts to awake "sleepy" Protestants in Quebec, and arouse satisfied Protestants in Manitoba, to conflict with those they have learned to respect, and let him learn from him whom he so long followed politically— and not from him only but from Mackenzie, Blake, Mowat and all the great leaders upon both sides of politics—that Canada's true national greatness can never be attained by force and coercion of large and important minorities, but by a spirit of fairness and sympathy—a sympathy which when it attains the ideal will mould all the religions of the world into one, all-embracing, religion of love.

My last words, I am glad to say are words of agreement with my learned friend in thanking you for the patience with which you have listened to this long, and, speaking for myself, I fear, very tedious argument.

Sir CHARLES HIBBERT TUPPER.—I would like to ask if you had considered the form of any remedial order ? You submitted a bill ; have you thought of any form of remedial order ?

Mr. EWART.—To some extent I have, and I would suggest the adoption of the form of order which proceeds from the Judicial Committee of the Privy Council. Rather this, at all events, than the form usually followed in Orders in Council of a report of the committee and the adoption of that report. I do not think it would be proper to proceed in that way, because I think the committee has no jurisdiction to hear us, but the whole Council had, and the whole Council has heard us.

Hon. Mr. IVES.—Can you give the Council anything like an accurate estimate of the children of school age in Manitoba ?

Hon. Senator BERNIER.—There are about 6,000.

Mr. MCCARTHY.—I have here the report of the Department of Education of Manitoba for the year 1893. I do not know that the figures are wholly accurate, but they will show approximately the school population in that year.

Sir MACKENZIE BOWELL. -The petition which Mr. Ewart asked for is upon the table for his use.

Mr. EWART.—I did not know that I was to have this petition this morning. As it is here, may I be allowed to say a few words in answer to the statement that I represent only the French element. I refer to the original petition put in, which contains 4,267 names. Reference to this document will show that it is signed by French and by Irish and English indifferently. And the names upon it, the Roman Catholic population of Manitoba being about fifteen thousand, represent more than 25 per cent of that whole Catholic population, men, women and children.

Mr. MCCARTHY.—I was going to suggest to the President that with regard to the so-called fourth list of rights, said to have been introduced at the trial of Regina v. Lepine, a certified copy of which is filed, it would be well if the Minister of Justice would have a copy of the evidence regarding it put in at the same time.

Sir CHAS. HIBBERT TUPPER.—You mean the evidence regarding it when it was put in ?

Mr. MCCARTHY.—Yes. When it was put in at the criminal trial. It might be of historical interest to know that.

Sir MACKENZIE BOWELL.—As the argument is finished this Council will now adjourn.

The Council then adjourned.

EXHIBIT A.

In the matter of the appeal of the Roman Catholic minority of the Queen's subjects in the Province of Manitoba to His Excellency the Governor General in Council, from two certain acts of the Legislature of said province, being chapters 37 and 38 of 53 Victoria, intituled respectively : "An Act respecting the Department of Education," and "An Act respecting Public Schools."

I, Noel Joseph Ritchot, of the parish of St. Norbert, in the province of Manitoba, parish priest of the Roman Catholic Church, make oath and say :

1. I was a resident of the Red River Settlement in and prior to the year 1870, and resided then as now about nine miles from the present city of Winnipeg.

2. I was one of the three delegates that were sent from the said settlement in that year to negotiate with the Government of the Dominion of Canada as to the terms upon which Rupert's Land and the North-west Territories were to be united to Canada. The other two delegates were Judge Black and Mr. Alfred H. Scott.

3. The instructions I received were in writing and consisted of three documents. True copies of two of these documents are hereto annexed and marked with the letters A and B, and the third was a bill of rights (Exhibit B), the seventh clause of which was as follows : "That the schools be separate and that the public money for schools be distributed among the different denominations in proportion to their respective populations according to the system of the province of Quebec."

4. I received these documents together and I never received any other bill of rights than the one aforesaid. The other delegates had with them at Ottawa bills of rights similar to the one aforsaid.

5. The said delegates had frequent and protracted conferences with Sir John A. Macdonald and Sir George E. Cartier who had been appointed a committee by the Canadian Government for the purpose of negotiating with us, which conferences extended to the second day of May.

6. During the said negotiations the said committee submitted to the delegates a draft of a bill containing the terms upon which they were prepared to consummate the union. This bill contained 26 clauses and the 19th thereof was an adaptation of section 93 of the British North America Act.

7. Upon the margin of the said draft bill I wrote my comments or remarks opposite each of the sections. Opposite the said clause 19 I wrote as follows :

"Cette clause étant la même que celle de l'Acte de l'Amérique Britannique du Nord, confère, je l'interprète ainsi, comme principe fondamental le privilège des écoles séparées dans toute la plénitude et, en cela est conforme à l'article 7 de nos instructions."

Which is equivalent in English to,—

" This clause being the same as the British North America Act, confers, so I interpret it, as fundamental principle, the privilege of separate schools to the fullest extent, and in that is in conformity with article 7 of our instructions."

8. I returned to the said committee the said draft bill with my remarks and comments written thereon as aforesaid and with the said memo. opposite the said clause 19.

9. After the conferences with the delegates were completed Sir George E. Cartier on the third day of May introduced into the House of Commons the bill which afterwards became the Manitoba Act.

10. Shortly afterwards I returned to the Red River Settlement carrying with me a copy of the said Act which on the twenty-fourth day of June I presented with some verbal report of my mission to the Legislative Assembly. After a short discussion the following resolution was amid cheering unanimously passed :—

"That the Legislative Assembly of this country do now, in the name of the people " accept the Manitoba Act and decide on entering the Dominion of Canada on the terms proposed in the Confederation Act."

11. The copy of the bill of rights which I received as aforesaid prior to my departure for Ottawa I retained in my own possession until the trial of Lepine in 1874 for the murder of Thomas Scott. At that trial I was called as a witness and did as such produce to and leave in the custody of the court the said copy of the bill of rights, since which time I have never seen it.

N. J. RITCHOT, O.M.I.

Sworn before me at St. Norbert, in the
province of Manitoba, this twenty-
first day of February, 1895.

G. CLOUTIER,
A Commissioner, &c.

MAISON GOUVERNEMENTALE, WINNIPEG.

Au Rev. Mons. Joseph N. Ritchot :

MONSIEUR,—Avec cette lettre vous recevrez aussi votre commission et une copie des conditions sous lesquelles le peuple de ce pays consentirait à entrer dans la confédération canadienne.

Vous vous rendrez aussi diligemment que faire se pourra en Canada, à Ottawa, et en arrivant en cette ville vous vous mettrez en compagnie de MM. l'honorable M. A. Scott et l'honorable John Black, pour entamer immédiatement avec le gouvernement de la Puissance du Canada les négociations qui font le sujet de votre commission.

Veuillez, s'il vous plait, observer que quant aux articles numérotés 1, 2, 3, 4, 6, 7, 15, 17, 19 et 20, vous pourrez, de concert avec les autres commissaires sus-mentionnés, les traiter librement et à discrétion ; mais n'oubliez jamais que puisque la confiance entière de ce peuple repose sur vous, on compte que, vous prévalant de cette liberté, vous ferez tout ce qui est en votre pouvoir, afin de nous assurer ces droits et libertés qui nous ont été jusqu'ici refusés.

A l'égard des autres articles, je suis chargé de vous informer qu'ils sont péremptoires.

Je dois en outre vous signifier que vous n'avez nullement le pouvoir de mener à conclusion finale aucun arrangement et que toute négociation conduite par vous auprès du gouvernement du Canada, devra préalablement recevoir la sanction du gouvernement provisoire.

J'ai l'honneur d'être, Monsieur et Révérend,
Votre très humble et obéissant serviteur,
THOS. BUNN
22 mars 1870. *Sect. of State.*

A MESSIRE J. N. RITCHOT, PTRE.

MONSIEUR,—Le président du gouvernement provisoire d'Assiniboïa en conseil vous met par les présentes en autorité et en délégation, vous, le révérend Messire J. N. Ritchot, en compagnie de Monsieur John Black, écuyer, et de l'honorable A. Scott, afin que vous vous dirigiez à Ottawa, en Canada ; et que là vous placiez devant le parlement canadien la liste qui vous sera confiée avec les présentes, liste qui contient les conditions et les propositions sous lesquelles le peuple d'Assiniboïa consentirait à entrer en confédération avec les autres provinces du Canada.

Signé ce vingt-deuxième jour de mars en l'an de Notre-Seigneur mil huit cent soixante-dix.

Par ordre,
THOS. BUNN,
Sec. of State.

Siège du gouvernement,
Winnipeg, Assiniboïa.

EXHIBIT B.

1. Que les territoires ci-devant connus sous le nom de terre de Rupert et du Nord-Ouest n'entreront dans la confédération de la Puissance du Canada qu'à titre de province et comme sous le nom de province d'Assiniboïa et jouissant de tous les droits et privilèges communs aux différentes provinces de la Puissance.

2. Que jusqu'au temps où l'accroissement de la population de ce pays nous ait donné droit à plus nous ayons deux représentants au Sénat et quatre aux Communes du Canada.

3. Qu'en entrant dans la confédération, la province d'Assiniboïa complètement étrangère à la dette publique du Canada et que si elle était appelée à assumer quelque partie de cette dette du Canada ce ne soit qu'après avoir reçu du Canada la somme même dont on voudrait qu'elle se rendit responsable.

4. Que la somme annuelle de quatre-vingt mille piastres soit allouée par la Puissance du Canada à la législature de la province du Nord-Ouest.

5. Que toutes les propriétés, tous les droits et privilèges possédés soient respectés, et que la reconnaissance et l'arrangement des coutumes, usages et privilèges soient laissés à la décision de la législature locale seulement.

6. Que ce pays ne soit soumis à aucune taxe directe à l'exception de celles qui pourraient être imposées par la législature locale pour des intérêts municipaux ou locaux.

7. Que les écoles soient séparées et que les argents pour écoles soient divisés entre les différentes dénominations religieuses au *pro rata* de leur population respective.

8. Que la détermination des qualifications des membres au parlement de la province ou à celui du Canada soit laissée à la législature locale.

9. Que dans ce pays à l'exception des indiens qui ne sont ni civilisés ni établis, tout homme ayant atteint l'âge de vingt et un ans et tout sujet anglais étranger à cette province mais ayant résidé trois ans dans ce pays et possédant une maison, ait le droit de voter aux élections des membres de la législature locale et du parlement canadien et que tout sujet étranger autre que sujet anglais ayant résidé le même temps et jouissant de la propriété d'une maison ait le même droit de vote à condition qu'il prête serment de fidélité.

Il est entendu que cet article n'est sujet à amendement que de la part de la législature locale exclusivement.

10. Que le marché de la Compagnie de la Baie-d'Hudson au sujet du transfert du gouvernement de ce pays à la Puissance du Canada, soit considéré comme nul en autant qu'il est contraire aux droits du peuple d'Assiniboïa et qu'il peut affecter nos relations futures avec le Canada.

11. Que la législature locale de cette province ait plein contrôle sur toutes les terres de la province et ait le droit d'annuler tous les arrangements faits ou commencés au sujet des terres publiques de R. Land et du Nord-Ouest appelé maintenant province d'Assiniboïa (Manitoba).

12. Qu'une commission d'ingénieurs nommés par le Canada ait à explorer les divers terrains du Nord-Ouest et à déposer devant la Chambre législative dans le terme de cinq ans un rapport sur la richesse minérale du pays.

13. Que des traités soient conclus entre le Canada et les différentes tribus sauvages du pays à la réquisition et avec le concours de la législature locale.

14. Que l'on garantisse une communication continue à vapeur du lac Supérieur au Fort-Garry à être complétée dans l'espace de cinq ans.

15. Que toutes les bâtisses et édifices publics soient à la charge du trésor canadien ainsi que les ponts, chemins et autres travaux publics.

16. Que les langues française et anglaise soient communes dans la législature et les cours, et que tous les documents publics ainsi que les actes de la législature soient publiés dans les deux langues.

(Raison exprimées en anglais.)

17. Que le lieutenant-gouverneur à nommer pour la province du Nord-Ouest possède les deux langues française et anglaise.

18. Que le juge de la cour Suprême parle le français et l'anglais.

19. Que les dettes contractées par le gouvernement provisoire du Nord Ou st soient payées par le trésor de la Puissance du Canada, vu que ces dettes n'ont été contractées que par suite des mesures illégales et inconsidérées adoptées par les agents canadiens pour amener la guerre civile au milieu de nous. De plus, qu'aucun des membres du gouvernement proviso re, non plus que ceux qui ont agi sous sa direction, ne puisse être inquiété relativement au mouvement qui a déterminé les négociations actuelles.

20. Que, en vue de la position exceptionnelle d'Assiniboia, les droits sur les marchandises importées dans la province, excepté sur les liqueurs, continueront à être les mêmes qu'à présent d'ici à trois ans à dater de notre entrée dans la confédération, et aussi longtemps ensuite que les voies de communication par chemin de fer ne seront pas terminées entre Saint-Paul et Winnipeg, ainsi qu'entre Winnipeg et le lac Supérieur.

A true copy of exhibit "N" in the trial of Lépine on record in this department.

L. A. CATELLIER,
Under Secretary of State.

A true copy :
DANIEL CASEY,
Clerk of Crown and Peace.

EXHIBIT C.

IN the matter of the appeal of the Roman Catholic minority of the Queen's subjects in the province of Manitoba to His Excellency the Governor General in Council, from two certain Acts of the Legislature of said province, being chapters 37 and 38 of 53 Victoria, intituled : "An Act respecting the Department of Education" and "An Act respecting Public Schools."

I, James Fisher, of the city of Winnipeg, in the province of Manitoba, barrister-at-law, make oath and say :—

1. I have taken an active part in the discussion of public affairs in this province for over ten years past, and am familiar with the course of provincial politics since the year eighteen hundred and eighty-three.

2. The present provincial government, of which Mr. Thomas Greenway is the head, took office in the month of January, eighteen hundred and eighty-eight. For many years before that time and up to about December, eighteen hundred and eighty-seven, the late Mr. John Norquay had been at the head of the government. He then retired and was succeeded by Dr. D. H. Harrison, who had been one of Mr. Norquay's colleagues and of the same political party with him, and who held office for only a few weeks, when he resigned, and Mr. Greenway became Premier.

3. Between the years eighteen hundred and eighty-three and the end of eighteen hundred and eighty-seven a very active opposition had been offered to Mr. Norquay's administration. This opposition was chiefly maintained by an organization of the Liberals of the province. That organization was at first particularly active in the city of Winnipeg, where a Liberal association was formed in eighteen hundred and eighty-four ; afterwards like organizations were formed throughout the province, and eventually a provincial organization.

4. I was for a number of years the president of the association at Winnipeg, as also of the provincial organization, and I was at the time the change of government took place in eighteen hundred and eighty-eight the president of the provincial association.

5. Amongst other things it was charged against the Norquay administration that there was a wasteful expenditure by government in the matter of public printing in the French language, and also that Mr. Norquay had failed to bring before the Legislature

a fair scheme for redistribution of seats in the House, it being charged by Liberals that in the old settlements along the Red River and lower Assiniboine the population had a larger representation than they should have, leaving the western and more newly settled part of the province without sufficient representation.

6. Amongst the electoral districts along the Red River and lower Assiniboine referred to, there were six constituencies which were usually spoken of as, and admitted to be French constituencies, that is in which the French-speaking population had a large majority of the votes, and the fact that the Liberal party were insisting upon a redistribution of seats coupled with their attacks upon the expenditure for French printing led to the Liberals being charged with political antipathy to the French and Roman Catholic population, the great majority of whom throughout the province were at that time supporters of the Norquay regime.

7. At the general election of eighteen hundred and eighty-six, of the six French electoral districts, five returned supporters of Mr. Norquay (three of them being elected by acclamation) and Mr. A. F. Martin, a Liberal, was elected to represent the sixth.

8. One of the districts that then elected a supporter of Mr. Norquay by acclamation was St. François Xavier, which returned Mr. Joseph Burke. The majority of the electors in that district were French speaking and Catholic as the Liberal leaders at all events understood, and they in fact controlled the seat.

9. When Dr. Harrison formed his government the said Mr. Joseph Burke accepted the office of Provincial Secretary in the administration.

10. The Liberal party were at that time confident that the Norquay Government had been considerably weakened as a result of the agitation of the past few years. Mr. Norquay's majority in the legislature was small; it was thought that one or two of his supporters in the House were ready to withdraw their allegiance when a convenient opportunity might arise, and it was the general opinion amongst Liberals that Mr. Norquay's retirement had been brought about and Dr. Harrison put in his place with the view of strengthening the Conservative party, and when the change took place the more active workers in the Liberal organization deemed it essential that a supreme effort should be made to defeat the new administration before it fairly got to work.

11. The opportunity that the Liberals desired seemed to be presented when Mr. Burke went back for re-election on taking office. It was recognized that he was in many respects peculiarly strong in his district. He was a resident merchant in the neighbourhood, and a Roman Catholic; and the French language, as we understood, was his mother tongue. The French-speaking electors in the district had been practically all supporters of the Conservative party, and it was quite impossible to carry the election without receiving a considerable portion of that vote.

12. At the same time certain reasons had led to the Conservative party being weakened in the district, and after full inquiry and consideration it was concluded that there was a fair chance of electing a Liberal candidate if the prejudice that was felt to exist amongst the French speaking and Roman Catholic population against the Liberals for the reasons already stated could be avoided.

13. Eventually Mr. F. H. Francis, an English-speaking merchant' resident in or near the district, and a Protestant, entered the field as the Liberal candidate.

14. The question of placing a candidate in the field was considered and the arrangements for the campaign were conducted in Winnipeg and I was present at several of the meetings that were then held for said purposes, and I was familiar with the different considerations which guided us in our conclusions and that led to our support of Mr. Francis.

15. I remember that Mr. Francis expressed himself very strongly during the campaign upon the question of the attitude of Liberals towards the French-speaking population, and especially as to their attitude on the question of interfering with the special privilege claimed by that population in respect to the use of the French language and schools. He gave us to understand, and we were fully convinced, that it was useless to contest the seat unless we could satisfy the electors that the Liberals were not to attack these privileges of the French and Catholic population in the event of their attaining power. It was well understood that this expressed the real attitude of

the party on these questions and I was informed that Mr. Francis was expressly authorized by the Liberal leaders to give a pledge to that effect.

16. During the progress of the campaign it came to the knowledge of the Liberal organizers in Winnipeg that a strong appeal was being made to the electors of the district to defeat Mr. Francis because of the fear that the Liberals would interfere with the privileges aforesaid and it was felt that this question must be promptly met.

17. At that time the leading representatives of the Liberals in the legislature were Mr. Thomas Greenway, who afterwards became Premier, and Mr. Joseph Martin who became the Attorney General in his administration, and they were undoubtedly the recognized leaders of the party, Mr. Greenway being the leader in the House. Mr. Martin was at that time resident in Winnipeg and Mr. Greenway was also in the city during the campaign and they both took a very active interest in it. Mr. Greenway chiefly taking charge of that part of the campaign which was conducted in the city, and it was left largely to Mr. A. F. Martin above named to organize and look after the work in the district and especially amongst the French-speaking population.

18. At the request of Mr. Joseph Martin I attended a meeting with him at the Roman Catholic school-house at St. François-Xavier on the evening before the election day. Our special object in attending there was to meet this particular charge as to the attitude of the Liberals towards those particular privileges of the French and Roman Catholic population.

19. It was then well known by the leading Liberals in Winnipeg who were interesting themselves in the campaign that at a meeting held some nights before in another part of the district Mr. Joseph Martin had been present, that Mr. Norquay had addressed the meeting and in very strong terms repeated this charge, and that Mr. Martin had effectively answered the charge by utterly denying that such was or would be the attitude of the Liberals and that he had squarely placed the Liberal policy before the electors as one entirely opposed to any such interference, as was suggested.

20. At the meeting at St. François-Xavier which Mr. Martin and I attended, the large majority of the electors present were at the time said to be and I have no doubt were French speaking and Roman Catholic. Mr. Burke was present and addressed the meeting, and according to my recollection he spoke before Mr. Martin did; at all events the same charges were made by our opponents against the Liberal party and the same appeals to oppose their candidate upon the grounds referred to. Mr. Martin then delivered a strong address to the meeting in which he characterized these allegations as to the attitude of Liberals as being utterly without foundation; he declared in the most positive terms that the Liberals had no thought of interfering with these institutions and made a positive declaration that if they attained office, they would not do so. He referred to my presence there as the president of the Liberal organization for the province, and said that if necessary, I would confirm what he said on the subject. I was not, according to my recollection, called upon to say anything, nor did I make any statement, but I would certainly have confirmed his statement had there seemed to be any occasion for it, and undoubtedly the statement of Mr. Martin, on the question and the pledges that he gave were entirely in accord with the position that I understood the Liberal party held, and they were in accord with what had been stated in Winnipeg at the meetings connected with the campaign, and our purpose in attending the meeting was to make a statement of that character with the view of satisfying the French and Roman Catholic electors.

21. It was never doubted amongst the Liberal leaders, and there is, I think, no doubt of the fact that the defeat at that time of Mr. Burke led to the resignation of the Harrison administration and the advent of the Liberals into power. I know that it was felt, throughout the whole campaign, by the Liberals who took charge of it, that the contest was a crucial one that was to decide which party should for some years in future hold office. We all felt that if Mr. Burke was elected and Mr. Harrison enabled to carry on the work of the session which had then actually opened, he would soon strengthen himself in power, and I have now no doubt that but for the result of that election the Conservatives would have still been in power in the province. It was also universally admitted at the time, and there cannot be a doubt of the fact, that the said election could not have been carried by the Liberals without a considerable number of

the French speaking and Roman Catholic voters, and the declaration of the Liberal policy was made, and the pledges as to the future action of the party given in order to secure that vote.

Sworn before me, at Winnipeg, in the
province of Manitoba, this 19th day
of February, A.D. 1895.

JAMES FISHER.

A. N. McPHERSON,
    A Commissioner, &c.

EXHIBIT D.

In the matter of the appeal of the Roman Catholic minority of the Queen's subjects in the province of Manitoba to His Excellency the Governor General in Council, from two certain Acts of the legislature of said province, being chapters 37 and 38 of 53 Victoria, intituled respectively " An Act respecting the Department of Education " and " An Act respecting Public Schools."

I, Alphonse Fortunat Martin, of the city of Winnipeg, in the province of Manitoba, Esquire, make oath and say :—

1. During the election contest between the Honourable Joseph Burke, as a member of the Conservative party, and Mr. F. H. Francis, as a member of the Liberal party, in the constituency of St. François Xavier, in the month of January, eighteen hundred and eighty-eight, I was the one appointed by the leaders of the Liberal party to organize and conduct the campaign on behalf of Mr. Francis.

2. I found in conducting the said campaign, that I was being constantly met with the assertion that the Liberal party was opposed to the further continuance of the Catholic schools and the use of the French language, and I thought it was necessary that in some public way, assurances should be given of undoubted character to the electors. For this purpose, I called two meetings, one on the seventh of January, eighteen hundred and eighty-eight, at the schoolhouse, at Le Petit Canada, and the other, on the eleventh of January, eighteen hundred and eighty-eight, at the school house at St. François Xavier, and both in the same constituency. I asked Mr. Joseph Martin, who was then one of the most prominent members of the Liberal party, to be present at both meetings, and to give assurances which I thought were necessary as above mentioned. He made upon each occasion a strong address to the meeting in which he characterized the allegations as to the attitude of Liberals upon the questions aforesaid as being utterly without foundation. He declared in the most positive terms, that the Liberals had no thought of interfering with those institutions ; and made a positive declaration, that if they attained office they would not do so ; and said that, if Liberals did such a thing he would leave the Liberal party for ever.

3. At the meeting on the eleventh day of January already referred to, Mr. James Fisher, who was then the President of the Liberal party in the province of Manitoba, was present during Mr. Martin's speech, and towards the end of Mr. Martin's address he pointed to Mr. Fisher as being the President of the Liberal party, and said that he (Mr. Fisher) would confirm, if necessary, what he had said as to the principles of the Liberal party.

4. The effect of these speeches was very great and to that alone can be attributed the fact that Mr. Francis was elected by the said constituency. Without these assurances given by Mr. Martin there can be no question that Mr. Burke would have been elected by a large majority.

5. The Joseph Martin referred to is the same Joseph Martin who became the Attorney General in the administration formed by Mr. Greenway, and it was under the auspices of the said administration and at their instance that the Acts referred to in the caption of this affidavit were passed.

Sworn before me, at the city of Winnipeg, in the province of Manitoba, this 20th day of February, A.D. 1895.

A. F. MARTIN.

HUGH ARMSTRONG,
 A Commissioner.

EXHIBIT E.

WINNIPEG, MAN., Feb. 21st, 1891.

To the Editor of the *Free Press*,
 Winnipeg, Man.

SIR,—For the reasons hereinafter given, I think the time has arrived when I should make the statement of facts in connection with the election contest between Mr. Jos. Burke and myself in St. François Xavier, in January, 1888, which has been the subject of discussion from time to time in the papers, and I beg that you will therefore publish the following statement of the facts in connection with that election as coming from me:—

I have been a resident of the village of Headingly, in the province of Manitoba, for the past sixteen years, and have there carried on for many years a general mercantile business. I was the Liberal candidate for election to represent the district of St. François Xavier in the legislature of Manitoba, in the election that took place in the month of January, 1888, my opponent being Mr. Jos. Burke, who had been elected to represent the constituency at the general election held in 1886, and who, having at the time referred to, accepted office in the administration formed by Dr. Harrison, had gone back for re-election by his constituents.

I entered into the said contest with the assent and approval of the leaders of the Liberal party in Winnipeg, including Mr. Greenway and Mr. Martin, and also Mr. Fisher, who, as I understand, was president of the Liberal Association for the province.

The election was looked upon as exceedingly important—one which, it was felt, was going to decide whether the Harrison administration should continue in power or not, as it was felt that the Conservative government had been weakened and that Dr. Harrison would be forced to retire should Mr. Burke be defeated.

The constituency was one of the French-speaking constituencies of the province, so called. About two-thirds of the electors in the district were French speaking and Roman Catholic in religion, and it was manifestly impossible to carry the election without securing the votes of a large number of the French-speaking electors.

Mr. Burke had been for many years also carrying on a mercantile business in the near neighbourhood, and was well known in the district. He is himself a Roman Catholic who came from the province of Quebec, and speaks French equally well with English.

Early in the campaign I found that a very serious cry was raised against the Liberal party on the ground, as it was alleged by Mr. Burke and his friends, that the Liberal party if they got into power were likely to pass legislation interfering with the rights and privileges of the French and Catholic population of the province in respect of the use of the French language and as to the schools, and because of my being a candidate of the Liberal party an appeal was made to the French speaking and Catholic electors to defeat me on that ground.

I had certainly never understood or supposed that it had ever been the policy of the Liberal party to interfere with these rights and privileges, and I would most decidedly have been opposed to such an interference, and I felt that unless I took a decided position upon this question it was utterly useless for me to continue in the field as a Liberal candidate.

Because of this, I waited upon Mr. Jos. Martin, then one of the Liberal leaders already named, who afterwards became the Attorney General of the province, and explained to him the situation, and I gave him to understand that unless the attitude of the Liberal party was made clear as not seeking to or intending to interfere with these rights and privileges, I should certainly not remain in the field.

Thereupon, I received assurances from Mr. Martin that satisfied me that the Liberals would not interfere with these rights and privileges, and which enabled me to take that attitude before the electors and to declare it as the attitude of the Liberal party, and I continued in the field and the result was that I was elected.

Mr. Martin himself came into the riding during the campaign and addressed certainly one, and possibly, two meetings at which I was present, and the principal object of his coming out was in order to refute and deny the allegations that were being made by our opponents, as to the alleged attitude of the Liberals upon the questions referred to, and certainly, at one such meeting, he spoke in strong terms denying that it was any part of the Liberal policy to interfere with these institutions, or that it was ever intended to do so, and I believe his statements went a long way to satisfy the minds of the French electors who were inclined to support me, and I believe that because of their being satisfied upon these points through my declarations and those of Mr. Martin, I received their support and secured the election.

It is beyond question that I could not have been elected had no such assurances been given to the electors as aforesaid, and there is no doubt that the immediate result of the election was the downfall of the Harrison administration and the advent into power of Mr. Greenway and Mr. Martin.

At the meeting that I particularly remember, Mr. Martin being present, Mr. Fisher, the president of the Provincial Liberal Association was also present and his presence was referred to as confirming what Mr. Martin stated, and Mr. Fisher either by silence or by nod or language gave consent to Mr. Martin's statements, at all events he was understood by the electors to concur in what Mr. Martin had said.

I have noticed from time to time statements that have been made in the press and in the legislature since the passage of the School Act of 1890, referring to the pledges given by Mr. Martin in St. François Xavier that I have referred to. I have not up to this time myself made any statement publicly on the question, and I desire to add in this statement that my silence hitherto arose that up to this time the question has been a legal one before the courts, and I deemed it better not to interfere in the matter. I desire also to add that my willingness to make a statement now arises not from a desire on my part so much to help one side or the other in the present contention as to put myself on record as entirely opposed to the agitation for the elimination of religious exercises from the public schools. I would also add that as a large number of the constituents were well known to me and customers at my store I think it just to myself to make the present statement.

Yours truly,

F. H. FRANCIS.

EXHIBIT F.

In the matter of the appeal of the Roman Catholic minority of the Queen's subjects in the province of Manitoba to His Excellency the Governor General in Council from two certain Acts of the legislature of said province, being chapters 37 and 38 of 53 Victoria, intituled respectively : " An Act respecting the Department of Education " and " An Act respecting Public Schools."

I, Joseph Burke, of the city of Winnipeg, but formerly of the parish of St. François Xavier, in the province of Manitoba, merchant, make oath and say as follows :—

1. At the general election for the Legislative Assembly of the province of Manitoba held in the year one thousand eight hundred and eighty-six, I was elected for the constituency of St. François Xavier, by acclamation, as a supporter of the then Norquay administration.

2. In the year one thousand eight hundred and eighty-seven, Mr. Harrison became leader of the government, and he asked me to take the portfolio of provincial secretary in his administration. I accordingly did so, and was sworn in as provincial secretary in such administration about the last of December, one thousand eight hundred and eighty-seven.

3. A writ was immediately issued for an election in my constituency which had become vacant by reason of my acceptance of office, and the election was fixed for the twelfth day of January, one thousand eight hundred and eigty-eight.

4. It was well known that the fate of the Harrison administration depended upon this election, and the Opposition placed in the field as opposed to me Mr. F. H. Francis, a store-keeper at Headingly, in the said constituency.

5. The large majority of the electors in the said constituency were members of the Roman Catholic church. I was a member of that church while Mr. Francis was a Protestant. The Harrison administration belonged to the political party commonly known as the Liberal-Conservatives. Mr. Francis was a candidate on the part of the political party known as Liberals.

6. At and prior to this period it had been frequently charged against the Liberal party that they were not in sympathy with the privileges enjoyed by the French-speaking part of the population and the Roman Catholics, and it was feared by many members of that nationality and religion that if the Liberals came into office that those privileges would be curtailed or entirely abolished. During the election to which I have above referred there was a great deal of discussion as to this attitude of the Liberal party and it was urged by me and many supporters and canvassers on my behalf that the Liberals were opposed to the privileges above referred to.

7. In order to meet these charges, two meetings were called on behalf of the Liberal candidate in the said constituency, one of which was held at a school-house at a place called Le Petit Canada, on the seventh of January, and the other was held at the school-house at St. Francois Xavier village, on the eleventh day of January. At both of these meetings Mr. Joseph Martin, who was then one of the leaders and one of the most prominent men of the Liberal party, appeared and made a speech to the electors of the said constituency ; he made upon each occasion a strong address to the meeting in which he characterized the allegations as to the attitude of the Liberals upon the questions aforesaid as being utterly without foundation. He declared in the most positive terms that the Liberals had no thought of interfering with those institutions ; and made a positive declaration that if they attained office they would not do so ; and said that if the Liberals did such a thing he would leave the Liberal party for ever.

8. At the meeting of the eleventh day of January, already referred to, Mr. James Fisher, who was then the President of the Liberal party in the province of Manitoba, was present during Mr. Martin's speech, and towards the end of Mr. Martin's address he pointed to Mr. Fisher as being the president of the Liberal party, and said that he (Mr. Fisher) would confirm, if it were necessary, what he had said as to the principles of the Liberal party.

9. The effect of these speeches was very great, and to that alone can be attributed the fact that Mr. Francis was elected by the said constituency. Without these assurances given by Mr. Martin, there can be no question that I would have been elected by a very large majority.

10. The said Harrison administration resigned office on the sixteenth day of said month of January, and such resignation was due entirely to the fact of my being defeated in the said constituency. Mr. Greenway, the leader of the Liberals, was immediately afterwards sent for, and undertook to and did form an administration which has remained in office till the present time.

11. The Joseph Martin above referred to is the same Joseph Martin who became the Attorney General in the administration formed by Mr. Greenway, and it was under the auspices of the said administration and at their instance that the Acts referred to in the caption of this affidavit were passed.

Sworn before me at Winnipeg, in the province of Manitoba, this 19th day of February, 1895.

JOSEPH BURKE.

ALFRED J. ANDREWS,
A Commissioner in B. R., &c., and Notary Public.

EXHIBIT G.

In the matter of the appeal of the Roman Catholic minority of the Queen's subjects in the province of Manitoba to His Excellency the Governor General in Council, from two certain Acts of the legislature of the said province, being chapters 37 and 38 of 53 Victoria, intituled respectively : " An Act respecting the Department of Education " and " An Act respecting Public Schools."

I, William Hogue, of the Parish of St. François Xavier, in the province of Manitoba, make oath and say as follows :—I was an elector of the constituency of St. François Xavier, at the election which took place at that constituency, in the month of January, eighteen hundred and eighty-eight, between the Honourable Joseph Burke on the one hand and Mr. F. H. Francis on the other.

2. I was present at the meeting held in the school-house at St. François Xavier East, in the said constituency, on the   day of the said month of January, and I heard Mr. Joseph Martin give assurances to the French and Roman Catholic electors with reference to the Catholic schools and the use of the French language. He said he heard that there was a rumour in the constituency that if the Liberals came into power they would abolish the Catholic schools and the use of the French language ; he could well understand why such a thing should be said in a Roman Catholic constituency ; but he absolutely denied it, and said there was not a word of truth in it, that it was a most absurd rumour. He positively assured the electors that the Liberal party would never interfere with the privileges aforesaid, and stated that if the Liberals came into power and made any attempt to interfere with their separate schools or the use of the French language, he (Mr. Martin) would leave the Liberal party for ever.

Sworn before me at St. François Xavier, in the province of Manitoba, this 22nd day of February, 1895.

WILLIAM HOGUE.

P. LAVALLÉE,
A Commissioner in B. R.

EXHIBIT II.

In the matter of the appeal of the Roman Catholic minority of the Queen's subjects in the province of Manitoba to His Excellency the Governor General in Council, from two certain Acts of the legislature of the said province, being chapters 37 and 38 of 53 Victoria, intituled respectively: "An Act respecting the Department of Education" and "An Act respecting Public Schools."

I, J. P. McDougall, of the parish of St. François Xavier, in the province of Manitoba, make oath and say as follows:—

1. I was an elector of the constituency of St. François Xavier at the election which took place at that constituency in the month of January, eighteen hundred and eighty-eight, between the Honourable Joseph Burke on the one hand and Mr. F. H. Francis on the other.

2. I was present at the meeting held in the school-house at St. François Xavier East, in the said constituency, on the   day of the said month of January, and I heard Mr. Joseph Martin give assurances to the French and Roman Catholic electors with reference to the Catholic schools and the use of the French language. He said he had heard that there was a rumour in the constituency that if the Liberals came into power they would abolish the Catholic schools and the use of the French language; he could well understand why such a thing should be said in a Roman Catholic constituency, but he absolutely denied it, and said there was not a word of truth in it, that it was a most absurd rumour. He positively assured the electors that the Liberal party would never interfere with the privileges aforesaid, and stated that if the Liberals came into power and made any attempt to interfere with their separate schools or the use of the French language, he (Mr. Martin) would leave the Liberal party for ever.

Sworn before me at St. François Xavier,
in the province of Manitoba, this 22nd day
of February, 1895.

JOHN P. McDOUGALL.

P. LAVALLÉE,
A Commissioner in B. R.

EXHIBIT I.

In the matter of the appeal of the Roman Catholic minority of the Queen's subjects in the province of Manitoba, to His Excellency the Governor General in Council, from two certain Acts of the legislature of said province, being chapters 37 and 38 of 53 Victoria, intituled respectively: "An Act respecting the Department of Education" and "An Act respecting Public Schools."

I, Norbert Todd, of the parish of St. François Xavier, in the province of Manitoba' make oath and say as follows:—

1. I was an elector of the constituency of St. François Xavier at the election which took place at that constituency in the month of January, 1888, between the Honourable Joseph Burke, on the one hand, and Mr. F. H. Francis, on the other.

2. I was present at the meeting held in the school-house, St. François Xavier East, in the said constituency, on the   day of the said month of January, and I heard Mr. Joseph Martin give assurances to the French and Roman Catholic electors with reference to the Catholic schools and the use of the French language. He said that he had heard that there was rumour in the constituency that if the Liberals came into power they would abolish the Catholic schools and the use of the French language.

He could well understand why such a thing should be said in a French Catholic constituency, but he absolutely denied it, and said there was not a word of truth in it, that it was a most absurd rumour. He positively assured the electors that the Liberal party would never interfere in the privileges aforesaid, and stated that if the Liberals came into power and made any attempt to interfere with their separate schools or the use of the French language, he (Mr. Martin), would leave the Liberal party for ever.

Sworn before me at the parish of St. François Xavier, in the province of Manitoba, this twenty-second day of February, 1895.

NORBERT TODD.

P. LAVALLÉE,
A Commissioner in B.R.

EXHIBIT J.

In the matter of the appeal of the Roman Catholic minority of the Queen's subjects in the province of Manitoba to His Excellency the Governor General in Council, from two certain Acts of the legislature of said province, being chapters 37 and 38 of 53 Victoria, intituled respectively : " An Act respecting the Department of Education" and " An Act respecting Public Schools."

I, Francis Walsh, of the parish of St. Frs.-Xavier, in the province of Manitoba, make oath and say as follows :—

1. I was an elector of the constituency of St. François-Xavier at the election which took place at that constituency in the month of January, 1888, between the Honourable Joseph Burke, on the one hand, and Mr. F. H. Francis, on the other.

2. I was present at the meeting held in the school-house, at St. François Xavier East, in the said constituency, on the   day of the said month of January, and I heard Mr. Joseph Martin give assurances to the French and Roman Catholic electors with reference to the Catholic schools and the use of the French language. He said that he had heard that there was rumour in the constituency that if the Liberals came into power they would abolish the Catholic schools and the use of the French language. He could well understand why such a thing should be said in a French Catholic constituency, but he absolutely denied it and said there was not a word of truth in it, that it was a most absurd rumour. He positively assured the electors that the Liberal party would never interfere in the privileges aforesaid, and stated that if the Liberals came into power and made any attempt to interfere with their separate schools, or the use of the French language, he (Mr. Martin) would leave the Liberal party for ever.

Sworn before me, at the Parish of St. François Xavier, province of Manitoba, this 22nd day of February, 1895.

FRANCIS × WALSH.
his mark

P. LAVALLÉE,
A Commissioner in B.R.

EXHIBIT K.

In the matter of the appeal of the Roman Catholic minority of the Queen's subjects in the province of Manitoba, to His Excellency the Governor General in Council from two certain Acts of the legislature of said province, being chapters 37 and 38 of 53 Victoria, intituled respectively : "An Act respecting the Department of Education" and "An Act respecting Public Schools."

I, Joseph Hogue, of the parish of St. François-Xavier, in the province of Manitoba, make oath and say as follows :—

1. I was an elector of the constituency of St. François-Xavier at the election which took place at that constituency in the month of January, 1888, between the Honourable Joseph Burke, on the one hand, and Mr. F. H. Francis on the other.

2. I was present at the meeting held in the school-house at St. François-Xavier East, in the said constituency, on the   day of the said month of January, and I heard Mr. Joseph Martin give assurances to the French and Roman Catholic electors with reference to the Catholic schools and the use of the French language. He said that he had heard that there was rumour in the constituency that if the Liberals came into power they would abolish the Catholic schools and the use of the French language. He could well understand why such a thing should be said in a French Catholic constituency, but he absolutely denied it and said there was not a word of truth in it, that it was a most absurd rumour. He positively assured the electors that the Liberal party would never interfere in the privileges aforesaid, and stated that if the Liberals came into power and made any attempt to interfere with their separate schools, or the use of the French language he (Mr. Martin) would leave the Liberal party for ever.

Sworn before me at the Parish of St. François-Xavier, province of Manitoba, this 22nd day of February, 1895.

JOSEPH + HOGUE.
his   mark.

P. LAVALLÉE,
A Commissioner in B.R.

EXHIBIT L.

In the matter of the appeal of the Roman Catholic minority of the Queen's subjects in the province of Manitoba to His Excellency the Governor General in Council, from two certain Acts of the Legislature of the said province, being chapters 37 and 38 of 53 Victoria intituled respectively : "An Act respecting the Department of Education," and "An Act Respecting Public Schools."

I, Gilbert Todd, of the parish of St. François-Xavier, in the province of Manitoba make oath and say as follows :—

1. I was an elector of the constituency of St. François-Xavier at the election which took place at that constituency in the month of January, eighteen hundred and eighty-eight, between the Honourable Joseph Burke, on the one hand, and Mr. F. H. Francis, on the other.

2. I was present at the meeting held in the school-house at St. François-Xavier East, in the said constituency, on the   day of the said month of January, and I heard Mr. Joseph Martin give assurances to the French and Roman Catholic electors with reference to the Catholic schools and the use of the French language. He said he had heard that there was a rumour in the constituency that if the Liberals came into power they would abolish the Catholic schools and the use of the French language ; he could well understand why such a thing should be said in a Roman Catholic constituency ;

but he absolutely denied it and said there was not a word of truth in it, that it was a most absurd rumour. He positively assured the electors that the Liberal party would never interfere with the privileges aforesaid, and stated that if the Liberals came into power and made any attempt to interfere with their separate schools, or the use of the French language, he (Mr. Martin) would leave the Liberal party for ever.

Sworn before me at St. François Xavier,
in the province of Manitoba, this
22nd day of February, 1895.

GILBERT TODD.

P. LAVALLÉE,
A Commissioner in B.R.

EXHIBIT M.

In the matter of the appeal of the Roman Catholic minority of the Queen's subjects, in the province of Manitoba to His Excellency the Governor General in Council, from two certain Acts of the legislature of said province, being chapters 37 and 38 of 53 Victoria, intituled respectively : "An Act respecting the Department of Education," and "An Act respecting Public Schools."

I, the Very Rev. Joachim Allard, O.M.I., of the town of St. Boniface, in the province of Manitoba, administrator of the Archdiocese of St. Boniface, make oath and say as follows : —

1. I was during all the year of our Lord one thousand eight hundred and eighty-eight, the Vicar-General of the said archdiocese of St. Boniface, having my residence in the episcopal residence at St. Boniface.

2. I distinctly remember that during the early part of the said year of our Lord one thousand eight hundred and eighty-eight, the Hon. Thomas Greenway, with whom I was not then personally acquainted, called at the said episcopal residence in St. Boniface, in company of Mr. W. F. Alloway, whom I personally knew, and the said Mr. Alloway then introduced the said Hon. Thos. Greenway to me, and the said Mr. Greenway then stated to me that he had called to see His Grace the Archbishop, personally, touching a confidential matter. His Grace was then sick and confined to his bed, and I so informed the said Mr. Greenway, and stated to him that as the vicar-general of His Grace I could receive any confidential communications and communicate the same to His Grace; and I then assured him that he could rely upon my discretion in any confidential communication that he wished to make, and that His Grace the Archbishop would also respect his confidence.

3. The Hon. Mr. Greenway then stated to me that he had been called to form a new government in this province, and that he was desirous to strengthen it by taking into his cabinet one of the French members of the legislature, who would be agreeable to the archbishop ; whereupon I remarked that I did not think that His Grace would favour any French member joining the new administration unconditionally, and without any previous understanding as to certain questions of great importance to His Grace. Mr. Greenway replied that he had already talked the matter over with his friends, and that he (Mr. Greenway) was quite willing to guarantee, under his government, the maintenance of the then existing condition of matters with regard :

    1. To separate Catholic schools ;
    2. To the official use of the French language ;
    3. To the French electoral divisions.

4. I received the assurances of the said Hon. Thomas Greenway, as above stated to me, and I promised him that I would convey the same to His Grace the Archbishop, and I further told him that I believed his assurances so made would give great satisfaction to His Grace. The said Hon. Thomas Greenway then proposed to come again on the

following day, to receive an answer as to the nomination of the French member of his cabinet ; but I told him that I would not put him to that inconvenience, but that I would meet him in Winnipeg on the following day for that purpose ; and it was then agreed between myself and him, that such meeting should take place on the following morning in Mr. Alloway's office at the hour of nine o'clock. This finished the first interview I had with the said Hon. Thomas Greenway.

5. During all the time that elapsed between the introduction of Mr. Greenway and the end of the said interview as above set out, and his departure from said residence on that day Mr. W. F. Alloway was personally present and heard all that took place between the said Hon. Thomas Greenway and myself, as above stated by me. In pursuance of my promise, I, on the said day of the interview, visited His Grace the Archbishop, in his bedroom, and reported to him fully and faithfully what had taken place at said interview.

6. His Grace expressed his satisfaction, and instructed me to answer the Honourable Thomas Greenway that he would throw no obstacle in the way of his administration, and that I could say to him that, His Grace would have no objection to Mr. Prendergast being taken into the new cabinet as a French representative, and His Grace particularly requested me to convey to Mr. Greenway the satisfaction given him by the assurance and promise made to me by the said Mr. Greenway.

7. On the following morning, in pursuance of the appointment so made, I attended at the office of Mr. Alloway in Winnipeg, and then again met the said Hon. Thomas Greenway, and I then communicated to him the message of His Grace so entrusted to me as above set out, and Mr. Greenway then expressed to me his personal gratification at the said message and attitude of His Grace, and he then assured me that faith would be kept by his government with His Grace ; and then again and in specific terms repeated to me the assurance that

First.—The Catholic separate schools ;
Second.—The official use of the French language ;
Third.—The number of French constituencies would not be disturbed during his administration.

8. I had promised not to violate the confidence of the Hon. Mr. Greenway by disclosing the particulars of said promises and assurances. But the said assurances have been denied by the said Mr. Greenway on the floor of the legislature, notwithstanding that he had violated the terms of the same before that time, and but for such open denial by him of such promises, and his misstatements of what took place, I would not have felt at liberty to now disclose the same.

9. Mr. W. F. Alloway was present at his office during the second interview with said Hon. Thomas Greenway, as above set out and remained in the room where we were closeted during much of the time during which said second interview lasted.

Sworn before me at Ottawa, in the county of Carleton, this twenty-sixth day of February, 1895.

J. ALLARD, O.M.I.
Administrator.

T. G. ROTHWELL,
A Commissioner in the H. C. J. and a Notary Public in and for the Province of Ontario.

EXHIBIT N.

In the matter of the appeal by the Roman Catholic minority of the Queen's subjects in the province of Manitoba to His Excellency the Governor General in Council from two certain Acts of the legislature of the said province, being chapters 37 and 38 of 53 Victoria, intituled respectively : "An Act respecting the Department of Education," and "An Act respecting Public Schools."

I, William Forbes Alloway, of the city of Winnipeg, in the province of Manitoba, banker, make oath and say as follows :—

1. In or about the month of January, in the year of our Lord 1888, the Honourable Thomas Greenway, then Premier of the province of Manitoba, with whom I was intimately acquainted had several interviews with me on the subject of the composition of his government which he was at that time forming, and especially as to the attitude of the Roman Catholic Archbishop of St. Boniface and the clergy and members of the Roman Catholic church towards his government ; and the said Greenway intimated to me that he was desirous of meeting the said Archbishop of St. Boniface with a view of discussing certain matters with him touching the formation of the government and especially as to the choice of a French speaking member of the government, and as he told me that he was not personally acquainted with the said Archbishop it was arranged that I should introduce him to His Grace for that purpose.

2. Accordingly I accompanied the Honourable Mr. Greenway to the episcopal residence at St. Boniface in said province shortly after said interview took place in order to wait upon the said Archbishop for the said purpose.

3. On reaching the said residence we found that the Archbishop was then unwell and confined to his bed, but we saw the Rev. J. Allard, the Vicar-General of the Archbishop who was informed by Mr. Greenway and me that Mr. Greenway had called to see His Grace the Archbishop touching a confidential matter, whereupon the said Vicar-General said, that as Vicar-General, he could receive any confidential communications and communicate the same to the Archbishop.

4. Thereupon a conference took place between the said Vicar General on the one part, and Mr. Greenway and myself on the other part, in which Mr. Greenway informed the Vicar-General, for the information of the Archbishop, that he had been called upon to form a new government in the province; that he was desirous of strengthening it by taking into his cabinet one of the French members of the legislature, and that he desired to consult the Archbishop as to the person who would be agreeable to him as such French member.

5. Thereupon the Vicar-General intimated that there were certain questions as to which probably the Archbishop would desire to have an understanding before he would favour any French member joining the new government. Mr. Greenway thereupon said that he had already discussed with his friends certain questions which they knew had created uneasiness amongst the French and Roman Catholic population in the province, and that he and his political friends forming the government were quite prepared to undertake that the feelings of the Roman Catholic section of the population upon these questions would be fully respected and that their position upon these questions would be fully sustained.

6. These questions were then talked over between Mr. Greenway and the Vicar-General, the same being questions that had been somewhat warmly discussed during an election contest that had recently taken place in a constituency in the province largely composed of the Roman Catholic and French population.

7. These questions were (first) that of the continuation or abolition of separate schools as hitherto enjoyed by Catholics, (second) as to the use of the French language as an official language in the province, and (third) as to changes in the representation in the legislature of the province which might affect the number of French electoral divisions.

8. Upon all of these questions Mr. Greenway assured the Vicar-General in my presence that his government was prepared to uphold the position of the Roman

Catholic section of the population and that they would neither interfere with separate schools nor the use of the French language as an official language or lessen the number of French electoral divisions.

9. The Vicar-General assured Mr. Greenway that he would communicate his statements to the Roman Catholic Archbishop immediately, and thereupon an appointment was made for Mr. Greenway and the Vicar-General to meet in my banking office in Winnipeg the following morning.

10. On the following morning pursuant to the said appointment Mr. Greenway and the said Vicar-General met in my office, when the Vicar-General reported that he had seen His Grace the Achbishop who had requested him, the Vicar-General, to convey to Mr. Greenway the satisfaction given him by the assurance and promise that had been made by Mr. Greenway to him in respect of these questions.

11. Some further conversation then took place between Mr. Greenway and the Vicar-General in which the assurance given the day before as to the attitude of the government upon these several questions was substantially repeated.

12. I was present during the whole of the interview on the first day at the episcopal residence in St. Boniface, and I took a particular interest in the discussion because I was very friendly to Mr. Greenway and desirous of seeing his government strengthened, and was desirous of securing the additional support of the Archbishop and the clergy and members of his church, and there is no doubt whatever than an assurance favourable to the position of the Roman Catholic party upon all of these questions was given by Mr. Greenway in the most positive terms.

13. At the interview in my office on the second day I was present the greater part of the time and heard the greater part of the conversation, and there is no doubt whatever that the promises and pledges of the previous day were substantially repeated and that there was a perfect understanding between Mr. Greenway and the Vicar-General as representing the Archbishop, that Mr. Greenway's government would respect and maintain the position of the Roman Catholic party upon all of these questions.

Sworn before me at the city of Ottawa, in the province of Ontario, this   day of
February, A.D. 1895.

W. F. ALLOWAY.

JOHN S. EWART,
A Commissioner, &c.

EXHIBIT O.

In the matter of the appeal of the Roman Catholic minority of the Queen's subjects in the province of Manitoba to His Excellency the Governor General in Council, from two certain Acts of the legislature of the said province, being chapters 37 and 38 of 53 Victoria, intituled respectively : " An Act respecting the Department of Education " and " An Act respecting Public Schools."

I, Thomas Alfred Bernier, of the village of St. Boniface, in the province of Manitoba, senator, make oath and say :—

1. In the year 1881 I became a member of the board of education for the province of Manitoba, and being a member of the Roman Catholic Church became also a member of the Roman Catholic section of the said board. In the same year I was appointed by the Lieutenant Governor in Council to act as superintendent of Roman Catholic schools in the said province. I retained my position on the Board of Education and my position as superintendent of Roman Catholic schools until the Education Act of 1890 came into force.

2. By the Manitoba School Act, passed in the year 1881, it was provided amongst other things that the sum appropriated by legislature for common school purposes should be divided between Protestant and Roman Catholic sections of the board of education in certain proportions.

3. Clause 90 of said last mentioned Act provided as follows :—" From the sum or proportion paid to each section there shall first be paid the incidental expenses of that section and such sum to the superintendent of education as the Lieutenant Governor in Council may deem just, and each section of the board may reserve for unforeseen contingencies a sum not exceeding ten per cent of its share of the appropriation," which clause remained in force until the year 1888.

4. In pursuance of the said clause of the said statute, the Roman Catholic section of the board of education did set apart for unforeseen contingencies from year to year a certain portion of the monies received by it from the government.

5. By the provisions of the Act of 1888, the provincial grant instead of being paid over to the different sections of the board were paid direct to the person or persons who might be entitled to receive the money upon the requisition of the respective superintendents of education.

6. Shortly after the passage of the Act of 1888, a demand was made upon me as superintendent of Roman Catholic schools for the payment over to the government of moneys which had accumulated by reason of the said board setting apart for unforeseen contingencies of a portion of the said grant from year to year.

7. The amount at the time under the control of the Roman Catholic section which had so accumulated as aforesaid was the sum of thirteen thousand eight hundred and seventy-nine dollars and forty-seven cents, and the said sum was on the twenty-second day of July, 1889, paid over by the Roman Catholic section to the Provincial Treasurer.

8. In the letter of the Provincial Secretary addressed to me as superintendent of Catholic schools asking that the amount should be paid over there were the following words : "this demand refers only to a detail of internal administration, and in no way to the property of the amount indicated, the amount is decidedly a vested right and will not admit of doubt at any time."

9. Before complying with the said demand the Roman Catholic section passed the following resolution, a copy of which was sent to the Provincial Secretary : "In accordance with the desire of the government expressed in the letter of the Hon. Secretary of State, of the 12th July, 1889, the Catholic section of the Board of Education authorizes its superintendent to hand over to the Provincial Treasurer the sum of thirteen thousand eight hundred and seventy-nine dollars and forty-seven cents being the reserve fund and the balance of all funds in hand for the schools under the direction of the said Catholic section of the Board of Education, in remitting the money the Catholic section takes the respectful liberty of observing :

"The reserve fund was raised and accrued in accordance with the dispositions of the educational acts then in vigour in the province ;

"2. This reserve has been made possible because the members of the Catholic section not only administered the school funds with the strictest economy, but also in many instances helped by personal sacrifice.

"3. The property of this reserve fund is a vested right to the Catholic schools of the province, therefore those who administered it until to-day are persuaded that the government will not change its destination and willnot on that account diminish the ordinary grants, in accordance with the positive assurance that the government has given us the above mentioned letter of the Honourable Secretary of State."

No part of the said sum of money was ever afterwards drawn by the Roman Catholic section or applied for the purposes of the Roman Catholic schools, but the whole amount remained with the provincial treasurer until the coming in force of the School Act of 1890 and the Roman Catholics have never received any benefit from the said sum of money whatever.

Sworn before me at the city of Ottawa, in the county of Carleton, and province of Ontario, this twenty-sixth day of February, A.D. 1895.

F. A. BERNIER.

T. R. ROTHWELL,
A Notary Public in and for the Province of Ontario.

131

EXHIBIT P.

AN ACT RESPECTING SEPARATE SCHOOLS.

HER Majesty, by and with the advice and consent of the Legislative Assembly of the province of Manitoba, enacts as follows :—
1. This Act may be cited as "The Separate Schools Act."
2. The Lieutenant Governor shall appoint, to form and constitute the Separate School Board of Education for the province of Manitoba, a certain number of persons not exceeding nine, all of which persons shall be Roman Catholics.
3. Three of such members, recorded at the foot of the list of the members of the board as entered in the minute book of the Executive Council of the province of Manitoba, shall retire and cease to hold office at the end of each year, which for the purposes of this Act shall be held and taken to be the second day of October annually, and the names of the members appointed in their stead shall be placed at the head of the list, and the three members so retiring in rotation and annually may be eligible for reappointment.
4. The Department of Education may, for the observance of the separate schools,—
(a.) Make from time to time such regulations as they may think fit for the general organization of the separate schools ;
(b.) Make regulations for the registering and reporting of daily attendance at all the separate schools in the province subject to the approval of the Lieutenant Governor in Council ;
(c.) Make regulations for the calling of meetings from time to time of the department, and prescribe the notices thereof to be given to the members (1881).
5. It shall be the duty of the Board of Education,—
(a.) To have under its control and management the separate schools and to make from time to time such regulations as may be deemed fit for their general government and discipline and the carrying out of the provisions of this Act ;
(b.) To arrange for the proper examination, grading and licensing of its teachers, the recognition of certificates obtained elsewhere, and for the withdrawing of license upon sufficient cause ;
(c.) To select all the books, maps and globes to be used in the schools under its control and to approve of the plans for the construction of school-houses. :
Provided, however, that in the case of books having reference to religion and morals they shall not be at variance with Roman Catholic doctrine :
(d.) To appoint inspectors who shall hold office during the pleasure of the board (1881).
(e.) To make regulations regarding the selection of school sites, the size of school grounds, and the formation and alteration of all school districts under its care.
(f.) To make and enforce regulations for the establishment and operation of departments in such of its schools as it may deem suitable for the preparation of candidates for the annual examination of teachers and for matriculating at the University of Manitoba, and for the doing of general literary work corresponding to the standard required for these examinations, and to give special aid to such schools from the funds at its disposal, not exceeding in the aggregate one-twentieth of its appropriation ; provided that no school shall be entitled to receive such special aid that does not comply fully with the regulations made by the board for its operation ; provided further that each such department shall be established only with the consent of the local board of school trustees.
(g.) The board may, whenever they shall see fit, appoint and hold a meeting of such board, in any part of the province, and such meeting shall be as valid as if held in the city of Winnipeg, which shall be the usual place of meeting of such board or section.

QUORUM.

6. The quorum of the board shall consist of a majority of the members.
7. Any member of the board absenting himself from the meetings of the board for six months, unless from sickness or absence from the province, shall be considered to have *ipso facto* resigned his position, and the superintendent of the board shall notify the Provincial Secretary of the vacancy so caused, and the member appointed to replace him shall hold office only for the unexpired term of the member whom he replaces.

SUPERINTENDENTS.

8. The Lieutenant Governor in Council shall appoint one of the members of the board to be the superintendent of the separate schools, and the superintendent shall be the secretary of the board.
9. In addition to the duties specified in other clauses of this Act, it shall be the duty of the superintendent, and he is hereby empowered,—

(*a*.) To call all meetings of the board, and also to call any school meeting required to be held under this Act when the parties who are otherwise invested with the power to do so, either neglect or refuse to exercise it ;

(*b*.) To have, as the executive officer of the board, the general supervision and direction of the schools, and of the inspectors that may from time to time be appointed ; and to have authority to take measures to enforce and carry into effect all the provisions of this Act and the regulations issued under its authority that relate to the schools within their respective jurisdictions ;

(*c*.) To give such explanations of the provisions of this or any other School Act, and of the regulations and decisions of the board, as may be required and to enforce the same ; and

(*d*.) To prepare during the first term of the school year a report to the Lieutenant Governor in Council upon all the schools under his supervision for the previous school year, accompanied with full statistical tables, showing among other things, the number of children of school age in each district, as shown by the census returns for that year, the number who have attended school and the average attendance as shown by the semi-annual returns of the different teachers, and such report shall also contain a statement of the receipts and expenditure of all government money furnished to the board for common school purposes.

10. In case of the absence of the superintendent, he may, with the sanction of the Lieutenant Governor in Council, appoint a member of the board to act for him.

11. It shall be the duty of the council of each municipality to establish, and alter when necessary, the school districts within their own bounds, and in case any school district or proposed district should be included in more than one municipality, its formation or alteration shall be made by the reeves or mayors of such municipalities, and the local inspector or inspectors of schools ; provided that the formation or alteration of school districts by municipal councils or by the reeves and mayors of municipalities and the local inspector or inspectors shall be made under the regulations that may from time to time be issued for that purpose by the Board of Education, and all by-laws and resolutions for forming or altering school districts, shall be submitted to the board and receive its sanction before they can be carried into effect ; provided also that upon the refusal or neglect of any council, or of the reeves and mayors and local inspectors of the municipalities concerned to establish or alter any school district, when petitioned to do so by at least five heads of families resident therein, or upon an appeal against the action of such body forming or altering any school district, the board shall be empowered to confirm or annul the action appealed against, or to form or alter such school district as they may think fit, within three months after their receipt of such appeal or petition ; provided further that no school district shall be organized under this Act unless there shall be at least ten children of school age living within the same, and situated not over three miles from a point that may in anywise be fixed as the first school site.

(*a*.) It shall be the duty of the clerk of each municipality within one month after the passing of this Act to transmit a description or map included in each school district within his municipality to the superintendent under a penalty of five dollars for neglect or refusal.

(b.) The reeves or mayors and the local inspector or inspectors of schools engaged in the formation or alteration of school districts extending within the bounds of two or more municipalities shall be entitled to the same remuneration per day with travelling expenses for their attendance as municipal councillors for attendance at meetings of their respective councils, and each reeve or mayor shall be paid by the council of his own municipality and the local inspector by all the municipalities concerned in equal parts. Provided that in no case the inspector shall be paid a less sum than two dollars and a half per day and ten cents per mile each way for travelling expenses.

12. In case of the readjustment of any school district subsequently to an issue of debentures by such district, and before the said debentures have been fully paid, all lands added to the school district by such readjustment shall thereafter be liable to taxation in common with the remaining portion of the school district for the purpose of meeting payments on such debentures as they become due; and all persons assessed for lands detached from any school district after an issue of debentures in such district and before the said debentures have been fully paid, shall in case of their assessment for the payment of debentures in any other school district, be entitled to receive back all sums for which they may hereafter be assessed for payments on debentures in any school district except that in which they then reside.

13. In all cases of readjustment, the inspector of schools for the district, jointly with one competent person to be appointed by each board of trustees, whose district the readjustment may affect, who shall be non-residents of the said district, shall form a board of arbitration, whose duty it shall be to value the existing school-houses, school sites and other school property or assets within the territories readjusted, and ascertain the respective debts and liabilities thereof; and the said board or a majority of its members shall thereupon adjust and settle in such a manner as they may deem just and equitable, the respective rights, claims and demands of the parties interested: and their award in writing, including their own reasonable costs and charges, may be enforced in the county courts of the province, and which said award shall in all respects be subject to appeal to the Court of Queen's Bench, the same as awards in civil matters.

(a.) The said arbitrators shall be entitled to receive for their attendance at the said arbitration the same remuneration with travelling expenses as paid to municipal councillors for their attendance at meetings of their respective councils, and such payments shall be paid equally by the school districts represented in the arbitration.

14. The school district of any incorporate city or town shall be the same as the territorial limits of the said city or town, except as hereinafter provided, but nothing herein shall prevent the union of a portion of the adjoining municipality or municipalities to a city or town or portion of a city or town for school purposes as provided in section eleven of this Act; and the first school meeting in any city or town or school district, including a city or town after its incorporation, shall be called by the city or town clerk within two weeks after the holding of the municipal elections, or, in case of his failure to do so, by the superintendent as soon afterwards as convenient.

(a.) It shall be lawful for the board to form or subdivide any city or town or any school district which includes or is included in a city or town, into wards for the election of school trustees, such number of wards not to exceed six in any one case, and to determine the number of trustees not exceeding two to represent each ward when the number of such wards is more than one, and to fix the date of the first election of trustees after such formation or subdivision; which election shall take place in each ward at the call of the superintendent, and in such case the trustees that may then be in office will so remain in office only until such election takes place irrespective of the date of their appointment: provided that the existing wards for municipal purposes shall be the wards for school purposes in any city or town until such formation or subdivision is effected by the board; provided further that the board shall have power to maintain its district as it existed before the incorporation of said city or town, or so to extend its district as to include Roman Catholics residing in the vicinity where no separate school is in operation, but in such cases the children of the residents within the city or town limits only shall be computed in the division of school taxes levied on the incorporated bodies within the city or town;

(b.) In portions of the province not organized into municipalities the Board of Education shall have authority to form and alter school districts under its authority, and the trustees of such school districts are hereby empowered to assess the same and to levy and collect taxes therein for the support of their schools.

SCHOOL MEETINGS.

15. All school meetings after the first shall be called by the respective boards of trustees, in accordance with the form of notice furnished by the Board of Education.

16. At every school meeting as authorized and required to be held under this present Act, the Roman Catholic ratepayers, or if it is a first meeting in a new district, then the Roman Catholic freeholders and householders present at such meeting, or a majority of them ;

(a.) Shall elect a chairman ; and the chairman of the meeting shall decide all questions of order, subject to an appeal to the meeting, and in case of equality of votes, he shall give the casting vote, but he shall have no vote as chairman, and the chairman shall take the votes in the manner desired by a majority of the electors present, unless a poll be demanded by any electors present, when he shall be the returning officer ;

(b.) Shall elect a secretary ; and the secretary shall record the proceedings of the meeting in a book kept for that purpose, and if a poll be held he shall record the names of the voters, and the candidate or candidates for whom each elector votes ; and such poll shall be held on the day of such meeting and shall be kept open until four o'clock in the afternoon, unless at any time one hour shall have elapsed without a vote being recorded ;

(c.) A copy of the minutes of all school meetings shall be transmitted to the superintendent within ten days after the holding of such meeting.

FIRST ELECTION OF TRUSTEES.

17. At the first meeting in any new school district such meeting being duly organized by the election of a chairman and secretary, the majority of the Roman Catholic resident freeholders, and householders present, of the full age of twenty-one years, shall elect three persons who shall be Roman Catholics to be school trustees for such district ; and

(a.) The first person elected shall continue in office for two years to be reckoned from the annual meeting next after his election, and until his successor has been appointed ;

(b.) The second person elected shall continue in office for one year to be reckoned from the annual meeting next after his election, and until his successor has been appointed ; and

(c.) The third and last person elected shall continue in office until the next ensuing annual school meeting, and until his successor has been appointed ;

(d.) Until a school tax has been imposed in any organized school district, every Roman Catholic resident freeholder, and householder, of the full age of twenty-one years shall be eligible for the office of trustee, and may take part in any school meeting.

18. In all school districts which include or may hereafter include a city or town not divided into wards for school purposes, there shall be elected three trustees who shall be Roman Catholics, at the first school meeting therein, whose term of office shall be the same as that of trustees elected at the first meeting in rural school districts ; and in all school districts divided or hereinafter to be divided into wards for school purposes, there shall be two trustees who shall be Roman Catholics elected for each ward at the first meeting, one of whom shall hold office one year from the next annual school meeting thereafter, and the other until the next annual school meeting, and in each case until a successor has been appointed ; the trustee to hold office for the longer term shall be the first nominated if no poll be held ; and in case a poll is held, the person obtaining the highest number of votes, and in case there be an equality of votes, the returning officer by his vote shall designate the person to serve the longer term, and afterwards there shall be elected at each annual meeting a number of trustees equal to the number

of those whose term of office has expired, and these newly elected trustees shall remain in office three years in towns and cities not divided into wards for school purposes, and two years if such are so divided, and in each case until a successor has been appointed.

SCHOOL MEETINGS.

19. On the first Monday in February in each year a meeting of the Roman Catholic ratepayers of each school district, of the age of twenty-one years, and upwards, shall be called by the board of trustees, by notice posted by them on the school-house, if there be one, or in three public places in the district, at least two weeks in advance ; and the majority of the electors present shall choose one or more persons (as the case may be) who are Roman Catholics, to be school trustees for the district, and two auditors, and shall receive and decide upon the annual report of the trustees and the report of the auditors, and transact such other business as may have been set forth in the notice calling the meeting.

(a.) All special meetings of the ratepayers in a school district shall be called by the trustees or the superintendent by posting up notices in at least three public places within the school district at least two weeks previous to such meeting ; the business to be considered at such meeting shall be plainly set forth in the notices calling the same, and no other business may be legally transacted at a special meeting but such as may be held in accordance with these provisions.

20. When in a district from any cause the annual meeting has not been held on the first Monday in February, the trustees shall appoint another day for the holding of such meeting ; provided that if the trustees fail to call such meeting the superintendent shall call it.

(a.) If within thirty days after the holding of a school meeting a complaint be made in writing to the superintendent regarding the legality or regularity of the proceedings at such meeting, he may cause an investigation to be held, and in his discretion declare the proceedings void, and cause another meeting for the same purpose to be called, or may ratify and confirm such proceedings, and any decision so rendered by s ch superintendent shall be final.

21. In incorporated cities and towns all annual meetings in each ward shall be held in the first Monday in February in every year, commencing at ten o'clock in the forenoon, and shall be called by the chairman of the board of school trustees. It shall be the duty of the said board to furnish the chairman of every such meeting with a copy of the Roman Catholic voters' list for such ward, and in all cases of cities and towns not divided into wards for school purposes, there shall be but one voting place in such city or town.

(a.) The ratepayers present at the said meeting shall elect a chairman and secretary and shall proceed to nominate a trustee or trustees, who shall be Roman Catholics, to take the place of those whose term of office has expired.

In case the number of nominations does not exceed the number of vacancies to be filled before the hour of eleven o'clock, the chairman shall declare the persons so nominated to be elected ; but should the number of persons nominated exceed the number of vacancies to be filled, a show of hands shall be taken and the person or persons having the majority of votes shall be declared elected should no ratepayer present demand a poll.

If a poll be demanded the chairman shall be the returning officer and shall record the votes given, and at four o'clock the poll shall be closed, and the person or persons having the majority of votes shall be declared elected, provided that if one hour elapses during such poll without a vote having been recorded, the chairman shall then declare the poll closed.

(b.) The first meeting of the board of trustees in a city or town shall be held on the day following the annual meeting.

22. Except as provided for in the first election of trustees and in the case of any person or persons who have been included in a school district after the last preceding assessment and levy of taxes within the same, no person shall be entitled to vote at any school meeting whatever, unless he shall have been assessed, and in case an objection be made to the right of any person to vote in a district, the chairman shall, at the request

of any elector present, require the person whose right of voting is objected to, to make the following declaration (or affirmation) :—

" I, A. B., do declare (or affirm) that I am rated on the assessment roll of that portion of the municipality of　　　　　　　　　now included in the school district ; that I am of the full age of twenty-one years, and that I am legally qualified to vote at this election."

Thereupon the person making such declaration shall be permitted to vote, and not otherwise.

23. In incorporated cities or towns no person shall be entitled to vote at any school meeting for the election of school trustees, on any school question whatsoever, except in the district to which he belongs, and unless his name be upon the revised municipal voters' list for the ward in which he offers to vote ; and in case any objection be made to the right of any person to vote in a ward, the chairman or returning officer of the election shall, at the request of any elector present, require the person whose right of voting is objected to, to make the following declaration :—

" I, A. B., do declare (or affirm) that I have been rated on the assessment roll of this school district and that I am legally qualified to vote at this election."

Thereupon the person making such declaration shall be permitted to vote.

SCHOOL ASSESSMENT.

24. For the purpose of supplementing the legislative grant it shall be the duty of the council of each municipality to levy and collect each year by assessment upon the whole of the Roman Catholic real and personal property within the municipality (as the case may be) that is liable to taxation under the Municipal Act, a sum equal to twenty dollars for each month that the trustees of each school district wholly or included within the municipality, may declare as hereinafter provided that they have kept and will keep a teacher under engagement at a salary in each of their schools during the current school year ; and for each school district partially included within the municipality, they shall levy and collect in like manner a proportionate part of twenty dollars per month, as fixed by the local inspector in the manner hereinafter provided for each of their schools, and the said council may in their discretion levy and collect in like manner an additional sum not exceeding twenty-five per cent of the amount hereinbefore required to be levied.

(*a.*) From the moneys so levied and collected the council shall, upon the first day of December following, pay over to each school district wholly or partially included in the municipality one-half the sum of twenty dollars per month or the proportion thereof allotted to each district as hereinbefore provided, and upon the thirty-first day of January following shall pay over the whole of the balance due to the said trustees, whether the necessary amount has been fully collected or not from the tax levied for the same. Provided that no board of trustees shall be entitled to receive a larger total amount for the school year than twenty dollars for each month within the same that they have actually had a teacher engaged at a salary in each of their schools, and in case of doubt or dispute as to the number of months, the certificate of the superintendent sha'l decide ;

Provided, further that all rural schools kept in operation over seven months of the school year which have not secured an average attendance of resident pupils of the period of operation equal to forty per cent of the enrolment for the same period, shall be subject, in the discretion of the council or councils concerned, with the consent of the proper superintendent of education and not otherwise, to a reduction not exceeding one-half of the amount otherwise payable for each month it was kept in operation over seven months ; and this percentage of attendance may be obtained on the application of any council from the proper superintendent after the close of the last half of the school year.

(*b.*) It shall be the duties of the trustees of each school district wholly situated in a municipality to lay before the council at its first meeting after the thirty-first day of July in each year a statement of the number of months in the current school year during which they have kept and will keep a teacher engaged at a salary in each of their schools, and before the thirty-first day of January following shall notify the clerk of the municipality if they have failed to keep a teacher engaged as so stated by them, and in such case give the actual number of months they have had such teacher engaged ;

(c.) It shall be the duty of the trustees of each school district that extends within the bounds of two or more municipalities or of a city or town and rural municipality to obtain from the last revised assessment roll of each municipality concerned a copy of that part of the said roll relating to the school district as included within the three miles limit as defined in this Act, and forward the said copies before the first of July to the local inspector with a statement of the number of months in the current school year during which they have kept and will keep a teacher under engagement at a salary in each of their schools, and the amounts of their estimates exclusive of the legislative grant required for the use of their schools, and the said inspector shall equalize the rate of assessment of the portion of each municipality included within the school district as hereinbefore described and shall allot to each municipality its due proportion of the sum of twenty dollars per month of the current school year that the said trustees have declared their school has been and will be kept in operation, and shall send notice thereof by mail to the clerk of each municipality concerned before the fifteenth day of July, and the said inspector shall in like manner allot the remainder of the trustees' estimate and return the copies of the rolls with his equalization and an allotment duly made out thereon to the trustees, and the said trustees if they fail to keep a teacher under engagement during the school year for the full time stated by them shall before the thirty-first day of January following notify the local inspector of the actual time, and he shall make another allotment based upon such time, and notify each council concerned, and the said trustees and the said inspector shall be entitled to receive from the trustees for each allotment made as hereinbefore required the sum of five dollars. And the said inspector shall be empowered, if he deem the amount of the trustees' estimate over and above the municipal levy to be excessive or improper, to demand an explanation thereof from the trustees, and in his discretion to reduce the said amount with the consent of the superintendent, and not otherwise.

(d.) Any board of school trustees that fails to notify their council or the local inspector (as the case may be) in due time of the number of months their school is to be kept in operation during any school year as hereinbefore required, shall not be entitled to receive a larger amount in such year from the municipal levy than the council or the local inspector (as the case may be) may in their discretion fix for them, and any board of trustees failing to keep a teacher under engagement the full time stated by them shall not be entitled to receive their second instalment of school moneys due on January thirty-first until they have notified the clerk of the municipality of the actual time such teacher has been under engagement, and any board of trustees wilfully making a false statement in regard to such time shall forfeit their second instalment.

(e.) Any moneys collected by a council from a general levy for school purposes that remain over in any year after all due payments therefrom have been made to the school districts entitled to the same, shall be deposited in some chartered bank by the said council and afterwards used only to pay or advance moneys to school districts within the municipality in the year or years following, unless the proper section of the Board of Education shall require the same moneys or any portion of them to be paid over at any time to any school district or school districts wholly or partly included in the municipality that the said board may consider in especial need of such assistance.

(f.) In levying an assessment for separate school purposes the council of each municipality shall assess all lands the denomination of whose owners as Catholics or non-Catholics cannot be ascertained before the time of making such levy in the manner provided in section 27 of this Act.

25. For the purpose of supplementing the legislative grant and the municipal levy it shall be the duty of the board of trustees of each school district wholly or partially included in a rural municipality before the first day of July in each year at a meeting of the said board, to make an estimate of the sum over and above the amount of the said legislative grant and municipal levy that they shall require for school purposes during the current school year, and resolve whether the said estimate shall be collected by the municipal council or councils concerned, or by a collector or collectors appointed by the said board.

(a.) In case the board of trustees resolve to levy and collect by their own authority the amount of their estimate, it shall be the duty of the said board, if their school district be wholly included in a single municipality, to obtain a copy of the last revised assessment roll of that portion of the municipality that includes all the lands liable for taxation for their school within their school district, and these lands shall be such within the district as are wholly included within a distance of three miles in a direct line from the school-house or site, and each quarter section or parish lot partially included within the same, except such as may contain a residence, the occupant of which must travel four miles or over by the public road from it to reach the school-house, and the said board of trustees shall then strike and levy a rate for raising the amount of the said estimate and place the amount of tax to be collected from each person or property included within the aforesaid limit opposite his name, or the description of his property, and place the roll in their collector's hands for collection, and such roll handed to him shall be his warrant for the collection of the taxes entered upon the same, and in collecting he shall possess and be vested with the same power and authority, and be subject to similar obligations and penalties as a collector employed by the municipality. The said collector may be the secretary-treasurer of the trustees or some other person not a trustee, and his remuneration shall in no case exceed five per cent of the amount collected ; and if the secretary-treasurer act as collector his remuneration for both offices shall not exceed the amount fixed for the office of the secretary-treasurer by this Act. The said collector shall give security to the satisfaction of the trustees for the faithful performance of his duties to the amount of the trustees' estimates, and if such security be not given the trustees shall, *ipso facto*, be his sureties.

(b.) The said collector shall pay over the taxes as collected to the secretary-treasurer, and shall return his roll to the trustees on or before the thirty-first day of January following his appointment.

(c.) In case the school district is included within the limits of two or more municipalities, whether city, town or rural municipalities, the trustees shall levy and collect the amount of their estimate according to the allotment made for them upon the equalized assessment rolls returned to them by the local inspector in the same manner, under the same conditions, and with the same powers given by this Act to trustees of school districts wholly included within the limits of a single municipality for the collection of their estimates.

(d.) In case the board of trustees resolve to have their estimates levied and collected by the council or councils of the municipality or municipalities in which their school district is wholly or partially included, they shall transmit a copy of such resolution with the amount of their estimate, or in the case of school districts included within the limits of two or more municipalities the proportion of their estimate allotted by the local inspector to the council of the municipality concerned, at or before its first meeting after the thirty-first day of July of the year in which such estimate is made, and it shall be the duty of the council of such municipality, employing their own lawful authorities, to levy and collect such estimate or proportion thereof upon the real and personal property within the three miles limit in each school district as hereinbefore described and pay the whole amount so collected to the trustees at the dates upon which they are required to pay them the amounts due from the municipal levy. Provided that in the case of any school district wholly situated within a municipality the council shall be empowered if it deem the estimate of the trustees for the special rate excessive or improper, to demand an explanation thereof from the trustees and in its discretion to reduce the said estimate with the consent of the superintendent, and not otherwise.

(e.) For the purpose of collecting the arrears of school taxes for any year, the trustees of any school district wholly or partially included in a city, town or rural municipality may, in any year, transmit a list of such arrears to the council of the municipality concerned with the estimate of the taxes to be collected for them, for the current school year, and thereupon the said council shall levy and collect the said arrears and pay them over to the trustees on the same dates as they are required to pay over their taxes collected for the current year. The trustees may, employing their own lawful authority, bring a suit in a court of competent jurisdiction for the collection of such arrears whether they had been assessed by the said trustees or by the council of the municipality.

(*f.*) In all cases where the assessment of personal property is mentioned in the Separate Schools Act it shall be held to mean personal property liable to assessment under the Municipal and Assessment Acts.

(*g.*) The whole or any portion of any school tax levied upon any land that has been due and unpaid for more than one year after the 31st day of December of the year when the rate for the same was struck, shall be liable to be sold for taxes in the manner provided by the Municipal and Assessment Acts, for the sale of land for taxes; and it shall be the duty of each municipal collector or treasurer, as the case may be, to include such lands in all lists of lands submitted by him to the mayor or reeve for authentication; provided that in cases where school trustees levy the school tax by their own authority, it shall be the duty of their secretary-treasurer to supply the council with a certified list of lands, liable to sale for arrears of school taxes from time to time, and it shall be the duty of each council, upon receiving the proceeds of any sale of lands, for school taxes, forthwith to hand the said proceeds over to the school trustees entitled to the sa ne, less the costs of such sale, interest and the excess over the amount of the school tax.

(*h.*) All the general school and the special school tax, actually collected remaining unpaid to the trustees by a council after date fixed by this Act for payment of the same shall be a debt due by such council to the trustees, except arrears of taxes levied by the authority of the trustees themselves.

26. The school assessment shall be laid equally according to valuation upon ratable real and personal property of Roman Catholics in the school district and shall be payable by and recoverable from the owner, occupier or possessor of the property liable to be rated, and shall, if not paid, be a special mortgage and not requiring registration to preserve it, on all real estate and a special charge and lien upon all personal property except live stock and farming implements to the value of five hundred dollars belonging to *bona fide* owners of real estate of at least forty acres.

27. The corporations situated in a locality where both public and separate school districts are established, shall be assessed only for the school district of the majority; yet out of such assessment the council of the local municipality, city or town, shall give to the school district of the minority a part of such assessment in proportion to the number of Catholic or non-Catholic children of school age, as the case may be, according to the census.

28. The following real and personal property shall be exempt from taxation under this Act:

(1). Real estate held in trust for Her Majesty, or for the public uses of the province;

(2). Real estate vested in or held in trust for the municipality, and used for municipal purposes;

(3). Real estate held in trust for any tribe or body of Indians;

(4). Every place of public worship, churchyard, burying-grounds, educational or charitable institution, public roadway, square, jail, hospital, agricultural and horticultural societies, with the land requisite for the due enjoyment thereof;

(5). Lands allotted by the Dominion Lands Act to half-breed children of heads of families under the age of eighteen years, not disposed of by them.

29. The Roman Catholic ratepayers of a school district including religious, benevolent, or educational corporations, shall pay their respective assessments to the separate schools; and in no case shall a non-Catholic ratepayer be obliged to pay for a Catholic school, or a Catholic ratepayer for a non-Catholic school.

30. When property owned by a non-Catholic is occupied by a Catholic and *vice versa*, the tenant in such cases shall only be assessed for the amount of property he owns, whether real or personal, but the school taxes on said rented or leased property shall in all cases, and whether or not the same has been or is stipulated in any deed, contract or lease whatever, be paid to the trustees of the schools to which the owner of the property so leased or rented ought to pay and to no other, subject to the exceptions aforesaid.

31. Wherever property is held jointly as tenants or as tenants in common by two or more persons, the holders of such property being non-Catholics and Catholics, they shall be assessed and held accountable to the two boards of school trustees for the amount of taxes in proportion to their interest in the business, tenancy or partnership respectively, and such taxes shall be paid accordingly.

32. In incorporated cities and towns no rate shall be levied at any general or special meeting, for the building, repairing or improving of a school-house, to exceed in any one year one cent on the dollar, on the ratable property in the district.

SCHOOL TRUSTEES.

33. The school trustees in each school district shall be a corporation under the name of "The school trustees for the separate school district of   number   in the province of Manitoba; and it shall be lawful for the Board of Education to assign a name and a number to designate each school district under its authority. The trustees of each school district shall have perpetual succession, and a common seal, if they think proper to have one; they may sue, and be sued, and shall generally have the same powers which any other body politic or corporate has or ought to have with regard to the purposes for which it is constituted.

34. Except as elsewhere provided the time of holding office as school trustee shall be three years. Provided that the trustees in any year elected shall remain in office until their successors are elected.

35. Every trustee after his election and before he shall be entitled to sit or vote as such at any meeting of the board, shall make before the chairman of the school meeting at which he was elected, or before a justice of the peace, a declaration, which he shall produce and deposit with the secretary-treasurer of the board, and which shall be in the following form :

"I., A. B., do solemnly declare that I will truly, faithfully, and to the best of my ability and judgment, discharge the duties of the office of school trustee for the Catholic school district of   to which I have been elected.

"Dated at   the   day of   18
"Taken before me, &c.,
    "C. D.
    J. P. (or chairman, as the case many be)."

36. The school trustees shall meet within ten days after receiving notice of their election for the purpose of choosing a chairman and a secretary-treasurer and transacting such other business as may be required.

(a.) In case of absence of the chairman from any meeting of the board, the then assembled school trustees shall elect one of their number to act in that capacity for the time being, who shall then be vested with the same powers and privileges as the ordinary chairman.

37. In the meetings of the school trustees all questions shall be decided by the majority of votes, and the chairman shall have the right to vote, but in case of an equality of votes the question shall be decided in the negative.

38. It shall be the duty of the board of trustees :

(a.) To take possession and have the custody and safekeeping of all school property which has been acquired or given for school purposes under this Act in their district, and such corporation shall be empowered to acquire and hold, as a corporation, by any title whatsoever, any land, movable property, moneys or income for school purposes, and to apply the same according to the terms on which the same was acquired or received, but they shall not, without the sanction of the board, have power to alienate or dispose of any school real estate ;

(b.) To do whatever they may judge expedient with regard to building, repairing, renting, warming, furnishing and keeping in order the school-house or school-houses in their district, its furniture and appendages, and the school land and inclosures held by them, and for procuring apparatus and school books for their school, and when there is no suitable school-house belonging to the district or when a second school-house is required, then, to build, rent, repair, furnish, warm and keep in order, a house and its appendages, to be used as a school-house;

(c.) To contract with and employ such teachers exclusively who hold certificates from the board, and such contract shall be in writing and signed by the contracting parties;

(d.) To provide for the salaries of teachers, and all other expenses of the school;

(e.) To visit the school once a month, for the purpose of seeing that it is conducted according to the prescribed regulations; and the school trustees, or any of them, shall, if necessary, make any suggestions in accordance with the said regulations, with a view to the more effectual working of the school, and should the teacher fail to act upon them, the matter shall be referred to the whole body of trustees, who shall report to the superintendent:

(f.) To see that the discipline of the school is properly enforced; at duly called meetings of the board of trustees to expel the unmanageable pupils on the complaint of the teacher; and hold meetings to inquire into the same;

(g.) To keep a record of their proceedings, signed for each sitting by the chairman and secretary, and also correct accounts of their receipts and expenditures, with reference to the school or schools under their control, mentioning especially what relates to each school, and such account shall be at all reasonable hours open to the inspection of the ratepayers of the school district;

(h.) To admit as pupils of the school any children whose parents or guardians are not assessed and do not pay the special tax for one-fourth of the estimated expenses of the school as provided in sections 24 and 25 of this Act, and to charge and collect a sum not exceeding fifty cents per month for each such pupil;

(i.) To have their schools in operation for at least six months every year when there are not less than ten children of school age in their district;

(j.) To transmit to the superintendent the half-yearly and annual reports and the census returns, required by him, on the forms provided, and to cause their books and accounts at any time to be laid open to his inspection, or to that of any person appointed by him for that purpose:

(k.) To call special meetings for any purpose whatever, whenever required to do so by the majority of the ratepayers or by the superintendent.

39. No act or proceeding of a board of trustees shall be deemed valid or binding on any party which is not adopted at a regular or special meeting of the corporation, of which notice shall have been given either by one of their body or the person chosen by them to act as a secretary-treasurer, to all the trustees, and a majority of the trustees at such meeting shall have full authority to perform any lawful business.

40. It shall not be lawful for any trustee to enter into a contract with the corporation of which he is a member, or to have any pecuniary claim on such corporation, except for a school site, or as a secretary-treasurer, and then only when he shall have been appointed by the other two members of the corporation.

41. No school trustee shall be teacher or inspector of any school in his school district.

42. Any person elected to the office of school trustee who refuses to serve as such shall forfeit the sum of five dollars for the use of the school district, and his neglect or refusal to take the declaration of office within one month after his election, if resident at the time within the district, shall be construed as such refusal, after which another person shall be elected to fill the place; but no school trustee shall be re-elected except by his own consent during the four years next after his going out of office.

43. Any person chosen as trustee may resign with the consent expressed in writing of his colleagues in office, and a continuous non-residence of three months shall cause the vacation of his office.

44. In all cases of vacancy another trustee shall be elected at a meeting called by the trustees or trustee remaining in office, and the person so elected shall hold office for the unexpired term of the trustee whom he replaces; provided that if the vacancy is not filled within one month, the superintendent shall appoint some qualified person to fill it.

45. In all cases of prolonged incapacity arising from sickness, no election or appointment to fill the said office shall take place unless the said incapacity has been established by the certificate of a physician, deposited with the secretary-treasurer, and the vacancy arising from such incapacity shall date from the day of the deposit of such certificate.

46. The board of school trustees or their secretary-treasurer shall have at all times during office hours free access to the assessment roll of the municipality, and they shall be permitted to copy therefrom that portion of it having reference to their respective school districts, together with the names and amount for which each individual is assessed.

47. If any trustee in cities and towns shall absent himself for three months from the meetings of the board of school trustees, without being authorized so to do by a resolution of the board, or if he ceases to reside in the school district for a period of three months consecutively, his seat shall thereby become vacant.

DISQUALIFICATION OF SCHOOL TRUSTEES.

48. Except as provided in clause seventeen, no person shall be eligible to be elected or to serve as a school trustee who is not a resident ratepayer of the district which he proposes to represent, and a Roman Catholic.

49. No person convicted of felony or of an infamous crime shall be eligible to be elected as a school trustee.

SECRETARY-TREASURER.

50. The trustees shall appoint as secretary-treasurer one of their own number, or some other competent person, and the duties of such secretary-treasurer shall include :

(a.) The correct and safe-keeping and producing (when called for) of the papers and moneys belonging to the corporation ;

(b.) The correct keeping of a record of all their proceedings in a book procured for that purpose ; and

(c.) The collecting, receiving and accounting for of all school moneys, whether from the government or otherwise, for the purpose of public school education within his district and the distributing of such moneys in the manner directed by the majority of the trustees.

51. Every secretary-treasurer shall before entering upon his duties as such give security to the school trustees by a bond signed and acknowledged before a justice of the peace, and such security shall be given by at least two solvent sureties, jointly and severally, to the satisfaction of the board of school trustees, and for the total amount of the moneys for which the secretary-treasurer may at any time be responsible, whether arising from the local school fund or from any particular contribution or donation paid into his hands for the support of schools, and such security shall be renewed or changed whenever its renewal or change is required by the school trustees.

(a.) In school districts in which the secretary-treasurer has not given such security the trustees shall be personally liable and responsible for any loss that may be caused through his default, except in case they shall, within three months from the date of their election as trustees or his appointment as secretary-treasurer, enter a written protest against the refusal of the majority to exact such security.

52. When the assessment is made by the trustees, the secretary-treasurer shall receive the assessment roll from the assessors, and shall thereupon notify each person whose name appears on said roll of the amount for which he is assessed, and such assessment roll shall be open at all reasonable hours to the inspection of any Roman Catholic ratepayer of the school district, and every such ratepayer shall be entitled to receive a copy thereof on payment to the secretary-treasurer at the rate of five cents per name on such roll ;

(a.) The secretary-treasurer shall notify each person whose name appears on the assessment roll of the date and the place fixed by the school trustees for the sitting of the court of revision ;

(b) The secretary-treasurer shall within one month after receiving the assessment roll from the assessors lay the same before the board of trustees, and after the said board have struck the rate he shall receive the roll from them for the purpose of collection.

53. Every secretary-treasurer shall prepare and submit to the board of school trustees annually, previous to the general meeting of the ratepayers, a detailed statement of receipts and expenditures of the school district for the current school year then expiring, and such statement after being approved by the school trustees shall be by them submitted at the annual meeting of the school district, and the secretary-treasurer shall on the payment to him of the sum of one dollar, furnish to any ratepayer a copy of such statement.

54. The remuneration of the secretary-treasurer may, in the discretion of the school trustees, be fixed at any amount not exceeding eight per cent on the moneys received by him in such capacity, but such remuneration shall include every service which the trustees may require from time to time from the secretary-treasurer, and shall cover all contingent expenses whatever, except such as may be specially authorized by rules and regulations of the Board of Education, and shall not in any case exceed the sum of one hundred dollars.

55. It shall be the duty of the board of trustees of cities and towns, and they are hereby empowered :

(a.) At their first meeting after the annual meeting of ratepayers, or at some subsequent meeting, to elect one of their number as chairman, and to appoint one of their number or some other person as the majority of the board may decide to be their secretary-treasurer, to determine the amount of salary to be paid to such officer, and to impose by by-law such additional duties as may be required of him by the board of trustees, and his appointment shall in all other respects be subject to the same duties, obligations and penalties as are imposed by this Act in the appointment of secretary-treasurers in rural school districts ;

(b.) To appoint, if they think proper to do so, a collector or collectors of school taxes for the city or town, who shall discharge similar duties and be subject to similar obligations and penalties and have the full powers and authority as a collector of a municipality ;

(c.) If they deem it advisable to do so, to make an estimate of the sum or sums required for educational purposes of the school district during the current school year ; to obtain a copy of the last revised assessment roll of the city or town that relates to properties liable to taxation for separate school purposes within the school district ; to strike and levy a rate for the raising of the amount of the said estimate upon such assessment, placing the amount of tax payable opposite the name or description of each person or property assessed ; and to place the said assessment roll in their collector's hands for collection, and he shall be empowered to collect the same in the same manner as any collector of a municipality ;

(d.) In case they deem it advisable to do so, to provide the clerk of the city or town before the 1st day of May in each school year, with their estimate of the amount required in such year by them for educational purposes, and accompany such estimate with a list of the names of the persons, or a description of the properties liable to be assessed for the support of the separate schools of which the board applying are trustees, and it shall be the duty of the council of such city or town to levy and collect the amount demanded and add a separate column for school taxes to their collector's roll, and to pay over such taxes monthly to the trustees as collected ;

(e.) To demand and obtain from the council of the city or town, if they deem it expedient to do so, a list of all uncollected school taxes for the current or for any previous school year, and it shall be the duty of the council to furnish such a list in compliance with such demand, and the said board may place such list in the hands of a collector appointed by them, whose powers, duties and obligations in collecting the same shall be the same as those of any collector of the municipality, and the said trustees may bring suit for the collection of all arrears of school taxes in a court of competent jurisdiction, whether the said arrears had been assessed by them or by the council of the municipality :

(*f.*) To collect at their discretion from the parents or guardians of children who do not reside or are not assessed within the school district, a sum not exceeding one dollar per month for each pupil attending their schools, and if they think proper so to do to supply all the pupils attending their schools with the necessary text books and other school requisites and to collect from their parents or guardians a sum not exceeding 20 cents per month for each pupil in payment for the same ;

(*g.*) To submit the books and accounts of their secretary-treasurer annually to the examination of the city or town auditor, or two auditors appointed by the board for that purpose, and to publish in one or more public newspapers or on printed sheets for the information of the public, on or before the 15th day of January in each year, a detailed statement of the receipts and expenditure of all school moneys for the current year and of the assets and liabilities of the board, with the certificate of the said auditor or auditors as to the correctness of such statement ;

(*h.*) To make all the returns required by the Department of Education or by the Board of Education upon the forms provided and within the time specified by the Department of Education or the board requiring the same ;

(*i.*) To require the officers and teachers to comply with the law and regulations of the Board of Education in the attendance and classification of pupils and the arrangement of their school exercises, the certification and duties of teachers, the arrangement of school rooms and their furniture, and the use of text books and apparatus ;

(*j.*) To purchase or rent school site or school premises, and rebuild, furnish, repair, warm and keep in order the school-houses and appendages, lands, inclosures, and movable property of the school district, and to provide registers in the prescribed form, suitable maps, apparatus, text and prize books for the schools, and if they deem it expedient, to establish and maintain school libraries ;

(*k.*) To determine under the direction and authority of the board the number, kind, grade and description of schools (such as male, female, infant, central or ward schools) to be established and maintained, the teachers to be employed, the terms upon which they are employed, the amount of their remuneration, and the duties in addition to those prescribed by the Board of Education, which they are to perform ;

(*l.*) To appoint with the concurrence of the Board of Education, an inspector or manager of the schools within the jurisdiction whose duty shall be, by frequent visits to the schools and in every other way to do all in his power to improve their character and efficiency ; he shall have control of the organization and management of the schools of such city or town, and report monthly to the trustees as to their condition and progress, but the schools of such city or town shall be under the supervision of the inspector appointed by the Board of Education for the county in which the city or town is situate except that in cities or towns in which a collegiate department is or may be established, the collegiate inspectors shall have such supervision and report half-yearly to the superintendent ;

(*m.*) To establish with the consent and not otherwise of the Board of Education and to conduct in accordance with the regulations of the same, a collegiate department for the preparation of students for matriculation in the University of Manitoba, for the preparation of students for first and second class teachers' certificates, and for the purpose of laying the foundation of a thorough education in the English or French language and literature ;

(*n.*) To exercise all the powers and perform all the duties not herein specified, and not inconsistent with those provisions that are given to the trustees of rural school districts by this Act.

PROSECUTION BY OR OF SCHOOL TRUSTEES.

56. The school trustees of any school district may institute suits, or prosecutions for the school assessments, assessment for school-houses, and for all arrears of the said assessments and monthly fees, and such suits or prosecutions may be instituted before the county court or before two justices of the peace of the county, and the justices may after judgment cause the amount of the judgment, together with the cost thereof, to be levied under warrant by the seizure and sale of the goods and chattels of the defendant,

such seizure and sale to be effected by the secretary-treasurer, who shall for that purpose have and execute the power of sheriff, and who shall be entitled for such services to the same fees as the said officer.

57. In all such suits or prosecutions judgment may be rendered with costs, and no judgment rendered on any such suit or prosecution shall be liable to be appealed from, nor shall any such suit or prosecution be removed by writ of certiorari.

58. No member of any board of school trustees shall engage in any suit at law as such trustee, as plaintiff, without a special authorization from the trustees, duly entered in the minutes, after deliberation : and every such action may be brought either by the chairman or by the secretary-treasurer, in the name of the corporation, as the board may see fit.

59. All persons entrusted in any manner with the carrying of this Act into effect, or qualified to vote at the election of school trustees, shall be competent to institute proceedings under this Act except in cases where it is specially provided to the contrary.

60. All contestation with regard to the election of school trustees and to the functions and powers assumed by school trustees or any of them, or their officers, or by any person or persons claiming to be such trustee or trustees, or officer or officers, may by any competent person be brought by a petition setting forth the case, of which a copy must have been served on the parties concerned, before the county court at its next sitting, and shall then be determined in a summary manner on the evidence adduced.

But no resolution, by-law, proceeding or action of any board of trustees shall be invalid or set aside by reason of any person whose election has been annulled or declared illegal having acted as a trustee.

61. Any school trustee whose election has been obtained by fraud or stratagem or by the votes of persons not qualified as electors, or any person usurping the functions of school trustee, or illegally holding that office, may be summarily prosecuted at the instance of any party interested or several collectively interested, before any one of the judges of the county court of the county in which such election, usurpation or illegal retention of office has taken place, for the purpose of declaring such election, or such retention of office, illegal and such seat vacant.

62. It shall be the duty of any judge of the Court of Queen's Bench or of the county court of this province, or any stipendiary magistrate, to investigate and decide any complaints which may be made in the manner provided by the statute in that behalf, in regard to the election of any school trustee, or in regard to any proceeding at any school meeting : provided always that no complaints in regard to any election or proceeding at any school meeting shall be entertained unless made in writing within twenty days after the holding of such election or meeting. The costs and expenses of such investigation shall be paid by the parties concerned in it, as such judge or magistrate may decide, but such judge or magistrate shall not be entitled for his own services, expenses to a greater sum than five dollars per day for each day actually engaged in such investigation.

63. The school trustees shall be constituted a court of revision for hearing and deciding any complaints that may be made against any assessment made under their authority, and shall sit as such at any time fixed by the trustees after eight days' notice given by posters in three public places of the district by the secretary treasurer; and the decision of the said court of revision shall be final when the amount to be paid shall not exceed twenty dollars ; and the members of the said court of revision shall be empowered to administer oath while sitting as such ; and every appeal from the decision of such court of revision shall be heard and determined finally at the next sitting of the county court within the jurisdiction of which the school district is situated.

QUORUM.

64. The quorum of any corporation, board or body constituted under this Act shall (unless otherwise expressly declared) be an absolute majority of all the members thereof; and the majority of the members present at any meeting regularly held at which there shall be a quorum may validly exercise the powers of the corporation.

ASSESSORS.

65. The school trustees may within twenty days after the annual school meeting, appoint one or more assessors from the resident ratepayers, provided the district is not included within a municipality, or the municipal council refuses or neglects to do so, and such remuneration shall be paid to such assessor as the board shall see fit.

66. Before entering upon the discharge of their duties such assessors shall be sworn before a justice of the peace to the faithful discharge of their duties, and they shall, within two weeks after their appointment, proceed to make out an assessment roll of the ratable property of each Roman Catholic ratepayer in the school district, and shall deliver the same into the hands of the secretary-treasurer of the school trustees within one month thereafter.

AUDITORS.

67. At every annual meeting of any rural school district there shall be appointed by the ratepayers two auditors, or persons to examine the accounts of the secretary-treasurer or of the school trustees and report thereon at the next annual meeting, and who shall certify to the correctness or otherwise of such accounts.

(a.) It shall be the duty of the secretary-treasurer to submit his books and vouchers to such auditors when called upon by them to do so. And their report shall be presented to the annual meeting next after their appointment.

68. It shall be the duty of every teacher employed by any board of school trustees—

(a.) To teach diligently and faithfully all the branches required to be taught in the schools according to the terms of his agreement with the school trustees, and in accordance with the laws of Manitoba relating to separate schools, or any by-laws or regulations issued under the same ;

(b.) To keep in the prescribed form the register of the school ;

(c.) To maintain proper order and discipline in his school ;

(d.) To keep a visitors' book (which the trustees shall provide) and enter therein the visits made to his school, and to present such book to every visitor and request him to make such remarks suggested by his visit ;

(e.) To give the trustees and visitors access at all times when desired by them to the registers and visitors' book appertaining to the school ;

(f.) To deliver up any school registers, visitors' book, school-house key or other school property in his possession on the demand or order of the board of school trustees employing him ;

(g.) To have at the end of every half year at least a public examination of his school, of which he shall give due public notice ;

(h.) To furnish to his superintendent or to the inspector any information which it may be in his power to give respecting anything connected with the working of his school, or in anywise affecting his interests or character.

69. All agreements between trustees and teachers to be valid and binding shall be in writing and signed by the teacher and chairman of the board of trustees employing him, and sealed with the corporate seal, if any, of the trustees.

(a.) Any teacher whose agreement has expired with the board of trustees, or who is dismissed by them, shall be entitled to receive forthwith all moneys due to him for his services as teacher while employed by the said board ; if such payment be not made by the trustees or tendered to the said teacher by them he shall be entitled to recover from the said trustees the full amount of his salary due and unpaid with ten per cent interest per annum until payment is made, by a suit in a court of competent jurisdiction, and upon his obtaining judgment therein, his case shall be a first lien upon all payments due the said trustees from any source whatsoever until the said claim is satisfied.

INSPECTORS.

70. The Board of Education shall have power to appoint inspectors who shall hold office during the pleasure of the board ; to define their duties and to provide for their remuneration ; and such inspectors shall visit the schools and report thereon at least twice a year.

VISITORS.

71. The visitor in each school district may be—
(a.) The resident Roman Catholic priest ;
(b.) The members of the Provincial Legislature ;
(c.) The judges of the Court of Queen's Bench and County Court ;
(d.) The members of the Department of Education ; and
(e.) The trustees of each school district in their own district.

72. In incorporated cities or towns, a general meeting of the visitors may be held at any time or place appointed by any two visitors, on sufficient notice being given to the other visitors, and the visitors thus assembled may devise such means as they may deem expedient for the efficient visitation of the schools, and in concert with the school authorities for promoting the establishment of libraries and the diffusion of knowledge.

SCHOOL ATTENDANCE.

73. The teacher of each school receiving public aid shall within ten days after the close of each semi-annual school term, transmit to his superintendent a correct statement of the names of the children attending such school, with their respective ages, and distinguishing between the sexes, together with the average attendance during the preceding school term, and a statement of the number of months during which the school has been kept open, with such additional information as the superintendent may from time to time require.

(a.) If any trustee or officer of a public school knowingly signs a false report, or if a public school keeps a false school register or makes a false return, that may thereby show a claim of such school to a larger sum than the just proportion of school moneys coming to the same, such school trustee, officer or teacher shall, for every offence, forfeit to the public fund of the municipality the sum of twenty dollars, for which any person whatever may prosecute him before a justice of the peace, and he may be convicted upon the oath of one credible witness other than the prosecutor.

ANNUAL CENSUS OF CHILDREN.

74. The school trustees in each school district shall between the first and thirtieth of November in each year cause to be made by their secretary-treasurer a census of the children in such school district from the age of five years inclusive to the age of fifteen years inclusive, giving the age in each case, and mentioning those who attend the school, and such census after being certified by the secretary-treasurer of the school district under oath signed by at least one of the trustees, shall, on or before the tenth of the month of December following, be presented to the superintendent, whose duty it shall be to forward the same to the Provincial Secretary within the eight days following, and no census shall be received by the superintendent after the said date of the 10th day of December in each year.

APPORTIONMENT OF PUBLIC MONEYS.

75. The sum appropriated by the legislature for school purposes shall be divided between the public and separate schools in the manner hereinafter provided in proportion to the number of children between the ages of five and fifteen inclusive, residing in the various public and separate school districts in the province where schools are in operation, as shown in the census returns.

76. The Provincial Treasurer and one other member of the Executive Council, to be appointed by the Lieutenant Governor, shall form a committee for the apportionment of education funds and legislative grant between the public and separate schools ; and the selection of a member of the Executive Council to act as a member of such committee, shall, when practicable, be so made, or from time to time changed by the Lieutenant Governor as to secure that one member of the said committee may be of the Catholic persuasion and one a non-Catholic.

10½

77. It shall be the duty of such committee on or before the fifteenth day of January in each year to apportion the education fund, and within two weeks after the prorogation of the session of the legislature at which the grant for education is voted, to apportion said grant between the schools, according to the aggregate number of children being respectively non-Catholic and Catholic between the ages of five inclusive and fifteen inclusive, who shall be found from the census hereinbefore described to be residing within all the school districts existing in the province.

78. If the census returns upon which such apportionment is at any time to be made, or any of them, be defective in any respect, the said committee shall have power to require school trustees to supply to the committee such information as will enable them to correct the same.

79. After such apportionment shall have been made the sum due to the separate schools shall be placed to the credit of the board in accounts to be opened in the books of the Treasury Department and in the Audit Office.

EXPENDITURE OF SCHOOL MONEYS.

80. (a.) From the sum so appropriated to the Board of Education there shall be paid such sums as may be provided by the Lieutenant-Governor in Council for incidental expenses and salaries of superintendent.

(b.) Then the sum of $75.00 shall be paid semi-annually to each school which has been in operation during the whole of the previous term, and a proportionate part thereof to each school in operation for a part of the same; and in the case of newly established schools, to those which have been in operation for at least one month of said term; provided that except in the case of new school districts no school shall be entitled to receive a larger amount than one-half the sum incurred by the trustees thereof for its current expenses during the term for which such grant is made; provided further that a reduction in the amount to be made may, in the discretion of the board, be made in the case of any school district in which the average attendance of the resident pupils enrolled for the term has been less than forty per cent of such enrolled number.

(c.) The residue remaining after all payments have been made as above provided shall be divided among all the school districts on the basis of average attendance of pupils at the schools of such districts. Provided that in reckoning such average attendance fifty per cent shall be added to the average attendance in rural school districts (being school districts outside the cities, towns and villages).

(d.) No school shall be entitled to receive any portion of the legislative grant whose trustees have neglected to transmit within the time provided by law in the preceding year the census returns which form the basis of the apportionment of the public funds, or whose annual or semi-annual returns are not transmitted as required by the regulations of the board, or whose school has not been kept in operation at least six months during the school year, unless with the sanction of the board.

(e.) No school district shall be entitled to receive any money from the legislative grant or the municipal levy in any year that does not contain at least ten resident children of school age, but the trustees of such may levy and collect from their school district the amount of any indebtedness that may fall due within the same during such year.

81. All payments to school districts shall be made to the order of the duly qualified teacher or teachers of the school, unless it be shown that the salary of such teacher or teachers has been paid in full.

(a.) All payments made by the Provincial Treasurer for the purposes of education shall be made direct to the person or persons entitled to receive the money. Provided no payment shall be made except upon the requisition of the superintendent of education.

82. Any school not conducted according to all the provisions of this or any Act in force for the time relating to separate schools or the regulations of the Board of Education in force under its authority, shall not be deemed a separate school within the

meaning of the law, and such schools shall neither participate in the educational fund nor in the legislative grant.

ARBITRATION.

83. In case of any difference between school trustees and teachers in regard to his salary or the sum due him or claimed to be due, or any other matter connected with his duty, the same shall be submitted to arbitration, in which case each party shall choose an arbitrator.

84. In case either party in the first instance neglects or refuses to appoint an arbitrator on his behalf, the party requiring the arbitration, may, by notice in writing to be served upon the party so neglecting or refusing, require the last named within three days exclusive of the day of service of such notice, to appoint an arbitrator on his behalf, and such notice shall name the arbitrator of the party requiring the arbitration ; and in case the party served with such notice does not, within the three days mentioned therein, name and appoint an arbitrator, then the party requiring the arbitration may appoint the second arbitrator.

85. The superintendent or a member of the Board of Education, to be nominated by such superintendent, shall be the third arbitrator.

86. The arbitrators may require the attendance of any or all the parties interested in the reference, and of their witnesses, and may direct them or any of them to produce all documents, books, papers, or writings bearing on the matter in question ; and the arbitrators may take evidence on oath.

87. The said arbitrators or any two of them may issue their warrant to any person named therein to enforce the collection of any moneys by them awarded to be paid, and the person named in such warrant shall have the power and authority to enforce the collection of the monies mentioned in the said warrant with all reasonable costs by seizure and sale of the property of the party or corporation against whom the same has issued, as any bailiff of the county court has in enforcing a judgment and execution issued out of such court.

88. In case of any dispute or difference arising between any two boards of school trustees in regard to any sum of money due or claimed to be due under any Act of the province of Manitoba, the same shall be referred to arbitration in the manner by this Act provided ; and, provided always, that in differences between any two boards of school trustees, the third arbitrator shall be chosen by the other two, and the decision of such three arbitrators shall be final.

MUNICIPAL OFFICERS.

89. It shall be the duty of the city or town clerk, or clerks of municipalities to furnish to the board of school trustees five days before the annual school meeting authorized to be held under this Act, a certified copy of the last revised municipal voters' list for each ward in the city, town or municipality in which such act is in force.

HOLIDAYS.

90. Every Saturday and every statutory holiday shall be a holiday in the public schools : subject, however, to regulations respecting holidays as the Board of Education may from time to time make for the schools.

BY-LAWS FOR COMPULSORY ATTENDANCE OF CHILDREN.

91. Every board of school trustees may, with the sanction of the board make, amend or revoke any by-laws for their school district, for any of the following purposes :

(a.) Requiring the parents or guardians of Roman Catholic children of not less than seven years nor more than twelve years of age, as may be fixed by the law, to send such children to school for a certain period in each year, unless sufficient evidence be produced by such parents or guardians, that they cannot do so; and any of the following shall be considered a reasonable excuse:

(1.) That the child is under instruction in some other manner satisfactory to the magistrate before whom the complaint may be brought:

(2.) That the child has been prevented from attending school from sickness or any unavoidable cause;

(3.) That such child has reached a standard of education of the same or greater degree than that to be obtained in such public school by children of twelve years of age:

(b.) Determining the time during which such children are to attend school;

(c.) Imposing penalties upon parents or guardians for the breach of any by-law;

(1). Admonition in the form of a note of warning, signed by the chairman of the board of school trustees;

(2). Summons to appear before the board of school trustees and to receive reprimand from the chairman, if merited;

(3). Complaints by the board of school trustees to any justice of the peace of the district, who may impose a fine not exceeding twenty-five cents for the first offence, fifty cents for the second, and so on, doubling the last fine for any repetition of the offence.

92. It shall be competent for any judge of the county or stipendiary magistrate to investigate and decide upon any complaints made by the trustees or any person authorized by them against any parent or guardian for the violation of any such by-law as by the previous section provided, may be enacted; and it shall be the duty of such judge of the county court to ascertain, as far as may be the circumstances of any party complained of, for not sending his or their child to school or otherwise educating him or them, and whether the alleged violation has been caused by poverty or ill-health, and in any such case the judge shall not award punishment but shall report the circumstances to the trustees making the complaint.

REGISTRATION OF SCHOOL TAXES.

93. Previous to the first day of August in each year the boards of school trustees, if they themselves collect the school taxes, shall cause to be made a list of the names of all persons in their district in arrears for school taxes, the amount due by them, the lot or lots on which such taxes are due; and if such taxes remain unpaid it shall be the duty of the said board of school trustees on or previous to the last day of August in each year, to register the said lots with the amount due on real estate only, with the treasurer of the municipality in which such lots are situated, and if such lots are not within a municipality then in the registry office of the county in which such lands are situated, by filing a copy of the tax list, after which such taxes shall become a first lien or mortgage on the lot or lots on which they are respectively due and payable, and any sale of property or transfer made thereafter shall be subject to such taxes.

94. In incorporated cities and towns the board of school trustees shall each have power to borrow money for the purchase of school lands or the erection of school buildings or other school purposes in the manner hereinafter provided.

BORROWING MONEY.

95. If the ratepayers of any school district at a public meeting duly called, require the trustees to borrow any sum of money for the purchase of school sites or erecting of school-houses and their appendages, or for the purchase or erection of a teacher's residence, or for the purpose of paying off any debt, charge or lien against such school-house, or residence, or against the trustees of any school district incurred by them as such trustees for any of the purposes aforesaid, the said trustees shall forward to the Lieutenant Governor in Council, a certified copy of the minutes of such meeting, and the Lieutenant Governor in Council may thereupon sanction such loans, and such sanction shall bind the ratepayers of the said school district to cause to be levied a sum sufficient for the payment of the principal and interest on any such loan at the times when the same shall become payable, as provided between trustees and the lender.

(a.) No loan under two thousand dollars shall be made for any term exceeding ten years nor for any amount for a period exceeding twenty years.

(b.) The principal on such loan shall be made payable by annual instalments unless with the sanction of the Lieutenant Governor in Council and the said annual instalments together with interest on the principal of such loan may be applied towards the immediate redeeming of the debt contracted by the issue of such debentures, and all school boards that have issued debentures not payable in instalments shall invest in a sinking fund annually, a sufficient sum to meet such debentures when due, and such investment shall be made with the consent and advice of the superintendent, and when so made shall not be payable to the order of the trustees without such order being countersigned by said superintendent until their debentures mature.

(c.) Notice of such meeting shall be given by posting up on the door of the school-house (if any) and in two or more conspicuous places within the school district for which such loan is sought to be obtained, at least two weeks previous to such meeting, a notice in the form or to the effect of that set forth in said schedule A of this Act.

(d.) A majority of the Roman Catholic ratepayers of any such schools present at such meeting shall be sufficient to authorize such loans, and the assent of the Lieutenant Governor shall be obtained before such loan is completed.

(e.) The assent of the Lieutenant Governor to any such loan shall be conclusive evidence of all the necessary formalities having been complied with, and that such loan is one which such school district may lawfully make.

(f.) Any school district having obtained the assent of the Lieutenant Governor to a loan, may issue debentures therefor in the form set forth in schedule B of this Act, to secure the amount of the principal and interest upon such loan, upon such terms as such loan can be obtained, and the said debentures shall be sufficient, when signed by the secretary-treasurer and countersigned by one or more trustees, to bind the said trustees and to create a charge or lien against all revenues of the school district for which such loan is made.

(g.) All debentures issued or to be issued under the authority of this Act and the coupons attached thereto shall create and be a charge and lien upon all school property then or thereafter acquired by, or granted, or given to the school district which shall issue the said debentures as well as upon all of the Roman Catholic property assessable in such school district for school purposes for the said district, and the amounts from time to time falling due upon such debentures and coupons (subject to any provisions for establishment of sinking funds for the repayment of any such debentures) shall be included in the amount required from time to time for school purposes for the said district, and shall be collected and received by and paid to the trustees of the said school district in the manner directed for the raising of money for school purposes.

(h.) Any writ of execution against the trustees for any school district which school lies wholly within one municipality, may be endorsed with a direction to the sheriff to levy the amount thereof by rate, and the proceedings thereon shall be the following:—

(1.) The sheriff shall deliver a copy of the writ and endorsement to the treasurer of the municipality in which such school district is situate, or leave such copy at the office or dwelling-house of such officer with a statement in writing of the sheriff's fees and of the amount required to satisfy such execution, including in such amount the interest calculated to some day as near as is convenient to the day of service.

(2.) In case this amount with interest thereon from the day mentioned in the statement is not paid to the sheriff within one month after the service, the sheriff shall examine the assessment roll of the municipality in which such school district is situate, and shall in like manner as rates are struck for general municipal purposes strike a rate on the assessable lands in said school district sufficient on the dollar to cover the amount due on the execution with such addition to the same as the sheriff deems sufficient to cover the interest and his own fees up to the time when such rate will probably be available.

(3.) He shall thereupon issue a precept or precepts under his hand and seal of office directed to the said treasurer, and shall annex to every such precept the roll of such rate, and shall by such precept after reciting the writ, and that the said trustees had neglected to satisfy the same, and referring to the roll annexed to the precept, command the said treasurer to levy or cause to be levied such rate at the time and in the manner by law required in respect of the general municipal rates.

(4.) At the time for levying the annual rates next after the receipt of such precept the said treasurer shall add a column to the tax roll of the lands in said school district headed " Execution rate of A. B. vs. The School Trustees for the Separate School District of   in the Province of Manitoba " (or, as the case may be, adding a column for each execution, if more than one) and shall insert thereon the amount by such precept required to be levied upon each person respectively, and shall levy the amount of such execution rate as aforesaid, and said treasurer, so soon as the amount of such execution or executions is collected, shall return to the sheriff the precept with the amount levied thereon.

(5.) The sheriff shall, after satisfying the executions and all fees thereon, return any surplus within ten days after receiving the same to the said treasurer for the general purposes of the said school trustees.

(6.) The treasurer shall for all purposes connected with carrying into effect or permitting or assisting the sheriff to carry into effect the provisions of this Act with respect to such execution, be deemed to be an officer of the court out of which the writ issued, and as such shall be amenable to the court and may be proceeded against by attachment, mandamus or otherwise, in order to compel him to perform the duties hereby imposed upon him.

(7.) The above clauses, one to six both inclusive, shall be applicable to executions against the school trustees for any district lying within more than one municipality, but in such case the said sheriff shall strike a rate on the assessable lands in said school district from the assessment rolls of the several municipalities in which said school is situate, and shall deliver to the treasurer of each of the municipalities the precept or precepts aforesaid, attaching a roll of said rate so far as it applies to the lands of said school district in the municipality of each of such treasurers.

SCHEDULE " A."

PUBLIC NOTICE.

Notice is hereby given that a meeting of the Roman Catholic ratepayers within the separate school district of   number   will be held at the   in the said district on   day the   day of   A.D. 18   at the hour of   o'clock in the   noon, for the purpose of considering the expediency of raising money by way of loan to (here state the purpose for which the loan is intended).

Dated this   day of   A.D. 18   .

Secretary-Treasurer.

SCHEDULE " B."

Debentures of the separate school trustees for the   separate school district of   number   in the   Province of Manitoba.

The school trustees for the separate school district of   number   in the province of Manitoba, promise to pay to bearer at the   at   the sum of   dollars of lawful money of Canada,   years from the date hereof, and to pay interest thereon during the currency hereof at the same place at the rate of   per centum per annum, to the bearer of the coupons hereunto annexed respectively, and numbered with the number of this debenture.

Issued at   this   day of   18   , by and under the authority of subsection *f* of section 95 of an Act of the Legislature of Manitoba, passed in the   year of Her Majesty's reign, chapter
S. H.

Trustee.

T. R.
Secretary-Treasurer.

Coupon No.

The school trustees of the separate school district of   number   in the province of Manitoba, will pay the bearer hereof at the   on the day of   18   , the sum of   dollars, being interest due on that day on school debentures, &c.

T. R.
Secretary-Treasurer.

The minutes of any section of the ratepayers of a school district called to consider the propriety of borrowing money as above mentioned shall be headed with a statement in the following form or to the same effect :—
 " Minutes of a public meeting of the Roman Catholic ratepayers of the separate
" school district of   number   in the province of Manitoba, held the
"   day of   18   in pursuance of a notice given as
" required by 'The Separate School Act,' and called for the purpose of considering
" (and advising the trustees of said school section in respect to) the question of raising
" or borrowing a sum of money for the purpose of (here state the purpose for which the
" loan is intended as is the public or posted notice).
 " The said meeting having been organized by Mr. A. B. as chairman, and Mr. C. B.
" as secretary, the following proceedings were had :
 " It was moved by Mr.   &c. (the motions and formal proceedings
" of the meetings to be then given, certified at the foot thereof to be correct, and signed
" by the chairman and secretary)."
 The said minutes shall also contain a list of the names of the ratepayers who voted at the said meeting upon the question of raising or borrowing money, distinguishing those who are freeholders from those who are not, and recording the vote given by each person " for or against the said question."

96. A copy of said minutes shall be given to the secretary-treasurer of the board of trustees of the district for the information of the said board and the original with a declaration endorsed thereon and attached thereto, taken before a justice of the peace or other person authorized to take declarations under the statute, with a copy of the notice calling such meeting, proving the posting of the said notice as required by the Act, shall be given or transmitted to the superintendent ; and it shall be the duty of such superintendent, with as little delay as possible after the receipt of such minutes and proof, to inquire and satisfy himself that the purpose for which the loan is required is a proper and necessary one, and having regard to the means of the ratepayers of such school district to repay the same ; and if such superintendent approves of such loan he shall transmit said minutes, proof, and other documents connected thereof to the provincial secretary together with a certificate or note of his approval endorsed thereon over his signature.

97. It shall be the duty of the secretary-treasurer of the board of school trustees of any school district, upon being made aware that a loan as aforesaid had been sanctioned by the ratepayers to at once transmit to the superintendent a statement duly certified under the hand of the said secretary-treasurer and the seal of the said board of trustees, to be correct, showing the amount of the assessed value of the real and personal estate of such school district, its debentures indebtedness including the amount proposed to be added under such by-law then being submitted for approval ; its indebtedness other than under said debentures ; the yearly rate in the dollar required to pay said debenture debt ; the total rate required for all purposes and the interest past due, if any, on the indebtedness of said school district.

98. A statement embodying the information mentioned in the last preceding section as to the assets and liabilities of the school section, shall be written or printed on the back of each debenture, issued under the authority of this Act, and following such statement shall also be written or printed the words " Issued under the provisions of the Separate School Act," viz. :   Vic., Cap   .

99. Upon the assent of the Lieutenant Governor being obtained to such loan and upon presentation within six months thereafter to the Provincial Secretary or Acting

Provincial Secretary of the debenture or debentures issued to raise the same the said Provincial Secretary or Acting Provincial Secretary (unless such assent has in the mean time been withdrawn) shall sign such debenture or debentures under the statement or endorsement thereon hereinbefore mentioned, and shall affix the seal of his office, or of the province thereto, and such signature and seal shall be conclusive that all the formalities in respect to said loan and the issue of said debentures have been complied with, and that the correctness of the statement or endorsement thereon, and the legality of the issue of such debenture shall be thereby conclusively established, and its validity shall not be questionable by any court in this province, but the same shall to the extent of the assets of the school district issuing the same, be a good and indefeasible security in the hands of any *bona fide* holder thereof.

100. The Governor General in Council, when the question of any school loan shall be before him for assent thereto, may take into consideration the effect of the proposed loan upon the security of any previous loan, in case the new proposed loan shall be repayable before a former one, or former ones, and may withhold such assent to such new loan if he considers that the security of the holder of any existing debenture loan of such school district was likely to be rendered insufficient by the reason of the date of payment of the proposed new loan being prior to that of any then existing debenture debt of such district.

101. The trustees of any school district may under the advice and with the consent of the superintendent, invest any money under the control of such trustee as a sinking fund for the payment of any loan, or otherwise held for school purposes and not required for expenditure within twelve months.

102. The trustee of any school district may with the consent and approval of the superintendent sell and dispose of any land or real estate, or any interest therein for the benefit and advantage of said school district and convey the same or any portion thereof in fee simple or for any less estate to any purchaser or purchasers thereof, or of any interest of freehold, leasehold, or other estate therein, by deed or other instrument as the case may be signed by the chairman and secretary-treasurer of such school district.

103. None of the provisions of this Act shall affect any suit pending in any of the courts at the date of the passing of the same.

104. In the case of any rural school district the trustees of which neglect or refuse to levy or ask the council to levy a special rate to meet their debentures indebtedness maturing within the school year, and in the case of any rural school district in which there is not a legally competent school board, the superintendent shall be empowered to act for such school board or school district in requiring the council or councils concerned to levy or collect the sums he shall designate as necessary to meet such indebtedness, and the council or councils shall levy and collect such sum and pay the same over to the creditors upon the order of the said superintendent. And it is further provided that upon the trustees of any rural school district becoming legally incompetent or unable to act from any cause and there being a sufficient number of ratepayers resident in the district to form a new school board, the superintendent shall thereupon be invested with the powers of the school trustees for such district, and shall be empowered to collect and receive all moneys due the said trustees from any source, to take possession of all their school properties, secure a proper title for all properties they may be entitled to, and in his discretion to dispose of or sell the same ; provided that all moneys received by the superintendent in any way in behalf of such district shall be paid over by him to meet the liabilities of the same that may become due from time to time.

LOANS.

105. At any time in any one year before the estimate of a school district has been prepared by a board of school trustees or handed to the clerk of the municipality, or before the moneys have been paid over to the board by the municipality, a board of school trustees in any city, town or local municipality, may borrow money upon the credit of the board and give the promissory note or notes of the board for the same, or for the moneys theretofore borrowed to such an amount as is legally authorized ;

provided, however, that no such money shall be borrowed or notes given to an amount exceeding in the aggregate one-half of the amount of the said estimate for the next preceding year, if such estimate has not been made for the current year ; and provided also that such moneys shall only be borrowed or notes given upon a by-law of the board, which recite the amounts previously borrowed and the notes previously given therefor and any sum paid thereon, but any error or omission in reciting such sums or notes shall not invalidate such by-law as against a *bona fide* lender or payee or holder for value of any such note having notice of such error or omission.

"(*a.*) Any such note or debt for money so borrowed may be enforced against the board of school trustees, and the ratepayers liable to contribute to its revenues in the same manner as claims against or debts of municipalities, may be enforced under the Municipal Act."

"(*b.*) Upon the payment to the board by a municipality of any portion of the sums to be levied for the trustees by a municipality it shall be the duty of the board of school trustees to apply one-half of such sum so paid to it for the reduction of the debt incurred for moneys so borrowed, or upon such note or notes, or in the event of no such debt or note or not sufficient thereof to exhaust the one-half of the sum so paid being then overdue, then to deposit such half, or the unexhausted portion thereof in some chartered bank and to apply the same to such debt or notes as may become due and payable."

(*c.*) All payments authorized by loan which are in the discretion of the Board of Education, shall be subject to ratification by the Lieutenant Governor in Council.

EXPROPRIATION.

106. It shall be the duty of the trustees of every school district to purchase or lease, and take with the consent, in writing, of the Board of Education in that behalf, the necessary land or real property for school-houses, teachers' residences and other buildings in connection therewith, and if necessary for the purpose aforesaid, to increase the extent of the school grounds, already in possession, by purchasing or leasing and taking lands adjoining the same.

(1.) No land or property may be taken for the purpose aforesaid without the consent of the owner, if, at the time of the application of the trustees for the same :

(*a.*) The said land or property is owned by any religious, charitable or educational corporation ;

(*b.*) The land or property required for a separate school is owned by a non-Catholic;

(*c.*) In a rural school district the land required is less than three hundred yards from the owner's residence or buildings or exceeds one acre in extent ;

(*d.*) In a city or town the lot required is not vacant ;

(2.) For the purposes aforesaid the school trustees shall first serve the owners of the land or parties empowered to convey the land required as aforesaid with a notice which shall contain :

(*a.* A description of the land to be taken :

(*b.*) A declaration of readiness to pay some certain sum or rent, as the case may be, for such land :

(*c.*) The name of a person to be appointed as the arbitrator of the school trustees if their offer be not accepted, and

(*d.*) Such notice shall be accompanied by the affidavit of one or more of the school trustees, setting forth that he knows the land, that the said land is required for school purposes, and that the sum offered is in his opinion a fair compensation.

(3.) If within ten days after service of the said notice the person owning the said land signifies in writing his readiness to accept the said sum for rent, then the school trustees shall cause the proper agreements and contracts to be made and entered into, and the price of compensation to be paid.

(4.) If within the time aforesaid, the owner or holder of the land does not signify his readiness to accept the said sum, but gives notice in writing, of the name of his arbitrator, then the two arbitrators shall jointly appoint the third, and if they cannot agree upon a third, the judge of the county court having jurisdiction in the division, in which the land is situate, shall appoint upon application such a third arbitrator.

(5.) If within the time aforesaid the said owner or holder of the land does not notify the trustees of his acceptance of the sum offered nor of the name of a person whom he appoints as arbitrator, then the judge of the county court shall, upon application appoint one in his stead, and the third arbitrator shall be appointed as aforesaid.

(6.) Where the person owning or holding the said lands or his agent or representative is unknown, or cannot be found with due diligence, or is incapable of receiving tender, then upon proof thereof to the county court judge, the said judge may dispense with such tender and notice; and in such case notice of submission to arbitration shall be published in a newspaper in or near the district in which the land lies, and subsequent proceedings may thereafter be taken as if such tender had been personally made and notice given.

(7.) The said arbitrators duly appointed, or a majority of them, shall value the land and make an award in writing and fix the amount of the costs of the arbitration not to exceed $3 per day for each arbitrator, and 10 cents per mile each way for travelling expenses, and they shall further direct which of the parties should pay the said costs, and if a portion, in what proportion.

(8.) An appeal to the judge of the county court shall lie upon application filed and served within ten days of the award for the revision of the costs taxed.

(9.) The compensation money agreed upon by the trustees or awarded by the arbitrators for any such land or property shall stand instead of such land or property, and any claim thereto or encumbrance, upon said lands or property shall be converted into a claim for such compensation money, or to a proportionate amount thereof, and shall be void as respects the land or property which shall by the fact of the making of said tender or award and of the payment of the money, become and be absolutely invested in the trustees for the purposes of this Act.

(10.) If the person owning such land is incapable of conveying the same, or the person to whom the compensation money is payable is incapable of executing or refuses to execute a proper conveyance and transfer of the said lands to said trustees or cannot be found, or is unknown or has no agent or representative, or the trustees have reason to fear any claim or encumbrance, they shall pay the compensation money agreed upon or the money awarded into the office of the clerk or prothonotary of the Court of Queen's Bench with interest thereon for six months at the rate of six per cent per annum, and deliver to the clerk or prothonotary of the court, a copy of the conveyance or agreement or award, or a certified copy of the agreement or award.

(11.) Notice in such form and for such time as the court appoints shall be forthwith inserted by the prothonotary in a newspaper in or near the district in which the lands are situate and shall state the facts under which such money is paid, and call upon all persons entitled thereto, or claiming the same or any part thereof, to file their claims, and such claims shall be received and adjudged upon by the court and such proceedings shall forever bar all claims to the compensation money or any part thereof, and the court shall make such order for the proper distribution or payment of said monies and for costs incidental to the application as may be proper.

107. No person suffering from any contagious or infectious disease, or who resides in a house in which any such disease exists shall be entitled to attend or enter any separate school during the existence of any such disease as aforesaid nor at any time thereafter, until he presents to the trustees of the school he wishes to attend a certificate of a physician that there is no longer danger of contagion or infection from his attendance to the other pupils of the school, provided that in rural school districts the trustees may, in the absence of a physician admit applicants for admission, without such certificate, if they are satisfied that there is no danger of contagion or infection from their doing so. And any parent or guardian of any child who knowingly sends such child to any public school in contravention of these provisions shall be liable, upon conviction before a justice of the peace, upon the complaint of the trustees or of any ratepayer of the school to a fine not exceeding ten dollars for each offence or imprisonment in the common jail for a period not exceeding thirty days.

FINES AND PENALTIES.

108. Any trustees or secretary-treasurer neglecting or refusing to discharge any duty assigned to him or them by this Act, shall be liable to a penalty of ten dollars for

each offence, and the said penalties may be recovered within three months of the time when such offence was committed.

109. Whenever any school trustee or secretary-treasurer, after his dismissal, resignation or ceasing to hold office, detains any money, book, paper or property belonging to the school trustees of any school, he shall thereby incur a penalty of not less than five dollars nor more than twenty dollars for each day during which he shall retain possession of any such money, book, paper or property, after having received a notice from the superintendent of education requiring him to deposit the same in the hands of some person mentioned in such notice.

110. If any trustee of a school, or other person, knowingly signs a false report, or if any teacher of a common school keeps a false school register, or makes a false return with a view of obtaining a larger sum than the just proportion of school moneys coming to such school, such trustee or teacher shall for each offence forfeit the sum of twenty dollars.

111. Every farmer, head of a family or guardian who refuses to give the trustees of any school district the information required by them to enable them to make up the census of children required by this Act, or who makes a false declaration, shall incur a penalty of not less than five nor more than twenty-five dollars.

112. Any justice of the peace, assessor, constable, or other officer neglecting or refusing to discharge any duty assigned to him by the provisions of this Act shall be liable to a penalty for each offence of a sum not exceeding fifty dollars.

113. If any person wilfully makes a false declaration of his right to vote, he shall be liable to a penalty of not less than fifty nor more than one hundred dollars.

114. The proceedings of every school meeting shall, within eight days thereafter be reported by the chairman of such meeting to the superintendent under a penalty of five dollars.

115. Any person who wilfully disturbs, interrupts, or disquiets the proceedings of any school meeting, or any one who interrupts or disturbs any school by rude or indecent behaviour or by making a noise either within the place where school is kept or held, or so near thereto as to disturb the order or exercises of the school, shall for each offence on conviction thereof before a justice of the peace, forfeit and pay a sum not exceeding twenty dollars, together with the cost of the conviction as the said justice may think fit.

116. Any person chosen as trustee who has not refused to accept office, and who at any time refuses or neglects to perform his duties shall forfeit the sum of twenty dollars.

117. Should the trustees of any school wilfully neglect or refuse to exercise all the corporate powers vested in them by this Act, or any other Act or Acts of this province, or the fulfilment of any contract or agreement made by them, any trustee or trustees so neglecting or refusing to exercise such powers, shall be held to be personally responsible for the fulfilment of such contract or agreement.

118. All such prosecution for fines and penalties may be instituted by any competent person before any justice of the peace who may convict the offender on the oath of one credible witness other than the prosecutor; and if upon conviction the penalty, with costs, is not paid forthwith, the same shall, under warrant of such justice, be levied with costs of distress, sale of goods and chattels of the offender; and such penalties, when so paid and collected, shall, by such justice, be paid over to the school fund of the district to which such delinquent belongs.

119. It shall be the duty of the superintendent in case of the loss of any school money or properties belonging to any school district through default, embezzlement or wilful neglect of any trustee or person connected therewith, to prosecute such trustee or person in his own name as such superintendent for the benefit of the district concerned, and to collect any costs that may be incurred by him in such prosecution from the school district or districts for whose benefit such prosecution was undertaken, by notifying the clerk of the municipality in which each such district is wholly or partly situated, and such clerk shall thereupon pay the said costs of the superintendent out of the municipal levy for the said school district, before paying any portion of the same to the trustees, provided that all such prosecutions shall be undertaken only when authorized by a resolution of the Board of Education.

NORMAL SCHOOLS.

120. The Board of Education is hereby empowered :

(a). To establish in connection with any separate schools which may be established at St. Boniface, normal school departments, with a view to the instruction and training of teachers of public schools in the science of education and the art of teaching, and to establish and provide for the conducting of teachers' institutes at any other schools within the jurisdiction of the board ;

(b.) To make, from time to time, rules and regulations necessary for the management and government of the said departments ;

(c.) To arrange with the trustees of such public schools all things which may be expedient to promote the objects and interests of the said normal school departments ;

(d.) To prescribe the terms and conditions on which students and pupils will be respectively received and instructed in the said departments ;

(e.) The determine the number and compensation of teachers, and of all others who may be employed in the said departments;

(f.) The select a suitable person as principal of the normal school under its management ; and the salary of the said principal shall be fixed by the Lieutenant Governor in Council and paid from the legislative grant.

121. The Lieutenant Governor in Council may direct that a sum not exceeding one-tenth of the amount of the grant for educational purposes be allowed for the maintenance of normal school departments as hereby established.

122. All moneys which on the 30th day of April, 1890, were held by the Government of the province of Manitoba for the use and benefit of the Roman Catholic section of the then Board of Education shall be by the said government held for the use and benefit of the Board of Education to be established under the provisions of this Act; shall be applied and paid out for the same purposes and under the same conditions as are provided by this Act in respect of other moneys which may be held by the said government for the use and benefit of separate schools.

123. In case of the establishment of any school district under the provisions of this Act with boundaries substantially similar to those of any Roman Catholic school district which was in existence on the 30th day of April, 1890 ; and in case the property or assets of the Catholic school district have been transferred to or taken by any board of school trustees which has been in existence under or by virtue of the Acts relating to education and public schools since the 1st day of May, 1890, then and in every such case the property and assets shall be transferred and delivered up to the new board of trustees established under the provisions of this Act.

EXHIBIT Q.

REPORT ON FRENCH SCHOOLS.

(A. L. YOUNG.)

I have the honour to submit the following report on the French schools of the province of Manitoba, for the year 1894.

From the records of the Catholic section of the old school board it appears that there were some ninety-one school districts under their control previous to the time when the present School Act came into force. A number of these districts, however, had been organized where the Catholic population was insufficient to support them, consequently several of them had never been put in operation, while others were maintained for a short time only.

The total number of districts disbanded for various reasons is twenty-four. In the majority of these cases the Catholic children attend the public schools where it is possible for them to do so.

Twenty-seven of these old districts, together with nine newly formed ones, have accepted the public school system ; making a total of thirty-six school districts now under government control.

Of the newly formed districts several are in mixed settlements, the French and English being about equally divided. In such cases I find that even when the Catholics have full control of the district they generally put in one English trustee. In one case the only Protestant in the district was unanimously elected a member of the school board.

Convent schools supported by voluntary subscriptions, fees, &c., are in operation at the following places :—Winnipeg, St. Boniface, St. Norbert, St. Jean Baptiste, Ste Anne, St. Pierre-Jolys, St. François Xavier and Brandon. In addition to these there are some thirty-eight schools throughout the province still conducted as separate schools and supported by voluntary subscriptions. The salaries paid in all such cases are very low.

In visiting the different French settlements throughout the province I find a growing interest in regard to educational matters.

I visited the Dauphin country for the first time in November last. Here I found a large number of half-breeds and French Canadians settled along the Turtle River. All were extremely anxious to have a school started, and eagerly signed a petition asking for the formation of a district at this point. Another petition was sent in at the same time by the French settlers in the vicinity of Elliott's stopping place on the Dauphin Road.

Owing to the lateness of the season I was unable to visit the French settlement on the Mossy River between Lakes Dauphin and Winnipegosis.

I also visited the French settlements along Lake Manitoba for the first time last fall. The Catholic Mission at St. Laurent is very thickly settled with half-breeds and a few French Canadians. The trustees take considerable interest in regard to school matters, and have engaged Alex. DeLaronde, B.A., who is at present attending the Normal School in Winnipeg, to take charge of the two schools which are located at this point. There are about sixty pupils enrolled in each one of these schools.

The French settlers in the vicinity of Oak Lake are now fairly well supplied with schools. Several new districts have been formed since my first visit in 1893.

The old Decorby school district at Fort Ellice was reorganized last fall, but owing to their territory having been encroached upon during the past five years, they are now limited to eleven sections of very poor land. The probabilities are that they will have a hard struggle to maintain a school at this place.

On my return from Fort Ellice I drove through the Hungarian settlement in Huns Valley. The school here had been closed for some time. Material is now being taken out and preparations are being made to build as soon as possible. I am in hopes that the new school will be opened early next spring.

The majority of the districts in the eastern part of the province require to be reorganized, as many of them appear to have no definite boundaries which are recognized by the municipalities.

With the exception of a very good supply of maps, the equipment of these schools leaves very much to be desired. The blackboard space is very limited and would be considered practically useless by any teacher who had taken a course of normal training.

A great drawback to some of the schools especially in the poorer districts is the lack of school books ; this difficulty is overcome in some cases by the trustees using the school funds for the purchase of books required, and supplying them to the children free of charge.

As a rule the teachers have the ability and energy to do good work, but they lack the normal school training. The different subjects are taken up and taught in the same manner that was done in the province of Quebec twenty years ago.

Very good work along a certain line is done in some subjects. For instance I have in my possession quite a number of letters received from French teachers, some of them written in English, which will compare favourably with correspondence received from English teachers.

I have seen a number of written engagements with teachers of schools which are in receipt of the Government grant, and in all cases it was agreed that no religious instruction should be given until four o'clock. As the school hours under the old system were from 9 to 11.30 o'clock a.m., and from 1 to 3.30 p.m., it is considered somewhat of a hardship by these teachers to put in an extra one and a half hours' work.

The constant agitation which has been kept up during the past five years has certainly had the effect of creating an increased interest in regard to educational matters; and I am satisfied that when the school question is finally settled this increased interest will have a very beneficial effect on the French schools of the province of Manitoba.

From my intercourse with the French and half-breeds Catholics of the province I have no hesitation in saying that the vast majority of them are prepared to abide by the final decision of the authorities in regard to the school question. They still cling to the hope that the separate school system will be restored to the province, but should this hope not be realized in the near future, it will only be a matter of a short time before the public school system will practically be universally adopted throughout the province.

Name of District.	Date receiving Grant as Public Schools.							
	1891.		1892.		1893.		1894.	
	1st	2nd	1st	2nd	1st	2nd	1st	2nd
St. Jean Baptiste North........................							1	1
Deux Petites Pointes...........................							1	1
St. Charles.....................................								1
St. François Xavier East.......................							1	1
St. Eustache....................................								1
Fairbanks.......................................						1	1	1
St. Leon Village................................	1	1			1	1	1	1
St. Leon East...................................						1	1	1
Theobald							1	1
Decorby						1	1	1
St. Alphonse South.............................								1
St. Laurent No. 1...............................							1	1
St. Laurent No. 2...............................							1	1
St. Boniface West..............................				1	1	1	1	1
St. François Xavier West, Martineau...........	1	1	1	1	1	1	1	1
St. Raymond...................................			1	1	1	1	1	1
St. Vital East...................................						1	1	1
Glengarry					1	1	1	1
Fannystelle								
Bernier...			1	1	1	1	1	1
Camper...	1			1			1	
St. Antoine.....................................			1		1	1	1	1
St. Hyacinthe..................................								1
Arsenault.......................................							1	
Deleau								
Maffam...					1	1	1	1
Routledge......................................								
St. Urbain...................................... formed since 1890								
Canadaville....................................								
Hamelin..								
St. Felix..								
Kinlough								
Huns Valley....................................							1	1
Total.............................	3	5	4	7	10	12	20	26

LIST of French schools in the Province of Manitoba, which have accepted the public school system :—

1. St. Jean-Baptiste, North..................St. Jean Baptiste Post Office.
2. Deux Petites Pointes....................Letellier   "
3. St. Charles............................St. Charles   "
4. St. François Xavier, East..............St. François Xavier "
5. St. Eustache...........................St. Eustache   "
6. Fairbanks ....Baie St. Paul   "
7. St. Leon Village.......................St. Léon   "
8. St. Leon, East.........................Manitou   "
9. Theobald...............................Somerset   "
10. Decorby...............................Fort Ellice   "
11. St. Alphonse, South ....St. Alphonse   "
12. St. Laurent No. 1.....................St. Laurent   "
13. St. Laurent No. 2.....................   "   "
14. St. Boniface, West ....St. Vital   "
15. Kinlough ....Starbuck   "
16. Martineau ....Water Hen River, Indian Reserve.
17. St. Raymond...........................Giroux Post Office.
18. St. Vital, East.......................St. Boniface Post Office.
19. Glengarry ....Ingleside, Scotch Catholics.
20. Fannystelle ....Fannystelle.
21. Bernier...............................St. Marks.
22. Camper ....Minnewakan, Mixed.
23. St. Antoine ....Ste. Agathe,
24. St. Hyacinthe ....La Salle,   "
25. Arsenault.............................Oak Lake,   "
26. Deleau ....Deleau,   "
27. Maffam ....Deleau,   "
28. Routledge ....Routledge,   "
29. St. Urbain............................St. Alphonse (school not yet built).
30. Canadaville ....Dauphin Road,   "   "   "
31. Hamelin ....Ste. Rose du Lac.
32. St. Felix ....Deloraine.
33. St. François Xavier, West.............St. François Xavier
34. Huns Valley ....Huns Valley (school building).
35. Gascon ....Clarkleigh.
36. Courchène.............................Oak Lake (organization not complete).

List of French Schools in Manitoba.

No.	Name.	Post Office.	Remarks.
1	Winnipeg	Winnipeg	Disbanded.
2	St. Boniface, Ville	St. Boniface	Separate.
3	St. Boniface, South	do	do
4	St. Vital	St. Vital	do
5	St. Norbert No. 1	St. Norbert	do
6	do 2	do	do
7	do 3	do	do
8	do 4	do	Convent.
9	St. Agathe	St. Agathe	Separate.
10	Provencher	do	do
11	St. Jean-Baptiste Centre	St. Jean-Baptiste	Convent.
12	do North	do	Public.
13	Deux Petites Pointes	Letellier	do
14	St. Pie	St. Pie	Separate.
15	Taché	St. Joseph	do
16	St. Joseph	do	do
17	Lorette East	Lorette	do
18	do West	do	do
19	do Centre	do	do
20	Ste. Anne West	Ste. Anne	do
21	do Centre	do	Convent.
22	do East	do	Separate.
23	St. Joachim	St. Malo	do
24			
25	St. Charles	St. Charles	Public.
26	St. François-Xavier, East	St. François-Xavier	do
27	do Centre	do	Convent.
28	do West	do	Public.
29	Baie St. Paul	Baie St. Paul	Disbanded.
30	St. Eustache	St. Eustache	Public.
31	Fairbanks	Baie St. Paul	do
32	St. Pierre, South	Jolys	Separate.
33	do Centre	do	do
34	do North	do	do
35	Iberville	do	do
36	St. Leon Village	St. Leon	Public.
37	do East	Manitou	do
38	Theobald	Somerset	do
39	Decorby	Fort Ellice	do
40	Brandon	Brandon	Convent.
41	Selkirk	Selkirk, West	Disbanded.
42	St. Alphonse	St. Alphonse	Separate.
43	do South	do	Public.
44	Marion	Oak Lake	Disbanded.
45	St. Daniel	Carman	do
46	P. La Prairie	P. La Prairie	do
47	Dufferin	Emerson	do
48			
49	Youville	St. Jean Baptiste	Separate.
50	St. Jean Baptiste, East	do	do
51	St. Laurent	St. Laurent	Public.
52	LaRivière	Deloraine	Disbanded
53	Lacombe	Cross Lake	do
54			
55	Maurepas	Fort Alexander	do
56	Darveau		do
57	Chenail		do
58	Brisbois	Minnedosa	do
59	Lac Plat	Shoal Lake	do
60	Caledonia	Ste. Anne	Separate.
61	Huns Valley	Huns Valley	Public.
62	Campeau	St. Alphonse	Separate.
63	St. Boniface, West	St. Vital	Public.
64	Kinlough	Starbuck	do
65	St. Boniface, North	St. Boniface	Disbanded.
66	Dupont	Lake Winnipegosis	do
67	Martineau	Water Hen River	Public.
68	St. Jean Baptiste du Lac	St. Jean Baptiste	Separate.
69	Stony Mountain	Stony Mountain	Disbanded.
70	Ste. Anne	Ste. Anne	Separate.

LIST of French Schools in Manitoba—*Continued.*

No.	Name.	Post Office.	Remarks.
71	St. Raymond	Giroux	Public.
72	St. Vital, East	St. Boniface	do
73	Ile des Chênes	Ile des Chênes	Separate.
74	St. Norbert, No. 5	St. Norbert	do
75	do No. 6	do	do
76	Riel	Grande Pointe	do
77	Glengarry	Ingleside	Public.
78	Ste. Marie	St. Alphonse	Separate.
79	Fannystelle	Fannystelle	Public.
80	St. Cuthbert	Lorette	Separate.
81	Varennes	Whitemouth	Disbanded.
82	St. Nicholas	St. Agathe	Separate.
83	Grande Clairière	Grande Clairière	do
84	Bernier	St. Marks	Public.
85	Camper	Minnewakan	do
86	Gascon	Clarkleigh	do
87	St. Joseph, No. 2	St. Joseph	Disbanded.
88	Courchene	Oak Lake	Public.
89	Vachon		Disbanded.
90	St. Antoine	St. Agathe	Public.
91	La Broquerie	La Broquerie	Separate.
	St. Agathe, No. 2	St. Agathe	do
	St. Hyacinthe	La Salle	Public.
	Notre-Dame de Lourdes	Lourdes	Separate.
	Arsenault	Oak Lake	Public.
	Routledge	Routledge	do
	Deleau	Deleau	do
	St. Urbain	St. Alphonse	do
	Maffam	Oak Lake	do
	Canadaville	Glen Smith	do
	Hamelin	Ste Rose du Lac	do

```
French school districts under Government control..............  35
    do          disbanded ..............................  22
                                                              —— 57
Separate schools ...............................................  44
                                                                 ———
                                                                 101
```

www.ingramcontent.com/pod-product-compliance
Lightning Source LLC
Chambersburg PA
CBHW030246170426
43202CB00009B/642